8-26-2-

8/26/2016 1:17 PM          Sales Receipt #56192
Store 1

# Reading Rock Books

Reading Rock Books

815-226-9401

We are on Facebook, Instagram & Twitter

Bill To
Judy Wight
Customer Program

| Title | Qty | Price | Ext Price |
|---|---|---|---|
| Reading Treasure Trove | 1 | $23.96 | $23.96 T |
| Kicking Bee | | 20% Off Reward | |
| | Subtotal | | $23.96 |
| Total Sales Tax | 9.75% Tax | | $2.34 |
| | RECEIPT TOTAL | | $26.30 |

Total Deposit Taken  $8.00
Balance Outstanding  $0.00

Total Rewards          $5.99
Total Savings          $5.99

*** Reward Program Reminder ***

Original Sales Order #56192

Return Policy: Exchanges only. No returns. Retail
may be returned for a Reading Rock book credit and
Exchanges require receipt and must be made within
30 days of purchase

56192

# The Fighting Sullivans

# The Fighting Sullivans

## How Hollywood and the Military Make Heroes

BRUCE KUKLICK

University Press of Kansas

Published by the University Press of Kansas (Lawrence, Kansas 66045), which was organized by the Kansas Board of Regents and is operated and funded by Emporia State University, Fort Hays State University, Kansas State University, Pittsburg State University, the University of Kansas, and Wichita State University

Library of Congress Cataloging-in-Publication Data

Names: Kuklick, Bruce, 1941– author.
Title: The fighting Sullivans : how Hollywood and the military make heroes / Bruce Kuklick.
Description: Lawrence, KS : University Press of Kansas, [2016] | Includes bibliographical references and index. Identifiers: LCCN 2016026155 |
  ISBN 9780700623549 (cloth : alk. paper) |
  ISBN 9780700623556 (ebook)
Subjects: LCSH: Juneau (Antiaircraft cruiser) | World War, 1939–1945—Naval operations, American. | Sullivan family. | Sailors—United States—Biography. | Brothers—United States—Biography. | Fighting Sullivans (Motion picture) | World War, 1939–1945—Motion pictures and the war. | Shipwrecks—South Pacific Ocean. | World War, 1939–1945—Search and rescue operations. | Waterloo (Iowa)—Biography. Classification: LCC D774.J86 K65 2016 | DDC 940.54/265933092277737—dc23
LC record available at https://lccn.loc.gov/2016026155.

British Library Cataloguing-in-Publication Data is available.

Printed in the United States of America

10 9 8 7 6 5 4 3 2 1

The paper used in this publication is recycled and contains 30 percent postconsumer waste. It is acid free and meets the minimum requirements of the American National Standard for Permanence of Paper for Printed Library Materials Z39.48-1992.

For My Brothers, Glenn and Eric
And for Our Descendants

*In rememberance of my late Dad - William Kermitt Cauthern, WWII - Army - European Theater.*

*Sep. 1942 - July 1945*

*and my late brother, Danny "Dan" Ray Cauthern, U.S. Marines Viet Nam.*

*Oct. 1968 - Dec 1971*

# CONTENTS

# ILLUSTRATIONS AND MAPS

Reputation is an idle and most false imposition, oft got without merit and lost without deserving.

—William Shakespeare, *Othello*

It is the summer of 1988 in Waterloo. With some promised funds for urban rehabilitation, the city fathers are making final plans to spruce up their municipality and stem its deterioration. Businesses and industries are failing, unemployment is up, and the town looks a little dilapidated. Waterloo is just one of the many casualties of the changes that have swept over the Midwest in the previous twenty-five years. For a long time Waterloo had staved off its decline, but since 1980 it had lost about one of every five residents. That year Frank Sinatra, expressing the feelings of an ambitious American moving out of the heartland for New York, sang about those "little town blues . . . melting away." "Start spreading the news, I'm leaving today."

In one small part of the fight to combat the exodus, Waterloo's leaders are calling for the remodeling and renaming of the old ConWay Convention Center. Politicians had earlier designed it to attract conventioneers from the northern tier of Iowa, but the ConWay Center had never really succeeded. Waterloo's elite proposed to smarten it up. They also wanted to give it a new name. "The Sullivan Brothers Convention Center" would highlight the region's most precious commodity: the five valorous sailors from Waterloo who died in World War II when the Japanese sank their ship in the South Pacific. This was the single greatest wartime sacrifice that any family in US history had made, and in 1943 President Franklin Roosevelt had sent a personal letter of condolence to the mother of the young men.

Waterloo had Sullivan Park, and a wing of the county hospital commemorated the boys. Donations had financed a statue in front of their old elementary school, and a special marker was placed in a cemetery. A great "Freedom Rock" in a nearby town would also honor them. In Washington, DC, a stand of trees outside the Capitol memorialized the five. The US Navy had launched a ship in their memory and would christen a second in 1995. Three years after that, in 1998, the block-buster movie *Saving Private Ryan* would recall the Sullivans. Indeed, the film took its inspiration from a Hollywood production of 1944, *The Fighting Sullivans*. This heartbreaking movie showed, during World War II, how intolerable adversity could invade the lives of even a god-fearing and well-thought-of American family. *The Fighting Sullivans* most conspicuously exemplified how the Sullivans had given Waterloo national prominence.

In 1988, the question did not appear to be: Should we rename the ConWay Center? Rather the question seemed: Why didn't Waterloo call it after the Sullivans in the first place?

Nonetheless, in that hot July, a public protest occurred. One headline from the local newspaper, *The Waterloo Courier*, read: RENAMING . . . A CLOSE CALL, while another announced: PROS, CONS TO BE HEARD. A poll by the paper, which always favorably reported on the Sullivan family, pointed out that about 45 percent of people in Waterloo did not want the change. The town called an initial open hearing in the large City Council chambers on the second floor of City Hall. One critic argued that the Sullivans already had a park. Some opponents did not want the brothers remembered in preference to other families who had lost loved ones and not been recognized. Don Miller, a longtime resident, stood up in the front row and said that he did not like to attack God, motherhood, and apple pie. *But,* he lectured community bigwigs, the "achievement" of the brothers was only "average." He had respect and admiration for the Sullivans, he went on. *But,* Miller added, gesturing to the World War II veterans sitting in back of him, "every man behind me did the same thing"—a strange claim to articulate since all of the veterans to whom he pointed were alive.[1]

Something strange was occurring in Waterloo. Hidden passions gripped this place forty-five years after a ghastly tragedy had destroyed a family and after Hollywood had given Waterloo stature all over the United States. The conflict was not a simple matter of where to plant some trees, or what to title a building. The debate reflected deeper issues.

In part this book is a collective biography of the Sullivans. It explores how misfortune transformed a family thought to be less than respectable—and transmuted five marginal young men into godlike beings. From the mid-1940s to the twenty-first century, various groups employed the deaths of the boys to promote a variety of political, commercial, and social causes, both in Waterloo and across the country.

Even if this old story is told without rose-colored glasses, why should it interest us today? Its central aspect concerns how the culture, and in this case also the government, manufacture heroes. How do we define an American hero? Because the United States has so often been at war from the 1950s on, the standard notion embraces men and women who have killed or been killed in the line of duty. But it can also encompass noncombatants lost in war, people murdered in random acts of violence, or those who surrendered their lives through natural disasters. We may also have living heroes—any veteran, even those who have only worked behind a desk. Civilians who have done altruistic deeds; endured some astonishingly dangerous experience; or simply participated in some significant or noteworthy events sometimes get counted as heroes. In many of these sorts of unusual or frightening circumstances, we have unmoored the heroic from the individual intrepid behavior that anchored its use in the past. People are often designated heroes in lieu of paying any further attention to them. In the most challenging cases, it is pronounced that someone who has been in the military is a hero. The person gets a "Thank you for your service" and is forgotten. Of those who are killed, no one is permitted to die "in vain."

This book shows how narratives of the heroic are constructed and why we need them. In looking at the Sullivans, I attend to a less than virtuous activity of the government, but also to the centrality of Hollywood storytelling and to the ambiguity of the movie capital's role. The tale of the Sullivans involves a chronicle of war, a family calamity, and a movie. It is, in addition to all these, an impressive example of how our history is made—and what it is made to mean.

# CHAPTER ONE

## GROWING UP SULLIVAN

From the southwest coast of Ireland the Beara Peninsula juts out into the North Atlantic. In the twenty-first century the area is still beautiful, but bleak and barren. In the first half of the nineteenth century, the male ancestors of the Sullivans lived there in the parish of Trafrask, near the tiny village of Adrigole in County Cork. The name Sullivan is a variant of O'Sullivan, the third most common Irish surname, and today the lore of County Cork sometimes refers to our five brothers as the "O'Sullivans." The Beara Peninsula has a long history of tenacious farming, but in the 1840s the potato blight and the famine drove many of these tribal and deeply Catholic people away from their homeland. In 1849 the starving and impoverished migrants included a Tom Sullivan, his wife, and his brother, all bound for Ellis Island, off New York City, and a new life in America.

Tom Sullivan traveled first to Oneida, in upstate New York, and then left the East Coast of the United States, settling at least for a time in the just-founded community of Harpers Ferry, Iowa. The state was immediately west of adjacent Wisconsin to the north and Illinois to the south, and Harpers Ferry was at the Wisconsin-Iowa line, north of the border between Wisconsin and Illinois. Tom and his brother built homes in Harpers Ferry, and in 1855 they helped to erect a Catholic church there.[1] But the town remained tiny, and the population never reached much more than 300.

The Sullivan family, however, obeyed the injunction—Be fruitful and multiply. Tom Sullivan and his wife had five children, and their oldest, Eugene, had nine more. Eugene's oldest boy, Tom, was born "about" 1883 or 1884, according to different censuses, and years later fathered our five Sullivan men and their sister Genevieve. (Kathleen, the Sullivans' second daughter and youngest child, died in infancy.) This Tom got four years of formal schooling in Harpers Ferry and at sixteen—about the turn of the twentieth century—set out to make his fortune hunting for precious metals in the western states. According to his obituary, he worked for some time in the silver mines of Colorado, a place then a magnet for ordinary men eager for the main chance.[2] Like most others Tom failed, and he also acquired a taste for alcohol, a dangerous craving that would mark his life. Some ten years later, he gave up his quest for mineral wealth and went back east, living 120 miles southwest of his relatives in Harpers Ferry in the larger settlement of Waterloo, Iowa. This town had over 12,000 people in 1900 and rapidly expanded, more than doubling in size over the following decade.

In his twenties, still a drinker but no longer an adventurer, Tom found in Waterloo hard if steady work. At the time the city offered two main options. One was the Rath Packing Company, which slaughtered and prepared pork, lamb, and beef for sale. Rath flourished when it began preparing food for the army in 1917 and 1918, as America entered World War I. The company's Waterloo plant grew up as the largest such facility in the United States. Tom chose the other option, the Illinois Central Railroad (the IC). In part because of Rath Packing, Waterloo developed into a rail hub, delivering livestock for butchery and sending processed meat east. The IC, later named "the Main Line of Mid-America," was the principal road between Omaha, Nebraska, 270 miles to the west, and Chicago, the king city of the Midwest, 300 miles to the east on the far end of nearby Illinois. Tom began as an unskilled worker in the railroad yards and worked his way up, taking up what would be lifetime employment with the IC.

The region of Waterloo had small rolling hills and low-lying wooded areas that, to the west, gave way to the prairie of the Great Plains. Settlers had built the town on both sides of the pretty Cedar River, which flowed south from Minnesota and snaked through Waterloo, cutting it more or less diagonally in two. Residents distinguished the (north) East and (south) West Sides. Locals considered the East Side, where Rath Packing and the IC had their headquarters, the more modest half, and the West Side the more affluent. Yet plenty of people of simple means inhabited the West Side. After World War I, the farm implement manufacturer John Deere bought up a small company in Waterloo to expand Deere's own production of tractors, and eventually it had a major plant in the city. Becoming the third large employer, Deere was located in a

**The Sullivans' Iowa**

low-income enclave on the West Side from which the company drew much of its help.

Thus, the industrial district straddled each shore of the river, as did the retail quarter. Historians date "modern" Waterloo from the opening of the James Black eight-story "Dry Goods Department Store" in 1916. Black's landmark building would be a foremost Waterloo success story for almost seventy years. Scenic bridges easily conveyed shoppers, businessmen, executives and workers, and pleasure-seekers—in addition to horses and buggies and a growing number of automobiles—from one bank of the Cedar to the other. The central 4th Street span led directly to Blacks.

The railroad works more unambiguously divided the town. The IC had a huge yard that split the East Side itself. Other railroads had subsidiary tracks that further isolated the prosperous and commercial downtown East Side from less elegant quarters on that side of the river.

A group of working-class Waterlooans lived around Rath's, behind some railroad tracks on the East Side near the Cedar. But the "North End" of the East Side close to the IC's yard was home to the most sizeable group of poorer people. Many of these manual and unskilled laborers called themselves Irish, but in the early part of the century, railroad management had brought in Croatian and Greek immigrants to replace troublesome Italians who worked for the IC. When a strike threatened in 1910, railroad executives imported African Americans from Mississippi to Iowa. In this North End lower-class mix, which finally included Mexicans, the blacks were the only significant Protestant group and the only significant nonimmigrants. Squeezed into their own segregated quarter, they lived between the IC's yard and other tracks farther east. Political leaders and the real-estate establishment in Waterloo referred to this area of some twenty square blocks as the "Black Triangle." West Siders, whose part of town was lily-white, might call it the "colored section." The white neighbors to the north of the African Americans might know it as "Niggertown," and some worried about its permeable northern border, which only restrictive housing covenants protected. The tracks and the covenants cut off the African Americans from poor whites, and the river cut both groups off from the upper crust.[3]

The blacks had the worst-paying and nastiest jobs on the railroad, even though their bosses had lured them from Mississippi by the promise of high wages and easy work. The white employers, however, had told the truth about housing. Waterloo had land to spare, courtesy of the retreat of the Indians across the middle of North America. The pioneers often laid out wide, tree-lined avenues with broad sidewalks. Even families with little money commonly lived in detached homes, which also had back and front yards. Beautifully positioned on the Cedar, the city did not get paved roads until the late 1920s and 1930s, and much through traffic was funneled to highways that skirted Waterloo. Cars did not create a nuisance downtown, where pedestrians abounded. Boosters proudly advertised the up-and-coming business and culture of this humming metropolitan area that also offered vistas of open countryside just beyond the city limits. Waterloo grew to over 60,000 by 1940, a bustling place set down in the middle of Iowa farms.

Tom Sullivan matured with the city. He had a small-town but urban mentality and was conscious of his workingman's status. He attached himself to the East Side and lived there for well over fifty years, although his early jobs often took him far from Waterloo to repair tracks. When he later rose from unskilled laborer to switchman, he often slept over somewhere and was frequently away in "hostels," the low-priced lodgings designed in the Midwest to give bed and board to trainmen. Tom's jobs gradually got better, and he finally landed in a responsible

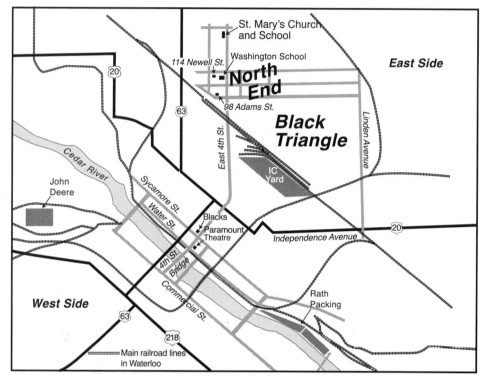

**Waterloo, 1920–1940s**

position as a conductor on the freight trains. This employment usually took him back and forth to Dubuque, Iowa—some ninety miles east of Waterloo at the Illinois boundary, and some seventy-five miles south of Harpers Ferry. On that run he still spent nights away from the East Side. At first alone with other single young males, Tom perfected his way of drinking—in Dubuque at Mrs. Joseph's Erie Café or the Huss House, and at Stone's Café in Marshalltown, another Iowa hub of the IC. Tom indulged only when he did not have to work, and although he habitually drank, he remained sober on the railroad and to that crucial extent controlled his habit. The liquoring-up went side by side with resolute skill as a railway hand untarnished by wayward performance in the yard.

Tom prospered with the Illinois Central. A union man, he benefited from early organizations of skilled hands and the "railway brotherhoods." Tom had a reliable paycheck and a good salary. Alcohol did not prevent him from achieving an unusually well-off life for an Irish American of little education in the early twentieth century. The common worker acquired valuable competencies.

Some of Tom's success derived from his friendship with George Abel, a man from a middle-class Waterloo family. Abel had a more senior position at the IC. He also had a capable wife, May, and a daughter, Alleta, who began seeing Tom Sullivan in 1913. George Abel may have recognized something in the hard-drinking but soft-spoken and dependable Tom. Abel may also have foreseen limited marital options for his daughter. She had not completed the elementary grades and could claim few of the graces that girls might achieve through a high-school education or a polite upbringing. Whatever youthful charm, beauty, and vivacity Alleta possessed vanished early in her life, although she retained a steady and driving concern for the respectability of her family. Tom and Alleta married at Saint Joseph's Catholic Church in Waterloo in early 1914. She was just nineteen; he was over thirty. After a Florida honeymoon, with the travel compensated by the IC, the couple settled in with May and George Abel.

Tom and Alleta's firstborn, George, named after George Abel, was born in December 1914. Less than a week later, on December 19, a rail yard accident injured George Abel, and he died three days later. May Abel was a thirty-six-year-old widow, only five years older than Tom. Now she would live permanently with her daughter and son-in-law, and their new family.

This family expanded rapidly, and Tom and Alleta named their other children after relatives, as they had George.[4] Francis, or Frank, arrived in early 1916; Genevieve, or Gen, a year later; Joseph Eugene (born in August 1918) was known as Joe or Gene and also Red because of his hair; Madison, or Matt, arrived less than fifteen months after Red. For the era, Tom Sullivan was a mature father—thirty-six when Matt was born. Nonetheless, three years later in 1922 Alleta delivered Albert, or Al, and nine years later in 1931 she gave birth to Kathleen Mae. We have no information about the couple's birth-control practices, but by then Tom Sullivan was pushing fifty. The appearance of a child so late

Tom and Alleta. The couple honeymooned in Fort Myers, Florida, in February 1914 (Collection of Michael McGee).

in their lives is noteworthy. After Kathleen died of pneumonia as an infant, Al remained the youngest sibling.

Alleta quickly lost her looks, as they said—and more. Frequent pregnancies did not allow women of that time and place and circumstance to have much concern for their physical attractiveness. Too short to carry extra pounds gracefully, Alleta was soon heavy and clumsy. Pictures of her from the late 1920s through the early 1940s show her squat, overweight, and unattractive. One hostile commentator described her as an "obese" woman who "waddled" around Waterloo.[5] Many testimonies pronounced Alleta withdrawn, but some also called her garrulous. I am convinced of her high intelligence, although she was peculiar and had little space to express her gifts. More important, Alleta was often depressed and incapable of functioning normally. When she had her "spells," she took to her bed for days at a stretch. When she was up, she would sometimes sit on the Sullivans' porch to watch the children, chewing tobacco and spitting it on the wood floor.

Tom's drunkenness may have increased Alleta's idiosyncrasies. She worried about what he was doing on the job, but he often used liquor at home, perhaps to make himself oblivious to Alleta. As time went on, passive-aggressive clashes occurred around the house, as wife reprimanded husband about boozing while Tom drowned out the reprimands with alcohol. Although a sociable drunk, according to reports, he did not talk much in his whiskey-infused encounters with his wife. Alleta would find secret stashes of drink around the house and, in the classic style of those close to an alcoholic, poured out the liquor and replaced it—with vinegar. Often Alleta informed the railroad that because Tom was "sick" he could not come to the yard. Yet his "illnesses"—inebriation or hangovers that prevented Tom's going to his job—only occurred when the IC contacted him at short notice for impromptu freight runs that might need him but that were unscheduled.

Sometimes the drinking did influence Tom's ability to manage the boys. We have evidence of what would now be called physical abuse, although the standards of the twenty-first century are not those of the American lower classes in the early twentieth century. A minimal example of paternal corporal punishment even appeared in the movie *The Fighting Sullivans*. When Tom slept during the day with the children in the house, he would sometimes wake up and yell to Alleta, "Keep those sons of bitches quiet!"

Tom's regular money and his calculation of his benders gave a rare twist to the lives of the family. We need to remember a decisive factor: financially secure if not prosperous, the Sullivans may have occupied a social but not an economic cliff.

In 1919 an amendment to the US Constitution outlawed alcoholic beverages, and laws to prevent their sale and consumption went into effect the following year. "Prohibition" dominated the 1920s, although we don't know exactly how it affected Tom Sullivan. Drink was still easy to come by, and nothing suggests that he stopped consuming. Bootleggers provided alcohol in the alleys off of the main streets of the downtown East Side. We also have indications that Tom built stills to manufacture alcohol and satisfied his habit with his own illegal brew. In 1933 the law sentenced an Oscar Christiansen, who at that point lived with the Sullivans, to thirty days in jail for illegal possession of alcohol.[6]

Alleta's mother, May Abel, kept the family together. People remembered her as a strong and optimistic woman. She took over when Tom was incapacitated or absent, or when Alleta was too down or blue to carry out her parental responsibilities. May organized the household and often meted out discipline to the boys.

The Sullivans moved frequently to accommodate a flourishing clan, the first time from May Abel's house in 1916. Tom's salary meant that May, Tom, Alleta, and the children could afford their own substantial place, but being comparatively well-off did not persuade Tom to give up his roots. He never resided in the fancy part of Waterloo, and we can trace the family's relocations around the East Side and, for most of the boys' abbreviated lives, literally on the "other side of the tracks" in the North End. In 1921—just about a year before Al was born—the family got a new address for a third time since Tom and Alleta's marriage: 114 Newell Street, not much more than a block from the trains. Here the boys would grow up. The location was great for Tom's job, and his sons had access to the backstreets of this fringe district and the lures of the railroad yard, not insignificant for these kids. They were also near the woods and fields of rural Iowa.

Nonetheless, the Sullivans lived unnervingly close to the African Americans, and only social barriers and not rail tracks defined the northern edge of the ghetto, a few blocks south of Newell Street. By the late 1920s, probably in an effort to put some distance between themselves and the blacks, the Sullivans moved again, to another part of the East Side; it was here that their youngest child, Kathleen, died in 1931. The next year the surviving Sullivans moved a final time, to 98 Adams Street. Each move had brought them a more valuable property.[7]

The Hollywood movie would make 98 Adams Street, at the corner of Adams and Ankeny, famous. Only a short distance from the old house on Newell Street and from where Tom reported for his conductor's duties, 98 Adams gave the Sullivans a comfortable home, although it still breathed on the Black Triangle. Marginal stores and shady undertakings lay within walking distance: drinking spots illegal during Prohibition; flophouses; betting parlors; pawn shops; pool halls; card rooms; pay-to-dance joints and more straightforward whorehouses; and various hangouts. The boys grew up largely unattended in a gamey neighborhood. The Sullivans would still be at Adams and Ankeny when the boys went off to war in 1942.

Frank and George were closer to each other than to their younger brothers. The two older boys were seven and eight years older than Al. Their experience of the world differed from his, and their connection to him during some periods was limited. George, Frank, and Genevieve started their educations in the early 1920s, and their parents paid a small tuition for them to go to the parish school of Saint Mary's Roman Catholic Church, near to their Newell Street home. The older children also may have attended Washington Public School. In the late 1920s and early 1930s it is possible that the younger brothers as well showed up at Saint Mary's.[8] But Tom and Alleta may have decided that a parochial classroom was not worth even the minimal price, and certainly after elementary instruction at Saint Mary's their offspring attended public schools. The grown-ups had so little interest in learning that they did not brood over where the siblings went.

The boys reflected their parents' values. None of them was a serious student; in fact, the reverse was true. One neighbor remarked that they were "not real bright"; the parish priest, who owned that he did not see much of them, described them as "pluggers."[9] One Waterloo researcher claimed that the boys may have been thrown out of Saint Mary's for truancy, failing grades, and discipline problems and that the nuns removed the records of their various violations as the 1940s exalted the brothers to secular canonization. Saint Mary's, however, has long since closed, and water had many times swamped the records stored in its basement when the school shut its doors.

The first part of the movie *The Fighting Sullivans* depicted a number of vignettes from the boys' lives. Friends and neighbors remembered that something similar to events shown on the screen, suitably dramatized, had actually happened. We cannot entirely trust these remembrances, because a viewing of the film, in all likelihood, influenced every one of them. But we have more reason to give some credit to the reports than not. Footage from the film had the boys climbing a water tower near the tracks to wave good-bye to Dad when his train went off for the morning; at least it seems the boys used to wait on the tower to monitor his arrival home after some days away. One time when Al was little more than a toddler, the boys found an old rowboat and made it seaworthy by filling some minor holes with mud. On the Cedar River, where African Americans were forbidden to swim, the Sullivans launched their vessel, which at once began to sink. The older boys abandoned ship, while nearby adults rescued Al.[10] The film featured a version of this incident. At another time, the Sullivans decided to build a box for firewood that would allow the family to deposit the wood on the kitchen porch and then extract it for the stove, on the other side of the wall inside the house. Before the children had finished the job, they had sawed through a water pipe in the kitchen and flooded the room. The movie illustrated this escapade, too.

People in Waterloo later recounted other stories about minor delinquencies. Banding together against other boys; driving more settled neighbors, usually older couples, to distraction; teasing girls; playing pranks on unsuspecting visitors to the neighborhood. All of this was expected conduct for children of their age and situation, and it was nothing to write home about. All the stories told after their deaths, and conversations conducted about them years later, inform us that the five boys were energetic, robust, and independent—if sometimes lowdown. For a few years as they were growing up, Alleta had forced them to Sunday Mass at Saint Mary's, which had become their home church, but they did not take to religion in part because of Alleta's own lack of commitment. When the youngsters reached adolescence, the church was irrelevant to their lives, although they did think of themselves as Irish and Catholic.

The distinguishing stories recounted by acquaintances and neighbors pointed to the advantage Tom's job gave the Sullivans in the economically constrained confines of the North End. They were uncommon in having an almost middle-class income combined with an underclass culture and set of attitudes. For a time the family had a large car for Sunday afternoon drives, a rarity in the alleys and streets near the tracks. On the Fourth of July Tom always purchased firecrackers and fireworks for the boys. Friends recalled that the siblings had store-bought kites. Because of Tom's work, the parents also got discounted tickets on the railroads and were unusually well traveled for people of their sort. In addition to the honeymoon in Florida, trains would take them to other parts of the country.

We need to mention a final aspect of the Sullivans' relative material comfort. When all the boys were in school by the late 1920s, summer vacations meant that May Abel and Alleta would have the boys on their hands all day, every day. Instead, they were sent east to Harpers Ferry, where Tom's family still had a farm and two younger unmarried brothers oversaw the land. But Tom and Alleta did not dispatch the boys to harvest the crops. They spent leisurely Julys and Augusts in the fields around Harpers Ferry. They roamed, fished, hunted game, and enjoyed the rough-and-tumble of the outdoors, all under the easy rule of Uncle Joe and Uncle George. Remarkably for working-class boys of this generation, they never learned much about work.

My educated guess is that Waterloo early on developed a bit of unease about the Sullivans. Many of the characteristics that the boys displayed or would display—pedestrian minds as measured by IQ, a disdain for contemplation, a taste for brawling and boozing, and an uneasy connection to the cops—were par for the course in their milieu and certainly not to be troubled over. Yet an ornery aspect that the boys displayed and that the parents did little to mitigate fueled some disquiet. It grew because the family appeared a bit arrogant on account of its relative affluence.

It is yet impossible to reconstruct in any detail or with great accuracy the family's history, including the biographies of the five boys before the war. There is not much evidence pertinent to the Sullivans and precious little that is reliable. Tom, Alleta, George, Frank, Gen, Red, Matt, Al; May Abel; and Al's wife, Keena Rooff Sullivan, whom he married in 1940, left few traces before the end of 1942. In the mid-1940s, when the Sullivans became important, commentators built narratives of the past from the memories of people who could not avoid having in mind the doom of the *Juneau,* the light cruiser that had taken the five brothers to their deaths in the South Pacific. Reporters and investigators interviewed remaining family members, friends, and Waterloo residents. The interviewers always had an agenda: to venerate a stricken family. All of those consulted had, naturally, different and sometimes conflicting stories, and the "oral histories" changed over the years. We have material from the mid-1940s, and also some from the 1980s and 1990s. All of it has a whisper-down-the-lane quality whose origins are in the 1920s and 1930s. Now all of the informants have themselves died, and we are left with disparate tales of almost every notable event in the lives of the Sullivans. Moreover, a famous Waterloo flood in 1961 destroyed much of what the family had in the way of memorabilia and documents.[11]

Easily the most significant piece of evidence dates from after their deaths—the 1944 movie; a series of conversations conducted in 1943 with the remaining Sullivans and with other people from Waterloo informed the script of the film. We cannot escape the movie, which influenced later recollections and even ostensibly more dispassionate studies. Life was shaped to copy art.

Any reconstruction of the lives of the Sullivans, including my own, is shaky and debatable. To remind readers of this aspect of the story, I have from time to time taken the unusual step of writing in the first person, not the conventional omnipresent third person of the historian; and I have sometimes alerted readers by using phrases like "maybe," or "in all likelihood" in telling the tale.

It is not enough to see that a big gap exists between the reality of the Sullivans and the perception of them based largely on the film. We commonly find such differences and regularly find them to be wide. We speak no ill of the dead but always remark on the disparity between eulogy and private knowledge. It will be no news that *The Fighting Sullivans* romanced the past. A more important enterprise is to understand *how* American culture transformed the boys and their family. We need to learn who specifically benefited from different Sullivan stories.

# CHAPTER TWO

## DEPRESSION TROUBLES

Even after the children reached adolescence, we have little sense of their personalities, and Tom and Alleta later stumbled in depicting the differences among the boys. "Georgy Porgie" was the leader, extroverted and gregarious; Frank, more serious and quiet; Red, easygoing, and later the ladies' man; Matt, another private person; and Al, the youngest, accustomed to being doted on, amiable and eager to please. Gen did not contribute to the ill-behaved activities of the boys. Her brothers, who took her as the arbiter of things feminine, protected her. That is the most we can say.

While they probably had a Roman Catholic grade-school experience at least in part, thereafter the Sullivan children began to show up at Waterloo East High School, which included junior high (seventh, eighth, and ninth grades) and senior high (tenth, eleventh, and twelfth grades).

In a period when the high school was a substantial institution in the United States, and when educators had not invented "social promotion," teachers did not fear to fail students or to stigmatize those who did not perform. A high-school diploma was worth something. George set an example for his brothers by being overage for his grade. When he was almost nineteen and left school for the last time in the fall of 1933, he had graduated only East Junior, at which time Genevieve had caught up with him. His age suggested he may have gone back and forth from school to lowly job to unemployment to school. Frank flunked eighth grade, then quit school after repeating. Red graduated East Junior, but he did not go on. Matt got in a year at East High School before leaving, and Al quit ninth grade at East Junior. As was not unexceptional in such families, Genevieve graduated from East High School in 1937 when she was twenty. Illnesses had interrupted her education, but she had studied the "commercial" program designed for young women to become receptionists, clerks, or typists in business firms.

The principal of a public elementary school later equivocally observed that the boys might have been good athletes "had they been interested in competitive sports."[1] Neither did they join extracurricular activities outside of athletics. Part of the reason for this was that they left the classroom too early to sign up for high-school baseball, football, or track. But they were not even involved in JV sports that boys could try out for in junior high, or in music groups, the debating society, various clubs, or student government.[2] And they avoided organized undertakings for young people outside of school—George was for a time a Boy Scout, but none of his brothers followed him. Nor did any of them go in for ball clubs or church groups.

The boys' carefree vacations in Harpers Ferry continued as they grew to an age when, ordinarily, they would have been expected to pick up at least summer jobs, with permanent employment the norm after they left school. Parental indulgence and Tom's paychecks may not have been doing the Sullivan brothers a good service. In addition, at the end of 1929, the stock market in New York City crashed. At first, the Wall Street collapse in Manhattan seemed to have limited consequences, but national unemployment increased each year thereafter. The financial crisis ultimately put millions of Americans out of work and discredited the Republican president, Herbert Hoover. In November 1932, near the bottom of the troubles, Hoover was defeated in the presidential election.

In early 1933, as Hoover's successor, Democrat Franklin Roosevelt, took over, the bottom *was* reached, and the Great Depression gripped Waterloo and the rest of the country. Despite Roosevelt's famous New Deal, which brought into being the rudiments of the welfare state, jobs and money were hard to turn up, and the miscarriages of the economy pervaded the 1930s. Overall, the business panic and the contraction of employment did not alter the Sullivans' status—Tom kept his job with the IC railroad, and the family weathered the fiscal trials of the decade. Nonetheless, the work previously on offer for the two older boys was now unavailable, and they had no training or experience.

After he left school, George joined the National Guard and drilled in nearby towns but avoided a steady job.[3] At some point, the IC employed him because of his dad, but George quit after a few months. When Frank flunked eighth grade, he too tried the IC but did not like it, and he also may have had some National Guard duties.[4] From time to time George and Frank took unskilled employment and may have worked in an early Depression-era relief program created by Roosevelt, the Civilian Conservation Corps. When the younger sons later joined the older siblings as school-leavers, they had slim pickings and little inclination to buckle down at dead-end or seasonal work. They too had only odd jobs—laboring at an ice house or caddying at a golf course. Red was exceptional. After his ninth-grade education, he learned the rudiments of auto mechanics at Schultz's Sunoco Service Station, a gas station and repair shop near Adams and Ankeny. Schultz used Red for low-level labor at the garage—he could fix a tire and bang out a fender.

Being jobless did not mean the Sullivan boys had nothing to do. In 1928 Tom had supported Al Smith, a Roman Catholic, whose bid for the presidency had failed. Smith was a "wet" Democrat and wanted to ease up on the laws prohibiting the sale of liquor in the 1920s. In 1933 when Roosevelt was inaugurated, the Sullivans celebrated his accession to power. The family was not political, but the adults saw FDR as a disciple of Smith and valued Roosevelt's attention to the working class and his support of unions. Additionally, soon after FDR's swearing in, leaders repealed the constitutional amendment and the legislative act that banned the sale of alcohol. After repeal, although Waterloo still had restrictions on drink, Tom could more easily get it, and so too his underage sons—the two older boys probably snitching their dad's moonshine, or shadowing him to the downtown backstreets where they might pick up booze. By the time Prohibition ended, the sons were copying Tom's drinking if not his work ethic.

Without employment, the young men loitered where drink was accessible. One place the brothers hung out was at Ray Hundley's. Throughout the 1920s and early 1930s Hundley flouted the law because he sold illegal liquor from his home some eight blocks from 98 Adams Street. After Prohibition, he opened a saloon, the Merry Garden, close to the popular Paramount Theatre on the river at East 4th Street. Adjacent to the Merry Garden was the Aragon Tavern, operated by Mary Hundley, who was convicted of furnishing liquor to minors.[5] Also popular with the boys were Carter's Pool Hall on East 4th, and a series of down-at-the-heels bars on Sycamore Street on the East Side as it ran east, including the Hi Ho Tap Room. The Sullivans frequented more proper dance halls such as the Farm Roof or the well-known Electric Park Ballroom, where they cultivated their interests in women. George for a time dated a wild girl, Ruth Leet, but others followed her, and his brothers trailed him. Red had some involvement with a "cross-eyed Susy," and Matt was worried that a "Nancy" was two-timing him.[6]

Another aspect of the lives of the boys may have contributed to what I believe was Waterloo's unease with the Sullivans. The brothers disliked the "snobs" who lived on the West Side. But 98 Adams Street, their home through the 1930s, was a stone's throw north of the black neighborhood. Like most whites, the white ethnic working class of the North End was not at all friendly to "the colored" and kept its distance. Not the Sullivans. Rumors had the boys prowling the African American slum to initiate fights; the siblings looked to create unpleasant racial incidents in which they would beat up black people. They "stirred the shit" and "really hated people the color of my grandparents." This was too much even for North End Waterloo; the Sullivan men were "mischief-makers" and had a malicious streak that they demonstrated a few blocks south of their home.[7]

The parents and children had limited horizons. By the 1930s, Waterloo had paved streets, and the houses had electricity and flush toilets. Promoters took pride in the city's more than respectable commercial district, with its upscale shopping and middle-class restaurants. Even in the 1930s the anchor department store, Blacks, operated at a profit, and its handsome building continued to be a central meeting spot downtown. But the Sullivans did not much participate in this gentility, and they ignored the outside world that the newspaper and radio brought them; they did not see much beyond their North End neighborhood. The boys walked its streets and haunted its trashy establishments. Beyond the town they knew only rural Iowa. George and Frank, however, got itchy feet.

In the early part of the twentieth century Hollywood films, in however simplified or distorted a fashion, introduced many citizens to exotic people, places, and ways of living. Throughout the century the American military found movies a powerful device to get young men to join the armed services. On its side, Hollywood profited from motion pictures showing exciting scenes, and studios often received technical and financial assistance from the army and navy. Emphasizing naval aviation and the submarine, the navy in the 1930s especially advertised the benefits of peacetime sailing for young men who might thus escape the dreary routines of the ongoing Depression. By providing facilities or advice, the navy nudged Hollywood in directions that would stimulate recruitment. The cinema showed prospective seamen the world with which they could come in contact. They could, in a movie house, get a sense of the fun and allure of travel, of opportunities to pursue women, and of the joys of drink and male camaraderie. These implicit benefits sold young males on the service.

The 1930s saw a run of films about sailors.[8] Some portrayed air maneuvers over the seas or underwater conflict in submarines. But audiences might have viewed these movies, dramatic and sensational, as giving a picture of dangerous and unappealing occupations—such as *Hell Divers* (1931). The cinema moreover portrayed the high-level Naval Academy in Annapolis, Maryland, and may well have represented a world to which the Sullivans could not aspire—*Shipmates Forever* in 1935, and *Hold 'Em Navy* and *Navy Blue and Gold*, both in 1937. Yet not all the movies depicted the unavailable. *Men Without Women* (1930) showed attainable women and featured run-of-the-mill "gobs," and so too did *Suicide Fleet* (1931), about three sailors interested in the same girl. *Here Comes the Navy* (1934), a comedy about regular guys, was in part filmed on the battleship USS *Arizona*, later sunk by the Japanese in their surprise attack on Pearl Harbor in Hawaii on December 7, 1941. In *Follow the Fleet* (1936) Fred Astaire and Randolph Scott played ordinary servicemen involved with gorgeous women of Hollywood fantasy, and an unworthy female attracted another two sailors in *Devil's Playground* (1937).[9]

Waterloo's movie palace, the Paramount on East 4th Street, catty-corner from Blacks, was tailored for large audiences and ran navy films. But so too did at least three other East Side theaters. In the mid-1930s, *Devil Dogs of the Air* (1935), about navy airmen, and *Shipmates Forever* were playing in East Side Waterloo. The submarine film *Hell Below* (1933) made two appearances in Waterloo in a single six-month period, and at least once patrons could catch two such films on a single day.[10]

In 1937 George and Frank, in one of the more decisive acts of their fleeting lives, joined the peacetime navy. They enlisted at the Naval Recruiting Station in nearby Cedar Falls in May 1937 and promptly went to Des Moines, Iowa, for their physicals. We don't know what motivated them, but there is educated speculation. They had been disinclined to search for and undertake hard-to-find low-level work and faced an empty future. The brothers were twenty-two and twenty-one when they went away for four years; Al would have been fifteen. Although the two sailors were not extraordinarily young for this experience, their independence is the first substantial piece of evidence to challenge the tales of the five boys unendingly "sticking together."

Standard practice in the navy when not at war allowed George and Frank to serve on the same ship, and they did. As Seamen Apprentices, they got ninety days of schooling at the Naval Training Station in San Diego, California, sent there by train from Iowa. The navy quickly fulfilled George and Frank's hopes of seeing distant shores. The boys left the confines of Waterloo for the West Coast, the Pacific Ocean, and finally berths on the USS *Hovey*, an American destroyer left over from the Great War of 1914–1918 (as that global conflict was known prior to World War II). The two Sullivans were much like other American sailors: white, uneducated, usually underprivileged men, with a disproportionate number of Roman Catholics, filled the navy. On his first liberty, with a few dollars to spend, George decided not on a prostitute but on a tattoo—an anchor with "USN" across it. His brother followed with the identical choice. The *Hovey* also disciplined them for drunkenness and an attempt to smuggle liquor onto the ship, although such infractions were common.[11]

Minimal military training took place on the water, and the destroyer usually anchored along the California seaboard. Nonetheless, George and Frank did cruise south along the coast of Mexico; along the shorelines of the Central American countries in the near Pacific; and through the Panama Canal at Balboa Harbor to the Caribbean and the South Atlantic. Moreover, three times the *Hovey* sailed west from California to the island chain of Hawaii, at that time a self-governing territory of the United States. The headquarters of the American Pacific fleet was on the island of Oahu, at the port of Pearl Harbor, just outside the much better known Hawaiian capital city, Honolulu. In Honolulu, as in other ports of call of the US Navy, the brothers, like so many others, frequented the bars, cheap restaurants, tattoo parlors, and houses of ill repute, all of which catered to American sailors.

At the same time, the military was "making men" of the boys, as families used to say. The brothers worked toward promotion from common seaman, and both succeeded. They became petty officers, low-ranking enlisted men with different duties that depended on their specialization. George was a third-class gunner's mate, Frank a third-class boatswain or cox (someone who worked with those actually sailing the ship). Both moved up to higher ratings. Frank joined the ship's boxing club as a welterweight, so we know that he tipped the scales at about 145 pounds. His team won the destroyer and squadron championship. Predictably, his shipmates nicknamed him "John L.," after the legendary John L. Sullivan of the late nineteenth century, the first heavyweight champion of gloved boxing. However, while in Hawaii, toward the end of this stint in the navy, Frank broke his hand and did not fight again as a sailor.[12]

In 1937, soon after the two Sullivans joined up, Tom and Alleta traveled to California to see their sons on the *Hovey* in San Diego. The next year the brothers took leave and returned home, just about when the Navy Mothers of Waterloo established Chapter 66.[13] Alleta was one of the founders. The boys visited Adams Street again in the winter of 1939–1940.

In September 1939, World War II broke out in Europe. It first pitted Britain and France ("the Allies") against Germany, as had occurred more than twenty years before. During World War I the three countries had shed much blood, and in 1917 the United States threw its support to the Allies to defeat the Germans. At the end of 1939 the Roosevelt administration sympathized with Britain and France in the new contest against the ferocious German Nazis, frighteningly led by Adolf Hitler, and the Fascists of Italy, perhaps more bumptiously led by Benito Mussolini. Would America again join forces with its old partners? Foreign war now made for a furious quarrel in the United States itself.

Some politicians, mainly Republicans, believed that American intervention in World War I under the Democratic president Woodrow

Wilson had been a major blunder. In the 1930s, they got labeled "isolationists," although it is probably better to call them "noninterventionists." They were determined that the earlier American intrusion in the affairs of Old World Europe should not be repeated. In Congress, many Republicans fought to stay away from what they saw as the unending extremist and imperial squabbles of Britain, France, and Germany. They had on their side the sentiments of most US citizens. Americans disliked the Nazis and their appalling anti-Semitism, but they did not want to get involved when the collapse of the international order after 1917–1918 had proved that the United States could not alter Europe's troubles.

For other statesmen, including those in Roosevelt's administration, the rise of an avenging Germany validated Wilson's notion that nations should pursue collective security. A way had to be found to have the American people accept this burden. For these statesmen, the looming second war had come to pass *because* the people had rejected (with Republican help) Wilson's plans for peace and his League of Nations that would banish war. The interventionists gathering around Roosevelt hoped to carry the day where Wilson had not, but they worried—more than worried, in fact—about how to secure the consent of the citizens.

The role of the Soviet Union, which had emerged as a revolutionary state after 1919, complicated the acrimony in American politics. The old Russian imperial regime had allied itself with Britain and France in the Great War but was overthrown at its end, and the Communists (or "Bolsheviks") took over and formed the new Union of Soviet Socialist Republics (USSR). The Soviets became a hated enemy of all the Western powers—the former European Allies, the United States, *and* the Germans. However, when the Great Depression swept over the world and capitalism was discredited, many politically active people in the United States found the Soviet experiment attractive and promising. Some people who supported Roosevelt's New Deal considered it a way station that would appropriately develop into the kind of system that was coming into existence in the Soviet Union. By the mid-1930s the Communists in Russia were the only ones explicitly opposed to Hitler. The "popular front" liberals in America, far to the left of Roosevelt, joined with the president and anyone else who stood against Hitler;

they became key proponents of the internationalism and collective security that would contain the Nazis and would also assist Germany's chief adversary, the USSR. These liberals promoted an overall alliance against fascism, a term that had the flavor not just of the Italians but of any evil government opposed to Bolshevik Russia. These pro-Soviet interventionists were sort of an embarrassment to conventional internationalists in the United States. For anti-interventionists, the association between the Soviet Union and Roosevelt's most extreme New Dealers was just another reason vehemently to reject any attempt to insert the United States into Europe.

Then, in the first part of 1939 before the new war started, a realignment in Europe had taken place. The USSR dropped its opposition to Hitler, and in August Hitler's Germany and Joseph Stalin's Russia signed the notorious Hitler-Stalin pact. In this disturbing alliance, the Communists would protect themselves from attack by the Nazis, and the Germans would be free to do what they wanted without having to worry that a major threat would come from their east. Thus, in September 1939 Hitler invaded Poland, and Britain and France, which had committed themselves to Poland's defense, declared war on Germany. World War II began. But communist Russia was not in it, nor was America.

For the foreign policy public in the United States, the fluctuating and confusing European groupings inflamed even more the shouting match between interventionists and noninterventionists. The connection of the Bolsheviks to the Nazis only convinced isolationists of the obscenity of the Old World and underscored why Americans needed to keep out. The popular front internationalists, who had previously pushed for the United States to defend the Soviets from Hitler, were at least embarrassed; some suspended their love affair with Russia; others robotically changed their tune and stopped denouncing the Nazis. They added to the political cacophony in America when they briefly joined with the noninterventionists. And yet, nine months after the war started, by May 1940, Hitler had overrun Western Europe, France had surrendered, and England fought alone. It was imperative, said Roosevelt's internationalists, that America get into the brawl to save the world from the scourge of the Nazis.

Almost certainly, the bewildering convolutions of international politics escaped the Sullivans in Waterloo and George and Frank on the California coast. But these convolutions inevitably had an impact on the US Navy in the Pacific area, where the two older brothers were on duty.

Tensions at first increased in the Atlantic for the American military. In the fall of 1939, despite the screams of the noninterventionists, Roosevelt and his officials were determined to favor Britain and France. US authorities offered supplies, arms, protection for shipping, and finally a silent partnership against the German navy in the North Atlantic. But troubles also burgeoned in the Pacific. There, Germany's friend of convenience, Japan, was making a bid for dominance in Asia and fighting a long war to bring China to heel. A United States unwilling to withdraw from the Western Pacific to California antagonized the Japanese. Americans had a long and paternal connection to China, although they did not really care much about the Chinese—except to prevent their immigration to the United States. By the late 1930s these issues disrupted Japanese American relations and embroiled diplomats on both sides. The United States did not want hostilities with Imperial Japan, but Japanese undertakings on the Asian mainland, which would exclude American interests, increasingly upset US decision-makers.

By the end of 1939, Hitler's aggressive policies in Europe inspired the Japanese to imitate Germany. But the conflict in Europe also agitated moralistic Americans who saw a worldwide danger to their democratic internationalism from the combined forces of German *and* Japanese militarists. American anxiety about Asia intensified. In 1940 and 1941, the United States amassed its naval forces around Pearl Harbor in the Pacific, and the two Sullivans shared in maneuvers that reflected evolving American concerns. In the spring of 1941, Pearl Harbor was almost on war footing, though the brothers still had little in the way of serious exercises in the arts of battle—and no combat experience; they also apparently showed little interest in pursuing careers in the navy.

While the wider world had dictated the movements of the *Hovey* in the last part of the enlistments of the Sullivans, the problems of international politics did not, from what we know, touch the two boys. With the end of their tour of duty in the spring of 1941, they returned to the life they had left.

George and Frank were away four years—a long time—and the escalating international fears had fostered a new prosperity in the United States. Various industries received armament orders, and businesses with any connection to defense were hiring. Employment in Waterloo picked up as new economic growth took place. "War-work" came to Rath Packing as the company prepared the processed, preserved, and canned meat that made its way into the mess kits of soldiers.

By the end of 1939, all three of the boys at home, including Al, who had left school when he was just sixteen the year before, had procured steady jobs at Rath's, or the "plant." They were being paid about $20 a week, about $1,040 a year, when the average salary was $1,368 a year—about 25 percent under the average. Tom, by contrast, was making $2,784 a year, more than $53 a week and double the average.[14]

With money in their pockets, the three brothers had novel ways to occupy themselves. The work at Schultz's Garage led Red to motorcycles and then to the Black Hawk Motorcycle Club. In the 1920s, souped-up bicycles had often raced against one another over outdoor courses laid down on wooden planks. The Indian Motorcycle Company of Springfield, Massachusetts, manufactured these vehicles, Indian Board-Track Racers. They made profits until the Depression, when the cost of maintaining the wooden courses hurt the manufacturer. By the mid-1930s, the Harley-Davidson Motor Company of Milwaukee had established commercial dominance over the Indians with its Cinder-Track Racers. "Gangs of bikers," as one writer put it, made the Milwaukee firm famous, and the motorcycle had evolved from a bicycle with a tiny engine to a machine that normal roadways could accommodate. Especially in the Midwest, certain customers expressed an enormous desire for Harleys, and bikers had begun to emerge as a social group that many believed could threaten middle-class propriety and civilized living.[15]

Waterloo was located in Black Hawk County. In 1932, the go-getting entrepreneur Paul Brokaw converted his bike and auto repair shop, which had sold Indians, into a Harley-Davidson dealership. He marketed motorcycles to the police, built a racetrack—Black Hawk Speedway—on a farmer's road near Waterloo, and advertised his vehicles one winter by riding a cycle with special runners at seventy miles an hour on the frozen Cedar River.[16] In 1934, he set up the Black Hawk

Motorcycle Club to attract business and to increase his customers' enthusiasm. It had about twenty-five members, overwhelmingly young males, but the "Black Hawks" additionally included girlfriends, a few wives, and some groupies unable to afford a machine. Brokaw had his garage on the nonelite West Side, near the John Deere Tractor Company, which employed some of the men with cycles. Most of the club members, however, worked at Rath's on the East Side. They went back and forth from the packing company to a nearby bar, the Tic Toc Tap, one of the many dives along the Sycamore Street corridor that eventually ran out behind Rath's. The Tic Toc became a main club headquarters.[17]

This was too early in the history of motorcycling to talk about "outlaw bikers." Yet when the Black Hawks sped around Waterloo wearing their heavy black goggles, they also dressed in a sort of costume—caps, leather jackets, and knee-high boots. Then they got military-style outfits of Italian fascist design—gray shirts with black epaulets on the shoulders; gray pants with black stripes running down the sides; black ties; and military hats. The membership organized rallies, trips as far away as Dubuque, races on the speedway as well as informal country tracks, and of course "meetings at the club house."[18] As one expert has written, "The massive consumption of alcohol and general good-natured debauchery" were biker pastimes from the earliest days of cycling.

Red began riding on the backs of friends' bikes, and with some money in his pocket from Rath's he joined the club after his two older brothers left for the navy. All of his earnings went to purchase a used motorcycle. He loved wearing his army-style attire, which is regularly in evidence in photographs that friends and family took of him. Even before Red's time, the Harley crowd in Waterloo bordered on the disreputable, and now the group around Red was over the top. He found the Tic Toc a place to drink and socialize.

The Tic Toc resembled what we might today call a biker bar. A number of cycles would be parked outside. Inside, beer, maybe watered down, would be on ice, along with a few varieties of inexpensive hard liquor. The Tap sold limited food—sandwiches, maybe some burgers. A pool table attracted an ever-changing clientele. The club members defined a part of the establishment as "theirs." They would be sitting

At the Tic Toc. Red Sullivan, right front, at his favorite hangout (Collection of Michael McGee).

in booths effectively reserved for them, or along one part of the bar, in their uniforms or in short leather jackets, boots, and various forms of outré headgear. Women pals hung out with waitresses, drinking and cursing with the men, and up for the sexual banter. Thick with cigarette smoke, the joint also smelled of stale alcohol. Club members listened to music from a radio or jukebox, or sang along when someone played the old piano. The board of health kept its distance.[19]

The more genteel folks in Waterloo did not witness the scene at the Tic Toc, where they never went. They did experience wild rides through the town by motorcyclists, along with the intimidation of a large group of men in soldiers' outfits.

Red frequented the Tic Toc and liked the roar of a biker outing, as well as the ninety-mile visits east to Dubuque and back. He got two other nicknames, in addition to Joe, Gene, and Red—"Crash Sullivan" and "Nine Lives," attesting to his fast and dangerous fashion of riding.[20]

At a motorcycle club event in the summer of 1939, Al—just seventeen—met Katherine Mary "Keena" Rooff from the West Side. The same age, they were soon going steady. People in Waterloo later corroborated one series of events from their whirlwind courtship, and it more or less faithfully appeared in the movie version of their lives. In an excess of male camaraderie, Red and Matt humiliated Al in front of Keena by pretending that he was handing her the same line that he used on other girls. After a family crisis, the middle sons apologized to the couple, and the romance continued. The Rooffs' parish, Sacred Heart, married Al and Keena on May 11, 1940. They were both seventeen. Al's two older brothers did not attend, nor was the date of the wedding made to coincide with their leave from the navy that occurred around the same time. Although Gen was the maid of honor, the best man was neither Red nor Matt but Keena's cousin, Leo Rooff. On February 2, 1941, Keena gave birth to a son, James—little Jimmy. The timing was so tight that Tom and Alleta would later fudge the dates to cover up what might have been and certainly looked like some kind of a shotgun wedding on the part of the youngest Sullivan boy. In November 1941, in another testimony to the family's material comfort, Al and Keena bought a West Side bungalow from Keena's uncle. But people were already saying that "the marriage was on the rocks." Al "had got her in trouble," and "the two teenage kids fought like cats and dogs, always having a ruckus." I repeatedly heard a story of this sort, but from people who could only have heard it from others. Did this mean that many people had known of problems in the marriage, or that some one person had spread the story? The reader can pick.

In May 1941, the navy discharged George and Frank. Neither their promotions nor the spread of the global conflict had induced them to stay on. Their enlistment over, the elder sons went back to Waterloo. National service may have left them fiercely patriotic. But while the perspectives of the two older boys may have expanded, four years abroad

Black Hawk Motorcycle Club, 1941. Red Sullivan is kneeling in the bottom row, third from the right (Collection of Michael McGee).

seemed to have left them remarkably untouched. By the summer of 1941 they were again living at 98 Adams Street.

George and Frank got jobs at Rath's, as American industries called for even more workers. Money in the pockets of George and Frank meant that they could spend, and having fixed employment meant that the boys could incur debts. George was attracted to Red's cycling interest and registered as a Black Hawk Club member. He bought his own machine and became "Ace" Sullivan—the number-one Sullivan.[21]

Al's connection with the Harley club may have been limited to his meeting Keena through its auspices, and we don't know about Matt. Red's life, however, centered on it, and George followed, with Frank close behind. By 1941 Red had sunk all of his money into a new Harley, and the older boys were partying with Red. Frank's skill as a former navy boxer assisted the brawling. Red was leading his group in the cycle club to minor dissipation and rowdy, drunken rides. One widely circulated story claimed that the boys filched gasoline to fuel their vehicles and also "refurbished" stolen cycles. Such stories were believable, although it is pretty clear that the brothers were never in serious trouble with the law.[22] But it is likely that a number of people who knew the Sullivan brothers were also more than willing to believe the worst.

No evidence suggests that the downward spiral of world politics attracted the interest of the family. But in June 1941, just after George and Frank returned to Waterloo, Hitler broke his agreement with Stalin and invaded Russia. For many this development was inexplicable; for the noninterventionists, it was yet another example of the lunacy in Europe. Nonetheless, as the force of a potent and virtually unstoppable Nazism exploded over Eurasia, the interventionists in the United States coalesced. Republicans such as Secretary of War Henry Stimson and Secretary of the Navy Frank Knox, both in Roosevelt's war cabinet created in 1940, thought in power-political terms about the threat of Germany. Administration Democrats, led of course by FDR, had both realistic and idealistic concerns. A small part of the electorate followed the president's wife, Eleanor Roosevelt, who had sympathies further left domestically than did her husband and who was disposed to fight international fascism, more widely defined, and anti-Semitism. Finally, there were clear radical American internationalists, that is to say, out-and-out backers of the Soviet Union; suddenly for these popular front liberals, it was again okay to oppose the Germans and to demand aid to the Soviet Union. Even without this pressure, New Dealers were determined to help Britain and now Russia, and the isolationists rightly worried about the drift of the United States toward a major war. The voices of anti-interventionists became more shrill.

Verne Marshall, editor of Iowa's *Cedar Rapids Gazette*, was a Republican isolationist and led an outfit called the No Foreign War Committee in 1940–1941.[23] In the months after the two older Sullivans came home, the *Gazette* was filled with warnings of the dangers of war. In September 1941, the newspaper proudly publicized the notable speech of Charles Lindbergh in Des Moines, not far from Waterloo and Cedar Rapids. Lindbergh was one of America's greatest heroes, the first person to fly across the Atlantic alone. His eloquent address was national news and showed the strength of anti-interventionist sentiment in Iowa. Speaking for the America First Committee, Lindbergh admonished Americans about the unnecessary war against Germany into which Roosevelt was dragging them. Lindbergh also told his listeners whom they could blame—not just internationalist Democrats but also Hollywood Jews promoting intervention. Lindbergh and the *Gazette* finally noted the foolishness of associating with Russia, as well as the untrustworthiness of England. The Sullivans were Irish, and whatever else they attended to about foreign affairs, they may have hated the English. But we have no evidence that any of these alarms penetrated Adams Street.

Moreover, people like Marshall and Lindbergh focused on the war in Europe, which now pitted Nazis against the English and the Communists. Interventionists too were absorbed with this contest, and in the North Atlantic the US Navy was provoking the Germans so that America could formally join with Britain (and less ostentatiously with Russia). The Nazis did not want full-scale belligerency from the Americans and avoided confrontation. America's navy was nonetheless directed to skirmish with German submarines under the sea-lanes between England and the United States. But neither internationalists nor isolationists put a priority on the Pacific, where tensions had been on the rise for almost two years—and where we might expect the Sullivans to have paid attention to developments.

Yet we draw a blank about the Sullivans even in respect to the ocean west of California, where the two boys had sailed. All we know is that by the end of 1941 George and Frank were back in the swing of things in Waterloo, immersed, with Red, in the Harley club.

# CHAPTER THREE

## IN THE NAVY

On December 7, 1941, the Japanese attacked the United States by air. They surprised the Pacific Fleet at its base in Pearl Harbor, Hawaii; sunk ships in the harbor; and killed almost 2,500 soldiers, sailors, and airmen. The next day Franklin Roosevelt engraved the events of December 7 in American memories as "a date which will live in infamy." He vowed victory in the Pacific "no matter how long it may take us." On December 11, Adolf Hitler declared war on the United States in support of his Japanese ally, with the belief that this second front in Asia would make the United States beatable. Pearl Harbor enabled the US president to lead a unified country into conflicts on two oceans. In its own way the attack was a godsend for the interventionists, who had previously struggled in duplicitous attempts to force the Germans into battle with the US Navy in the North Atlantic.

In the Pacific the United States shared the blame for war. The Americans had been unwilling to defer to Japanese plans for racial and commercial hegemony in Asia, especially in China. From 1939 on the United States had coupled exhortation about Japan's moral failings with growing economic sanctions that choked the Japanese. American officials had a hard time getting it into their heads that Japan might respond militarily, and certainly they underestimated the abilities of a nonwhite armed force. Thus, the United States recklessly pushed its adversary. December 7, 1941, displayed the aggression of the Japanese but also the meddlesome self-righteousness in the American national character and its results.

No matter about duplicity in the Atlantic, or complicity in the Pacific. The events of December 7 to December 11 launched the United States on a great crusade, and all across the country citizens rallied to the flag. In Waterloo, as in most towns across America, complexity and reflection took a backseat to action.

On December 7—a Sunday—George, Frank, and Red spent the day

at the Tic Toc with a friend. Later that afternoon, on two bikes, the four-some rumbled up to Adams Street, where they learned the news. Two of the Sullivans were navy veterans, and the bombing energized all five brothers. Moreover, they had a personal connection. Gen was romantically attached to Bill Ball from Fredericksburg, Iowa, some forty miles from Waterloo. He had taken her to dances and concerts and had visited the Sullivan house on Adams Street in 1937 and 1938. Then, in 1938, after he had graduated from high school, Bill and his brother Masten enlisted in the navy, like the older Sullivan brothers. The friendship between the two navy families, the Sullivans and the Balls, continued. In the early part of 1941, when the *Hovey* had called at Pearl Harbor, George and Frank had gotten together with the Ball brothers, stationed in Hawaii on the battleship USS *Arizona*. Bill and Masten were still there on December 7.

Although Masten survived the air strike, the Ball family soon learned that Bill had lost his life aboard the *Arizona*, sunk by the Japanese. Almost 1,200 men on the ship went to the bottom, including Bill Ball and other acquaintances of the Sullivans. At once the boys decided to enlist in the navy. A desire to avenge Bill's death animated the brothers, including Al, whom the military would have protected even from a draft because he was a husband and father. Fear of a draft, however, does not seem to have been much of a motivating factor for any of them. They had nondescript jobs in Waterloo, and war has much appeal to young men who know nothing about it. Moreover, this conflict was urgent to everyone.

We have evidence that father Tom agreed to square all their bills and mortgaged the house to do so; but we also have evidence that the boys paid off debts themselves.[1] Whatever the truth, Pearl Harbor had galvanized the Sullivans; the war gave direction to these five at-sea siblings. Why did Al go with his four brothers? We really don't have much of an answer to this question, except that Waterlooans told and retold tales about troubles in the family of Al, Keena, and their baby. He had "knocked her up . . . and then wanted a way out."

Why did the five serve together? Alleta gave conflicting accounts to newspapermen in the public aftermath of the deaths of her sons. We also have written records at variance with Alleta's narratives.

The Five Movie Sullivans. This publicity still shows the film brothers with their enrollment officer (Everett Collection).

*Ward Bond*

To the extent that the army and navy thought about the deaths of more than one member of the same family at the start of World War II, officials recalled the violent Civil War of 1861–1865, which killed brothers and relatives—sometimes on opposite sides. That war had seared the country's conscience, but it was eighty years distant. The Spanish-American War of 1898 and the Great War in Europe of 1917–1918 were more recent, but the death tolls had not risen to the levels that produced the cultural trauma of the Civil War. American military men of the later 1930s, in their democratic society, had limited familiarity with mass death in a nonprofessional armed force. Leaders mainly did not think through the problem of siblings wanting to be with each other, even though that could mean they might all die at once. The armed forces had only ad-hoc ideas regulating how relatives might participate as one and never adopted a policy. The navy did not prohibit such service on vessels, although it was discouraged in wartime, and the admirals did issue instructions on the "impractical" nature of transferring family members *to* ships with close kin. Nonetheless, the service allowed family members to remain together; the navy accommodated them. The need for men and the positive publicity attendant on multiple enlistment of family and friends overrode worries about joint death.

In December 1941, naval enrollers, according to the standard story, put off the Sullivans. A first attempt to enlist may have come to nothing because the boys insisted on going as a unit, as George and Frank had on their first tour of duty. All the branches of service were eager for men, but the navy may have thought that the wave of feeling that swept the United States at the end of 1941 and into 1942 would bring them enlistees who made less problematic demands than these five brothers. On their side, the Sullivans may have elected to defer individual commitments to the navy or to try other ways to get into the fight.

Then, on Friday, December 26, the boys joined the navy en masse at the Waterloo Post Office, which was functioning as a recruiting station. Within the week the five brothers appeared at Saint Mary's. Al brought Keena and baby Jimmy—almost a year old—and asked to have his son baptized. The family went to a Mass and received a blessing.

At some point during the same week George wrote an extraordinary letter to the Department of the Navy:

> G. T. Sullivan
> 98 Adams
> Waterloo, Iowa

Dear Sir:

I have four brothers and 2 buddies from my Motorcycle club. I talked them into going into the U.S. Navy for the U.S.A. As a bunch there is no-body that can beat us. There is nothing that can back us up. I had 4 years training in the Navy and four in the National Guards. My brother had four years in the Navy and a couple years military training. Otherwise, anyone of our brothers which there are five of us and our 2 buddies would like to stick together. We would all do our best to be as good as any other sailors in the Navy. We would appreciate it very much if you could, if possible keep us together. We will all leave for enlistment Jan 2, 1942. I think we will go to the Great Lakes Training Center near Chicago Illinois we would appreciate it very much if you could keep our 5 brothers and 2 buddies together. Our names are

*G. T. Sullivan
*F. H. Sullivan
*J. E. Sullivan
*M. P. Sullivan
*A. L. Sullivan
Five brothers and two buddies
Arnie Ray
Eddie Feuer.

We will make a team together that can't be beat. I have qualified as a First Class Gun Captain before I left the Navy and I know I can make a first class team out of them. I thank you dearly. We had 5 buddies killed in Hawaii. Help us.

/s/ G. T. Sullivan
Formerly U.S.S. Hovey[2]

The letter bears analysis. The individuals, including Al, had enlisted but appealed to the navy to treat them as one. They wanted to "stick together," though not entirely just as brothers: a group of seven was moved to go into the navy as a team. Not only George, Frank, Red, and Matt but also Al and two Sullivan friends. The team's members had legally obligated themselves as individuals to the service, although they had a preference to sail on the same vessel. Later, in an interview, father Tom said: "When they joined the navy," they requested that they be put "on the same boat." An official navy spokesman later said, "It was the desire of your five sons that they might serve on the same ship, and the navy respected that wish."[3]

Contrary to what the government later stated, the enlistment of the Sullivans did not depend on their serving on one ship, and the navy had the final say on what ship or ships they would be on. The navy assigned the brothers to the same warcraft. Togetherness was not a condition of service; responsibility for this decision lay with the admirals. On Friday, January 2, as George's letter stated, the seven left for their physicals and induction at the Des Moines recruiting headquarters. The newspapers reported their "hope" that the navy would not split them up.[4]

The next day at the recruiting station, some 130 miles from Waterloo, the doctors passed the Sullivans and the two other motorcycle club members. The *Des Moines Register* wrote that "five husky Waterloo brothers" who had lost a friend in Hawaii were accepted as recruits. "You see," said George, "a buddy of ours . . . Bill Ball . . . was killed in the Pearl Harbor attack." Frank added, "That's where we want to go now, Pearl Harbor." The others nodded.[5] That night, Saturday, January 3, the group took the train east to the Great Lakes naval training facility in Illinois, just outside Chicago. The Sullivans spent only a month at the Great Lakes "boot camp" —two months less than George and Frank had spent at the training center in San Diego during peacetime in 1937. In 1942 the seven learned (or relearned) basic military discipline and duties, how to fill out papers, and how to care for their uniforms and gear. But the boys received superficial preparation for war making.

The training began less than four weeks after the declaration of war, and the navy was unready and ill equipped for what it was supposed to accomplish. One sailor who underwent "basic" with the five brothers related that the first night the veterans George and Frank had to show the recruits how to sleep in hammocks. The two oldest siblings promptly fell to the ground themselves. But at Great Lakes, the navy soon separated George and Frank—middle-aged and experienced from the viewpoint of the service—from the men with no prior skills. Although George and Frank theoretically reverted to common seamen when they joined up again, their re-enlistment gave them some higher status, George as second-class gunner's mate, and Frank as a third-class boatswain. Yet officers who often had no familiarity with fighting on the seas guided even the two senior Sullivans—as well as the raw enlistees who included three Sullivan boys and two other Harley club members. Naval officers had vague plans that aboard ship new men might pick up battle skills from old hands.[6]

The brothers wrote at least two letters home telling friends that it was not yet clear if they—the seven team members—were to serve as a group. Frank and George, who trained independently from Matt, Red, Al, Arnie, and Eddie, also did not know "when they were going to leave," but Red crossed his fingers that the seven would "all [be] . . . going on the same ship." When the rudimentary training ended in early

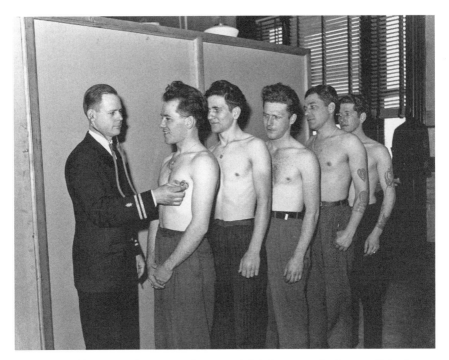

The Five Sullivan Brothers Join the Navy. This is a staged picture of the boys
when they passed their physicals in early 1942 (AP).

February, no guarantee had come that the three younger brothers and
Arnie Ray and Eddie Feuer would be together, or that the two older
brothers would join these five.[7]

Few parents could match the contribution of Tom and Alleta Sullivan
to American solidarity. As soon as the boys went off in early 1942, Tom
and Alleta followed the convention and put a banner of five blue stars
in their window—one for each family member in the service; one star
was store-bought, the other four homemade.[8] Just before the brothers
left Great Lakes, Tom, Alleta, and Gen visited the just-hatched sailors.[9]

The navy being built in the late 1930s consisted first of battleships
designed to pummel enemy vessels and the shores of enemy lands. By
1940, however, aircraft carriers that unleashed planes to assault targets
on land or to destroy enemy ships had become crucial. The carriers
became increasingly important not only because the Japanese had sunk
older battleships at Pearl Harbor but also because carrier-based aviation

could now deliver enough ordnance to sink an enemy's battleship. But planes also occupied naval theorists because no independent air force existed. The service was developing its own capabilities but also competed with the traditional air bases of the US Army Air Forces located on Pacific islands.

Moreover, in addition to the carriers, the more common and smaller destroyers (or torpedo-destroyers like the old *Hovey*) provided protection for battleships and carriers. The superior speed and maneuverability of destroyers allowed them more effectively to use depth charges against submarines, as well as torpedoes against larger surface ships.

The cruiser was a medium ship of war with more speed and maneuverability than the battleship. The novel class of light cruiser had less overpowering weaponry than the cruiser and even more speed. The navy designed the many guns of such light cruisers to bring down planes, not to sink ships. Ships with more speed weighed less, and so planners cheated on the armor around a light cruiser's hull and deck; the steel shield was not thick enough to prevent damage from the weapons of other vessels. Cruisers were fast and might outrun or outflank other ships, certainly slower submarines. With a great array of antiaircraft guns, light cruisers could spray the air with lethal material and protect the fleet from enemy planes.

The navy was experimenting with the sorts of warships that might be effective, but the brass could not foresee which evolving operational approaches would prove useful. Since the time of the navy's last encounters with an enemy in 1917 and 1918, almost twenty-five years before, neither Americans nor their ships had fought enough to test the conjectures that before the war emanated from the old State, War, and Navy Building in Washington, DC. The navy did want the light cruisers to be more than antiaircraft ships, and in thinking up additional functions, planners expected too much. According to theory, the quick-moving cruisers might serve as flagships for groups of destroyers and also carry depth charges. In fact, a cruiser could be a death trap if called upon to attack surface vessels or if put in their way. The insubstantial armoring that gave light cruisers speed made them dangerously vulnerable to the shells of destroyers and battleships—and to the torpedoes of submarines. Many authorities have testified that these cruisers were high-speed ammunition dumps that ship-to-ship combat could easily wipe out.[10]

Construction had begun on such a light cruiser, the USS *Juneau*, at the end of May 1940 at the Federal Shipbuilding Company in Kearney, New Jersey. In the fall of 1941, before the United States went to war, the navy launched *Juneau*, named after the capital city of Alaska, then an American territory, and it was commissioned on February 14, 1942.

The navy had assigned the Sullivan "team" to the *Juneau*, although illness prevented Eddie Feuer from taking up the placement. On February 3, 1942, after one month's training, the remaining six were sent east to the vessel in New York City at the Brooklyn Navy Yard, across the East River, south of Lower Manhattan. The Sullivans were onboard on Valentine's Day as the captain commanded, "Man our ship and bring her to life."

That February day the navy used the brothers to extol national service. They had gotten some exposure when they enlisted together and made the papers; now the commissioning of the ship brought them more status. A photographer took a picture of the five of them that became a publicity shot for the navy—and later a famous emblem of sacrificial American devotion. That day the Sullivans shared the limelight with the four brothers of the Rogers family from Connecticut, also sailing on the *Juneau*. The military profited from the newspaper stories that proclaimed family loyalty—four Rogerses and five Sullivans—and downplayed stories that aired official concerns about relatives serving collectively. The navy put out of its mind that kin who stayed together could also easily be killed together. The service emphasized instead how the military kept families—two, three, four siblings—whole.

In movie houses at that time, in addition to two feature-length films—a shorter B-movie and a more respectable A-movie—theatergoers might watch a hodgepodge of other material, including a weekly compendium of important events from all over the world—a newsreel. Evincing the interest in enlistments (and the interest of the navy in on-screen publicity), the movie news now showcased the brothers. Alleta saw her sons on *Juneau* at the Strand Theater in Waterloo.[11]

In March 1942 the Sullivan parents got their first letter from Secretary of the Navy Frank Knox. He asked Alleta to "sponsor" a ship, which would call attention to the children's patriotism and the good cause for which the brothers were fighting. She agreed to christen a fleet tug, the USS *Tawasa*. Its construction would begin in the summer of 1942 in Portland, Oregon, and in April the *Courier* announced the tribute on page one. The family in fact now regularly made the front pages in Waterloo, and the city knew Alleta's children as "the navy's five Sullivans."

Tom had joined the Ancient Order of United Workmen, a fraternal lodge based in the Midwest. It had a women's auxiliary, the Degree of Honor Protective Association. After the navy requested that Alleta commission the *Tawasa*, the Degree of Honor asked Waterloo's mayor to salute her at a war-bond drive with an eagle-shaped brooch with five stars. Alleta wore this piece of jewelry to all of her subsequent public appearances.[12] The boys then sent a letter thanking the mayor for the tribute to their mother. "Keep your chins up" and "Keep 'em flying," the boys advised their hometown. In May the host of a stage show sponsoring Naval Relief introduced the now VIP parents, and in June Alleta chaired a Navy Mothers charity sale. By that time, the Navy Mothers in Waterloo had eighty-five members, doubled in size from when she had helped to found it four years before, in 1938.[13]

As if sent from on high, the war, the common enlistment, and the navy allowed Alleta to remake the standing of her nearest and dearest. At last, so far as the wider world knew, the Sullivans were well thought of, and the family had a cleaned-up image. We may only make surmises about what the Sullivans at home thought of their new look, or what Waterloo thought of them as just-folks celebrities.

Meanwhile, George, Frank, Red, Matt, and Al participated in the drinking and partying of sailors. Unaware that they were in a dangerously vulnerable ship, they were proud of their spanking new cruiser whose hustle was generally touted and whose decks bristled with weapons. They spent some time carousing in New York and its environs, the first taste for the younger boys of the off-duty revelry available to American servicemen. The navy started to record punishments to the Sullivans for more or less minor infractions on their shore leaves; these violations mainly concerned liquor, as well as infirmary treatment for possible infections—their "own misconduct."

Jack Dempsey, the famous former heavyweight boxing champion of the 1920s, had opened an eatery in Manhattan, Jack Dempsey's Broadway Restaurant. In the late winter of 1942, the Sullivan boys had their picture taken with the champ at his establishment. Dempsey made his money greeting and glad-handing patrons, but only the chosen. The picture with the Sullivans testified to the recognition that the boys had received by enlisting together.

Toward the end of March, the *Juneau* moved from the Brooklyn Navy Yard to nearby Gravesend Bay, a little farther south at Coney Island, to be loaded with machine-gun cartridges and armor-piercing shells. Then *Juneau* had a "shakedown" cruise along the Atlantic coast, first to the Norfolk Naval Base on the Virginia coast, to test the performance of the ship and to acclimate the new crew. This was not a cakewalk, for just offshore German U-boats were sinking merchant shipping, and in the Delaware Bay the ship anchored one evening as a deterrent to these enemy submarines. Two days later the *Juneau*'s crew responded with depth charges to chasten a nonexistent submarine. This embarrassment began the real training the Sullivans would have for the next month—antiaircraft drills, firing at fixed targets, and damage-control exercises.

At the beginning of May, *Juneau* departed Norfolk, Annapolis, and the Chesapeake and headed north again to New York. But before the men could enjoy another liberty in the city, the *Juneau* instead sailed down the East Coast and into the Caribbean to San Juan, Puerto Rico, and its first mission on May 3. The cruiser patrolled the French islands of Martinique and Guadeloupe in the Caribbean to prevent ships of the pro-German Vichy government in France from escaping the islands. Were these ships to break out, they could become part of the German fleet. Negotiations at Martinique avoided a fracas with the French, but not before, once again, the *Juneau* set off depth charges against a foe that was not under the sea. In the Caribbean George and Frank showed the ropes to the three younger boys, who got their first taste of the honky-tonk and the tawdry but absorbing pleasures that sailors might enjoy on leave in ports of call outside the United States.[14]

Via Saint Thomas and Puerto Rico, the *Juneau* returned to Gravesend Bay and then the nearby Brooklyn Navy Yard for another refurbishing. This time, in the last week of May, the boys got a home leave. Matt and

Al, and then George, briefly went back to Waterloo for what turned out to be a last visit. The *Courier* put a picture of Al and Matt in the paper, along with Tom and Alleta and grandson Jimmy.[15]

At the same time, Frank and Red "didn't get a chance" to make the trip: "Something had turned up, that kept us from coming," and they traveled to Pittsburgh for the weekend. Twenty-two-year-old Marge Jaros had written to Red after seeing his picture in a newspaper when the wire services picked up the navy's February publicity photo. He had written back, and she later recalled that they had met face-to-face in March. At the end of May, instead of going to Waterloo, Red rendezvoused with Jaros for a second time in Pittsburgh. Red's older brother went along for protection as did Bob McCann, a pal from the *Juneau* who lived in the city. According to Jaros, the second meeting did the trick: she and Red went to a movie on Friday night; on Saturday evening Marge and a friend of hers attended a party at the home of McCann's family; on Sunday afternoon, the two girls were again at the McCanns. When the sailors left later on Sunday, Red asked Marge to wait for him. Back on the *Juneau*, he sent her a ring and announced they were to wed. He wrote his parents that they should arrange to meet Marge and even suggested that she move to Waterloo at once and get a job at Rath's; eventually he wanted "to tie the knot" in Waterloo. Jaros visited May Abel and the Sullivans—Tom, Alleta, Gen, Keena, and Jimmy—in Waterloo at the end of October, but Red never saw her again.[16]

Matt followed Red in exploiting the fame of the Sullivan boys and succumbing to the frenzy of romance that American entry into the war had induced. All across the country young men and women who barely knew one another were declaring eternal love. Matt too had corresponded with a forward eighteen-year-old from Jersey City, Bea Imperato. As soon as Matt returned from his Iowa leave, Frank accompanied another brother on a date that began at Times Square. Matt and Bea stepped out several more times before the *Juneau* weighed anchor. He gave her an engagement gift of a silver and jade bracelet. They had been acquainted in person for a week when Matt waved good-bye to her for the last time at the end of May.

On June 1, all five Sullivans were back on the ship. One was married; two had fiancées; the two oldest boys were unattached. The *Juneau* had

The Sullivan Family. This was a partial, and last, reunion (from the archives of the Grout Museum of History and Science, Waterloo, Iowa).

its full crew of almost 700 and sailed from New York for Bayonne, New Jersey, where a large shipping terminal stuck out into New York Bay. Here workers strengthened the hull of the *Juneau*. Then, for almost two months the ship had duties in the North Atlantic, at first for ten days in June around Argentia, a city on the island of Newfoundland off the northeastern coast of Canada; and next along the Atlantic coast of North America, calling at US ports, including the Boston Navy Yard, where experts fitted the ship with the latest naval radar.

By July the ship had patrol and escort obligations in the Caribbean and South Atlantic. *Juneau* first sailed to Port-of-Spain, the capital of the holiday island Trinidad, off Venezuela in South America. The vessel protected the maritime commerce between North and South America and assisted in convoying supplies to England across the South Atlantic. The USS *Juneau* traversed the waters off northeastern Brazil with other American and English ships to discourage German submarines. The first part of this exercise ended with a stop and liberty toward the end of July on the Atlantic coast of Brazil at Recife, a vacation city more exotic than Port-of-Spain. The three younger boys were getting a good taste of navy life, and George and Frank were enjoying their status as navy veterans. MPs caught Red smuggling liquor into the ship before it took its place in a convoy. The *Juneau* and its partners headed east into the Atlantic, where they handed over merchant vessels to the British Royal Navy, which would squire them to England. *Juneau* then swept through the middle of the south-central Atlantic to the Cape Verde Islands, off north-central Africa, before a planned return to Recife and more convoy duty.

From the time they had left Waterloo, the boys and the family at home relied on the mail to stay in touch, as we have seen. Families sent off letters and packages to a central military postal depot. Almost always this material eventually made its way to the fighting men, even and often when they were in combat. In return, millions of servicemen, most not used to writing, composed brief and simple letters, always subject to censorship but part of a vital lifeline to home.

We must look to the Civil War for the primary antecedents to this wartime alteration in the postal service. Eighty years before, the Rebellion had also turned inarticulate farmhands into hesitant but straightforward writers and produced a notable literary effort by ordinary people in the United States, north and south.[17] In World War II the volume of letters so overwhelmed the government that it introduced a microfilming process called V-Mail. It was an extraordinary experiment in saving paper and reducing air shipping.[18]

After the *Juneau* had sailed from New York, and was rightly believed to be heading into danger, missives back and forth became even more important. The boys overseas and family and friends at home treasured these documents. Americans were fortunate compared to the families and men at war in Russia, Germany, and Japan, where the losses were so much greater and where the government's concern for the feelings of citizens and soldiers was so much less than in a sentimental and democratic culture like the United States. Unaccomplished Americans learned writing skills that previously only the privileged had possessed.

War transformed face-to-face connections that had been formal and polite at home, and the relationships of masses of Americans were reduced to—or celebrated on—paper. For millions, the written word surprisingly came to represent thought and feeling. Dispatches from the front became public circulars.

In thousands of households in the United States—and at 98 Adams Street—relatives recited for all to hear. They passed letters from hand to hand, and some commented as individual family members read silently. Then moms and dads and siblings again read the letters aloud. Neighbors were informed. The mail was the opposite of great literature. "How are you all?" letters would ask. "Is everyone OK?" "I hope you are all fine." "Do you have an address for . . . ?" "Have you by any chance seen . . . ?" "We are all good here." "The food is OK." "Last nite we were under attack, but it was not much." "I cant wait to come home." "We will beat these Japs" (if such an indication of location got through the censor).

In Waterloo, Alleta, Gen, and Keena—and occasionally even Tom and May Abel—corresponded. In return, the boys wrote all the time, though not at length, to family and to Waterloo friends. Five sailors; five immediate grown-up relatives at home; many motorcycle buddies. A lot of mail was generated—and saved. At 98 Adams Street, a "large dossier" existed by the end of 1942. On the ship, at one point, Red alone got fifty-three letters when the mail caught up with him. The letters that reached the Sullivan brothers have not survived. Most of the correspondence that the five boys sent to Waterloo has been lost. Red never received the letter of late October that his sister wrote him about meeting his fiancée. Gen told Red that she liked Marge a lot. In late February 1943, the post office returned this letter, marked "address unknown," to Adams Street.[19]

The extant letters home display a genuine affection on the part of the Sullivan sons for their parents and Gen. We have no sense of the boys' ideas before their enlistment, and it is unlikely that any of the five brothers ever wrote down connected thoughts about the world before they went away. Yet it is not romanticizing to see the effect on them of the huge errand that entangled them. They talked about coming home "if I ever do"; they reflected, even if minimally, "on politics and the war," after having been lectured to on issues of the conflict aboard ship; they were sad and nostalgic about what they called—five months into their enlistment—"the old days." National service in a great cause was altering the moral sensibilities of the Sullivan men.[20]

On joining up in January, the boys had announced that they wanted to go to Pearl Harbor in the Pacific to avenge their friends, but for some months they had been at the periphery of the naval combat against Germany in the Atlantic. In mid-August, however, the navy abruptly ordered *Juneau* to the Panama Canal for passage to the Pacific. In a hasty stop at Port-of-Spain in Trinidad the ship refueled and reached the Panama Canal on August 19, where the cruiser immediately made the transit through the canal. In Balboa Harbor, on the Pacific side of the Americas, where a few years before George and Frank had enjoyed its cheap amusements, the ship had minor repairs. The navy restocked *Juneau* while her crew relished liberty for two days; this time, the navy punished Al and not Red for drunkenness.

On August 22, *Juneau* set sail for the southwestern expanse of the Pacific, where most of the fighting was taking place. The boys journeyed almost 7,500 miles in waters that dwarfed the Atlantic, but got only marginally closer to Pearl Harbor, far off in the northeastern Pacific. Because the enemy controlled a huge area of the North-Central Pacific, the *Juneau* like many Allied ships took a far southern route to its destination. The ship sailed in the direction of Australia and New Zealand, both part of the British Commonwealth. *Juneau* first stopped at Tongatabu, the capital of a cluster of 176 small bits of property, the Tonga Islands. Britain protected the Tongas, a sovereign nation, but Tongatabu still lay 1,200 miles away from New Zealand to the southwest. The only well-known pieces of geography in the region were the Fiji Islands, 500 miles northwest. *Mutiny on the Bounty* with Clark Gable and Charles Laughton had made the Fijis memorable. This movie about an incident that left English seamen in Polynesia won the Academy Award for Best Picture in 1935. In Tongatabu, where the Sullivans arrived on September 4, their final port of call remained 1,800 miles to the north—the Solomon Islands, another clutch of English assets. The Solomons were at that very moment under attack from the Japanese. Here, the United States was fighting. In the Tongas, at the border of the

South Pacific, the Japanese Empire did not endanger the *Juneau*, but the ship was a long way from where it needed to be.

Vast distances, unpronounceable or unfamiliar names, alien geography, miles and miles of enigmatic ocean—what did the five brothers, the great majority of their provincial uniformed comrades, and almost all other Americans wonder about this enormous stage? What did they pick up about the Pacific war? There was California, the US West Coast, and to its west in the Pacific the American base at Pearl Harbor, which the Japanese had sneak-attacked. The Sullivans had wanted to go there to even the score for people like Bill Ball. From Pearl Harbor, the five might have imagined they would advance farther west—closer to Tokyo—to fight the Japanese. Now the boys would fight, but they would do battle some 3,500 miles southwest of Pearl Harbor and 3,400 southeast of Tokyo! It is unlikely that the Sullivans and their comrades could map out their mission—probably all they knew was that they were not on their way to Hawaii to punish the Japanese.

In its entirety, to servicemen and families at home, the Pacific appeared as an uncharted zone, a mysterious and gargantuan military chessboard. At the same time, back in Waterloo, Tom and Alleta would have had a vivid sense of the dangers that lay in wait for their offspring. By August 1942, as Americans marked up their world maps, the public could read almost every day about battles in the South Pacific and about a place called Guadalcanal, the chief of the Solomon Islands. In September 1942, John Ford's propaganda-documentary film about the Pacific War arrived at theaters across the United States. One of America's most accomplished movie directors, Ford was responsible for some of the famous cinema of the era, including *Stagecoach* (1939), *The Grapes of Wrath* (1940), and *How Green Was My Valley* (1941). In 1942 he was making movies for the military, and his eighteen-minute short subject, *The Battle of Midway*, won the Academy Award for Best Documentary that year. Earlier in 1942, the Americans had defeated the Japanese in a major clash, both unforeseen and unique. Midway—at least it had a name and location Americans could understand—was in the Central Pacific west of Hawaii and far from the Solomon Islands. Although the victory did not portend a straightforward rush west to Japan, it did make vivid the ocean violence. The electrifying documentary, which

Ford filmed in part himself, contained unedited footage of the Imperial Japanese assaults on the American navy—dogfights in the air; naval guns in action; airmen rescued in the water after being shot down; burial in the ocean. The film screened in Waterloo in the early fall.[21] The Sullivans at home had plenty to worry about when they thought about their boys.

In the Southwest Pacific the Sullivan men had involved themselves in a breathtaking world-historic conflict.

# CHAPTER FOUR

## GUADALCANAL

In the aftermath of Pearl Harbor, many Americans feared that the Japanese would invade the West Coast, but Imperial designs, although grand, did not include the continental United States. Japan initiated some desperate moves with the attack on Hawaii. A sanctimonious and powerful America had confronted a proud and militaristic Imperial people with two alternatives—a junior partnership with the United States in Asia and the relinquishing of China, the jewel in the Japanese crown of empire; or war. In crippling the fleet at Pearl Harbor and compromising American naval power, the Japanese anticipated the creation of a rough shield that would allow them to preserve a new Pacific realm. It was more or less a throw of the dice. They did not intend to go on the offensive in North America.

On the mainland of Asia, Japan colonized Korea to the north; substantial parts of the coast of China; Indochina—Vietnam, Cambodia, and Laos—in Southeast Asia; and Burma in South Asia, surrounding the southwestern coast of China with Japanese satellites. After the island city-state of Singapore fell in British Malaya, the Japanese Empire included this peninsular domain. In addition, the Japanese controlled collections of islands off the Pacific rimland, primarily the Dutch East Indies. Next, to the north, was the Philippines, a spread of islands to which the United States had granted independence in 1939. There the American general Douglas MacArthur had commanded the military. After Pearl Harbor and the subsequent loss of the Philippines, he had fled to Australia, much farther south.

The island acreage—and more to the east in the Central Pacific—formed a large arc. The ring of properties protected a gigantic and far-flung sphere of influence and the home islands of Japan, chief among them Honshu, where the imposing city of Tokyo embodied the glory of the Empire of the Rising Sun. A weakened American navy, Japan's strategists both hoped and reasoned, would not be able to penetrate Japan's Pacific holdings.

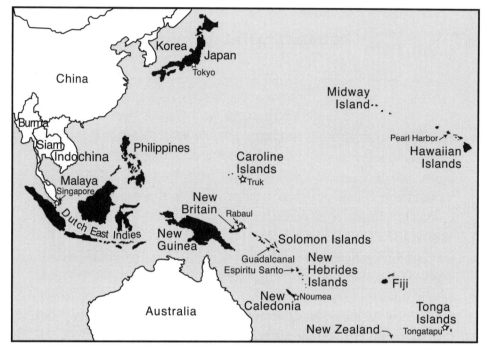

**Asia-Pacific Theater**

An extreme Japanese element wanted to follow up the attack on Pearl Harbor and to threaten American rule in Hawaii. In the northern Pacific, Midway Island, a minor American protectorate about two-thirds of the way from Tokyo to Honolulu, was to form Japan's spear point. The amazing American victory at Midway, about which John Ford had produced his documentary, taught that the Empire could not easily move farther east and predisposed the Japanese to concentrate their efforts elsewhere. At the same time, while the victory convinced American strategists that the security of Hawaii need not be the only priority, the victory did not make appealing a direct assault from Midway on essential Japanese assets in the northwestern Pacific.

The United States was pitiably ill equipped for war on the two widely separated Atlantic and Pacific fronts. Despite the public fear and hatred of Japan, top policy makers regarded the war against Germany as more important than the war against the Japanese. In the early going, aggressive American navy leaders did claim for the Pacific theater and the South Pacific the lion's share of the scarce but growing US resources. But in 1942 the untried American naval forces in the Pacific would, in costly encounters, only slowly gain superiority against the Japanese. Moreover, the United States did not have many choices. No army invasion, with the help of the navy, could be launched against German-occupied Western Europe, and the navy could not move west from Midway. Necessity drove American operations.

The United States would mount an offensive in the region of Australia and New Zealand. Australia in the far South Pacific, where MacArthur retreated, was the redoubt of the West. Among alternative routes to Tokyo the United States had no other place realistically to contest Japan but the deep south. Because the Japanese took to fortifying positions in the south after Midway, they invited combat with the United States "down under," at the bottom of the world. Australia's viewpoint instructs us of the Pacific. A great curve of island territories, large and small, governed by different powers, formed a belt around the north of Australia. Command of these regions by the Japanese, especially those in the great northeast, would encircle the roof of Australia, and Japan might extend its dominion to this British commonwealth.

The enemy intended at least to prevent Commonwealth and American troops from moving north and west, and to contain the Allies. Or the Japanese might cut off supply routes from the United States to Australia and the huge island of New Guinea to Australia's north, complexly administered by various Western powers. The Americans rightly worried about an Imperial assault. In 1942, the fighting off the Australian northeast in which the Sullivans participated would create bases from which Japan would expand, or bases from which the Allies would destroy Japan.

The Japanese held some high cards. They operated from the Japanese territory of the Caroline Islands, site of a major naval base on the island of Truk, north of Australia and New Guinea. In early 1942, the Empire captured the port of Rabaul, the capital city of the island of New Britain, off the coast of New Guinea. The Japanese turned Rabaul into a hub of operations and next landed on mainland New Guinea, where they gained a foothold. Japan hoped to bomb New Guinea into submission from a forward base and had some success using the nearby island of Bougainville to the south, at the northern extreme of the Solomon Islands, controlled by England. By May 1942 the Japanese had established their presence in the Solomons themselves and, in June, set up an airfield on the most important property in this chain, Guadalcanal, located at the southern end. A Guadalcanal airstrip would allow the Japanese to rule the airlanes to New Guinea. From the American perspective, the enemy had moved from Truk, to Rabaul, to New Guinea, to Bougainville, to Guadalcanal, advancing southeast to the safe havens of the beleaguered United States.

The US Navy had designated what amounted to a southern headquarters in Auckland, New Zealand, distant from the Japanese-dominated Pacific but also out of the action. Then Tongatabu in the Tongas, to the northeast of New Zealand, became a bastion; it had been the point of departure for *Juneau* and the Sullivans on their way to the emerging Pacific theater. By March 1942, Noumea on the island of New Caledonia, a former French colony north of New Zealand, had become the navy's South Pacific command post. Almost 1,100 miles west of Tongatabu, New Caledonia still lay far to the south of the Japanese although closer to the fighting. While the navy had formally chosen Noumea as headquarters in early November, in July the United States established another base, on Espiritu Santo, the foremost of the New Hebrides Islands, run by the British and French. North of Noumea, Espiritu Santo was still south of the Solomons. In the first part of 1942, the Americans had inched closer to sustained encounter with Japan—from Auckland to Tongatabu, to Noumea, to Espiritu Santo. They wanted to guard Australia and to stake out locations for an offensive against the Japanese.

Initially, as a noted participant and historian of the conflict has written, the navy knew no more than the American people about the Solomon Islands. If naval higher-ups "had been embarked on a voyage to the moon . . . [they] would have been only a little more ignorant of their destination."[1] The Americans concentrated on the great Japanese center of Rabaul, but the stepping-stone to Rabaul became the Solomons' Guadalcanal, which would take on its own singular importance.

In August 1942, less than two months after the Japanese had begun their airfield on Guadalcanal, Allied forces—mainly American Marines assisted by the navy—landed on the island. They drove off Japan's small contingent working on the airstrip, and completed their own, Henderson Field. In time a considerable presence of some 20,000 troops defended Henderson Field. The Americans dug in, and they organized attacks on Japanese transport vessels and ships of war in the area. But the United States had only a precarious air superiority. A major embarrassing defeat of the American navy had accompanied the insertion of the Marines on Guadalcanal: on the night of August 8–9, around nearby Savo Island, the Japanese had sent US warships to the bottom. The rout weakened the American presence and prompted the deployment of *Juneau*—and other ships—to the South Pacific to bolster the navy. On Guadalcanal itself Japan besieged Henderson Field. The United States had regularly to resupply and reenforce the airstrip because its critical position attracted the Japanese. Moreover, soldiers of the Imperial Army already on Guadalcanal gave the enemy traction and constantly endangered the Marines. Both the United States and Japan had a foothold, and they constantly fought on and around the island. Yet without new forces after the disaster at Savo Island, the navy could not protect the Americans on Guadalcanal.

On their way to the Solomons, the Sullivans did not differ much from compatriots who had also been summoned to this part of the globe. The American ships assembling thousands of miles from home included men from across the United States, previously tucked away in towns large and small, with little jobs and little plans. Taken singly these sailors were ordinary fellows like the Sullivans—lower socioeconomic groups of unschooled whites. But together they once again, as in previous conflicts, provided the manpower that fueled war, operated huge machines, and consumed resources extravagantly. A terrible and lethal contest enmeshed all of these young men. The sparring in the air, at sea, and on land around Henderson Field was one of the most ferocious encounters the navy had during World War II. The five Sullivans had spent most of their lives in the North End of Waterloo, but their bones would be spread over endless reaches of the South Pacific.

Attempts by the Japanese in the late summer of 1942 to overrun the airfield had failed but continued into the fall, when the big push culminated. *Juneau* arrived in the Tonga Islands on September 4, and by September 10 the ship had traveled the 1,200 miles from the Tongas to Noumea and undertaken convoy duties. The cruiser assisted in the delivery of men, planes, and supplies to the embedded Americans on Guadalcanal. In defense of aircraft carriers, light cruisers such as the *Juneau* warded off the Japanese air force. On September 15, the Japanese torpedoed the carrier *Wasp*. When the ship was hit, some 200 seamen died and some 400 were wounded. As a member of *Wasp*'s task force, the *Juneau* rescued some of the carrier's crew, taking them to Espiritu Santo the following day. Although the *Juneau* had neither fired nor been fired upon, the Sullivans got a taste of conflict at sea. In troubled waters, the brothers would have seen the screaming men in the ocean and the wounded while they were taken to the makeshift hospital on Espiritu Santo. The reality of the war was coming home. Back in New Caledonia's Noumea on September 17, the *Juneau* refueled and replenished its ammunition.

After the *Wasp* went down, the navy assigned *Juneau* to a task force that the carrier *Hornet* led, and these warships were involved in further inconclusive skirmishes. Then, for more than a month, the *Juneau* had no contact with the foe, and the ship and the boys were still receiving mail from home and sending back letters. On October 24 the *Juneau*, with the *Hornet*, left Noumea. The ships steamed north, where the Americans found a fight near a desolate collection of four volcanic mounds, the Santa Cruz Islands, some 250 miles southeast of Guadalcanal. While other elements of the Imperial military pounded Henderson Field, Japan's navy surrounding the Santa Cruz Islands intercepted the Americans. This time Japan bloodied *Juneau*, although the cruiser had a minor role in the battle. When enemy planes attacked the *Hornet*, the *Juneau* did the job it was devised to do, and its sailors brought down planes with antiaircraft fire.

Red, Matt, and Al loaded shells into the *Juneau*'s guns, while Frank, a boatswain, would have been on the bridge. Manning the depth-charge rack, George would have awaited orders in case Japanese submarines were spotted. In the end, the carrier *Hornet* followed *Wasp* to the bottom. The Japanese navy so severely damaged *Hornet* that Admiral William "Bull" Halsey, now in charge in Noumea, ordered it scuttled, although the Japanese sank it on the early morning of October 27.

The *Juneau* suffered only minor losses, and its executive officer noted that while the conduct of the crew was "without exception, praiseworthy," no member was "sufficiently outstanding or remarkable" as to merit special recognition.[2] Yet the *Juneau* had destroyed several enemy planes and again pulled American airmen from the Pacific. The Sullivans had been in combat. By October 31 the ship docked in Noumea and was resupplied and cleaned up. The men enjoyed a short leave in the town, which still had some of the character of a provincial French colonial enclave, although war had overrun it with mountains of equipment, servicemen, bars, and prostitutes.

Just at the end of George and Frank's first tour of duty in early 1941, the navy had converted their ship, the USS *Hovey*, from a destroyer to a minesweeper. During the war she had escort duties around Guadalcanal before the Japanese sank her in January 1945; the two oldest boys may have met some of their former shipmates at the end of 1942.[3] On November 7, 1942, Robert Madaris and Paul Tharp from Waterloo passed the *Juneau* in Noumea's port, on a launch from their own ship. They haled seamen on the *Juneau*, and the five brothers clambered out on the deck. For a few minutes they reminisced with the other two sailors from Waterloo.[4] Two days before, back in Iowa, Madaris's mother had spent the afternoon with Alleta Sullivan working together in the Navy Mothers charity.[5] Later, on November 8, when the boys sent their last letters to Waterloo, their mail vaguely referred to the "Jaybirds" (Japanese planes). Tom and Alleta might at least have had an inkling of what war was like for the *Juneau* in treacherous seas.

During this early November layover, at the urging of their officers, two of the four Rogers brothers left the *Juneau*. After the transfer of the Rogers siblings, the Sullivans apparently agreed to split up when the navy would next be able to reassign them. Although George and Frank planned not to stick together with their three younger brothers, the two older boys never got the chance to leave the ship. In addition to the remaining Rogers brothers, seven other families had two brothers on the vessel, plus the five Sullivans and the remaining motorcycle club member, Arnie Ray.

On November 8, the *Juneau* set off from safe harbor for the last time. Noumea gave the squadron of ships a full-court farewell. Four days later the ship got into a minor fight chaperoning transport vessels that were landing men and supplies near Henderson Field. The *Juneau* opened up its guns once more against enemy planes. The antiaircraft weapons foiled the attack, and the *Juneau* was unscathed. Yet again the brothers came under fire on November 12.

Although several indecisive matchups involving air, sea, and land forces took place in September, October, and November—and continued into February 1943—both sides looked to end the stalemate. In retrospect, we can see that the crucial battles took place in the four days following the daytime dust-up of November 12.

In the late evening and early morning of November 12–13, with a large convoy from New Britain's Rabaul, the Japanese attempted to land supplies and some 7,000 infantry troops who would retake Henderson Field. Off the coast of Guadalcanal, a US force that included the *Juneau* approached from the south. The United States had two heavy cruisers, three light cruisers (counting the *Juneau*), and eight destroyers—thirteen ships in all. The Japanese had fourteen. Overall, the matchup was pretty even, although the Japanese outclassed the Americans. Both sides made mistakes that the near-total darkness and bad weather magnified. While Japan outgunned the less-experienced and barely trained Americans and put them at a disadvantage, the chaos of the night fighting, with both sides at times shelling their own vessels, may have helped the United States.

The hostilities, which commentators have found the most brutal the US Navy faced during the war, lasted only some forty minutes. Yet when the senior officers on each side disengaged, commentators have also agreed that the Japanese, although not unscarred, were positioned to overrun Henderson Field and land a large number of their own forces. The Americans had suffered crushing losses. Now for a third time the brothers had participated in the dreadfulness of sea warfare.

*Juneau*, designed only to bring down enemy airplanes with its guns, fought in a real ship-versus-ship contest for which it was unsuited. Although the role of the light cruiser in this fight is still indeterminate, the Sullivans witnessed serious injury to their boat, its steering and guns crippled by a torpedo. The "fish" hit forward and killed some twenty men, including a member of the Sullivan "team," Arnie Ray. The keel

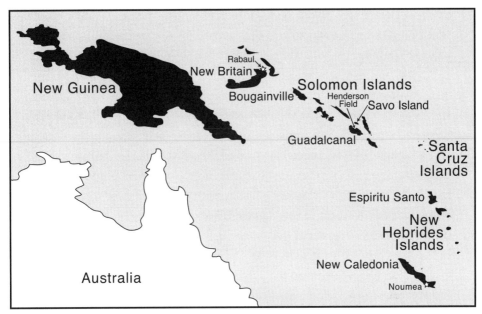

# Battles of Guadalcanal, October–November 1942

buckled, and the propellers jammed; the ship listed to its port side with its prow up; the stink of fuel made it difficult to breathe below deck. During the battle sailors vomited and wept on the ship; others tried to claw their way into the steel belly of the vessel to hide from the barrage.[6] George Sullivan suffered a mild injury to his back; he had been thrown on the deck of the ship when the submarine's missile struck. After a fearful time of only ten to fifteen minutes, *Juneau* fell out of action, and its captain awkwardly navigated it east.

What did the experience and distress do to the five young sailors? Combat makes some men permanently incapable of living again in a peaceful social order. Violence transfigures still others, and they come to a level of maturity in meeting existential problems that they would never have reached in civilian life. Did any of the boys think of the great struggle in terms other than personal revenge? Did any one of them meditate on the mysteries of life? Or think about going home and making a different path for himself? We will never know the answers to these questions. If the war altered only one—George, Frank, Red, Matt, or Al—the conversion would have given new meaning to their early years.

At the end of the firefights in the early hours of November 13, the American defenders of Henderson Field had only one light cruiser (*Helena*) and a destroyer (*Fletcher*) able to go at it again, while the Japanese had a battleship, a cruiser, and four destroyers. Nonetheless, each side disengaged, and when the Imperial commander retired, the Japanese effectively postponed their invasion of Guadalcanal and Henderson Field. The American navy had lost two rear admirals and seven ships. Captain Gilbert Hoover of the *Helena* became the senior officer of the only US forces that had been in the battle and that could function cohesively, although they were in no condition to scuffle. Captain Hoover led the *Helena* and the *Fletcher,* as well as the heavily damaged cruiser *San Francisco* in addition to the smashed-up destroyers, *Sterrett* and *O'Bannon*, and finally the gravely hurt *Juneau*, which had just been able to creep out of the area. In the immediate aftermath of the fight, *Juneau*'s captain first thought of finding a nearby cove to make repairs but was able to do enough patching to permit the cruiser to join Hoover's flotilla. Although the torpedo did not fully disable *Juneau*, the ship was probably the most endangered among Hoover's six. By early morning, this maimed group was crawling from the scene toward the comparative safety of Allied bases to the south.

Hoover sent *O'Bannon* ahead. Without giving away the position of the other ships to the enemy, *O'Bannon* would radio a report on the battle and request air cover. The remaining ships were in no condition for another set-to with the Japanese and desperately needed assistance. They made agonizingly slow progress, with the *Juneau* moving very slowly at the rear. In addition to the damage to *Juneau*'s structural integrity, fumes from the torpedo hit continued to foul the air belowdecks. Crowded together topside were sun-blistered comrades, hoping to get to Espiritu Santo alive. We can bet they did not display the same bravado as when the *Juneau* was commissioned in February 1942, just ten months before. The Sullivans were again adrift, but never in greater peril. We cannot know what they felt, but surely they understood the hazards of their situation.

By 10:45 A.M. that morning *Juneau* was some 125 miles from where it had been disabled, 25 miles southwest of San Cristobal (now Makira), the most southern of the Solomons and nearly 500 miles from even a comparatively safe harbor. About 11:00 A.M. a Japanese submarine, tracking the ailing vessels, aimed to sink the *San Francisco*. The sub missed its target and at 11:01 A.M. hit instead the already off-kilter *Juneau*.

The *Juneau* did not subside slowly. Instead, a sudden and furious eruption took her into the deep, and underwater explosions followed, probably the result of boilers bursting. In the eruption the ship broke in two, and the forward part of *Juneau*, where the torpedo struck, at once disappeared. Then the sea swallowed up the stern. The blasts shot up into the air an array of material. Fragments of the cruiser struck her sister ships, the *Helena* and the *San Francisco*. The turret from a huge antiaircraft gun flew from the vanishing vessel to within 100 yards of the *Fletcher*. One witness wrote that there was a "large single explosion" and a "cloud of black, yellow black, and brown smoke." Another officer related in the aftermath: "It is certain that all on board perished. Nothing could be seen in the water when smoke lifted."

Sailors belowdecks in *Juneau* were almost certainly drowned at once. The explosion might have sucked most of those on deck to the bottom while it blew others to bits—body parts fell from the sky. Some sailors, however, were tossed clear of immediate destruction, although reports and stories by survivors concerning what happened disagree.

By 11:30 A.M., within a half-hour of the torpedo hit, an American B-17 bomber appeared overhead the ships. *Helena* and the plane exchanged signals about the loss of *Juneau*, as the remains of the task force left the area of the attack. Hoover may have asked if there were any men who had not gone down with the ship. He also asked the plane to inform headquarters of the event so that *Helena* would not have to relax its order of radio silence, although since the Japanese had already struck, the concern for such silence seems beside the point. Apparently a short time later, a message came back from the airplane telling of survivors. It is uncertain if Hoover at this point knew that not all of the *Juneau*'s sailors had died, for, according to his immediate report, *Juneau* was "completely destroyed" and had "completely disappear[ed], and "no search was made" for anyone who might have lived. The detonation may have convinced him that just a couple of men, or even none, were still breathing. A rescue attempt risked the lives of hundreds of Americans on the other ships, limping along to escape further attack. The five ships would travel more quickly to Espiritu Santo because they did not have to slow down to accommodate the *Juneau*. Indeed, Hoover ordered the *Fletcher*, which had turned to look for men in the ocean, to resume its southerly course. Hoover probably thought that the B-17 would notify Espiritu Santo and, perhaps, that headquarters would send aid to anyone left. But, again, we lack clarity on these critical issues.[7]

When the B-17 located the men who did not sink with the *Juneau*, the airplane crew saw that Hoover had been dramatically wrong, if he thought no one had escaped. From what we can estimate, about 500–600 sailors drowned at once. But another 100–200, in all likelihood those who had been on the deck of the ship, were pitched clear. Many of these soon died of injuries, or of poisoning by the black fuel oil, or from scalding. The sailors were in pitiful shape—scared in the deep sea or in shock, injured from the blast, cut from flying metal, burned from the fire of the blowup, covered with thick oil, belching saltwater. Yet for an initial period, perhaps over 100 clung together using the debris from the cruiser—mattresses, life jackets, tarpaulins, and three oval rafts, 10 feet by 5 feet, with floors of wooden slats and attached ropes to accommodate hangers-on. Around the living floated dead friends and shipmates, the quickly dying, and assorted human carnage. The plane overhead estimated how many—60? 100?—in the rafts and many more thrashing in the ocean. In a huge oil slick, as one of the airmen wrote in his diary, men were drifting, hugging wreckage, or swimming to preservers, "floating in the mess like peanuts in brittle." An air-force gunner waved to the stressed and injured, and while they were dispirited at seeing their convoy move away, they rightly thought that the B-17 had signaled that help was on the way. According to one testimony, the plane not only informed *Helena* of those in the sea; it went back and again circled the pathetic collection treading water near where *Juneau* had disappeared.[8]

Nonetheless, navy officers did not have *Juneau* on their minds. A new group of American ships was being put together, and the Japanese too planned a further strike against Henderson Field. At about the same time as *Juneau* went under, in the late morning off the coast of Guadalcanal, other American warcraft were undertaking a cleanup of the night before: they sank a floundering and nearly destroyed Japanese ship, assisted their own vessels in the area, and rescued sailors who were adrift. The next day, November 14, US naval and airpower pounded Japanese transports still attempting to land troops and supplies on the island, and by the evening Admiral Halsey had assembled his second force just in time to ward off yet another big assault by Japan. On the night of November 14–15, some Japanese soldiers landed, but Allied planes and the new collection of ships destroyed most of the Japanese supplies and stymied the disembarkation of the troops.

This loss shattered Japan's crusade to recapture Henderson Field. By early December the Empire did not dispute American domination of Guadalcanal, though fighting continued off and on for the next three months. In the eyes of many experts, the disastrous US losses of November 13, when the *Juneau* and other ships were trounced, had given the Americans a needed extra day. The US sacrifices diminished the strength of the enemy just enough and caused the Japanese to lose essential time. From now on, the United States would have a forward base. The Japanese significantly drew back in consequence of the bloodletting of November 14–15.[9]

During this time, in the ocean, the survivors of *Juneau* waited for help. The aircraft that had spotted them on the late morning of November 13 patrolled for several hours, returned to the area, dumped some supplies, and later filed reports at Espiritu Santo. In the next couple of days on other missions, the B-17 continued to note *Juneau*'s men in the water, and a second plane also dropped an inflatable raft. But the information on the plight of the *Juneau*'s sailors sat in a pile of messages and did not at once reach Noumea, farther south where Halsey had his headquarters. Later, Captain Hoover and other officers themselves described the loss of the *Juneau* when they got to Espiritu Santo. As soon as Halsey learned what had happened, he ordered an immediate air and sea search of the area in which *Juneau* had sunk, although this expedition did not take place instantly. Halsey at once stripped Hoover of his command for not trying to rescue the men in the Pacific.[10]

The Japanese submarine's destruction of *Juneau* was in some measure a footnote or afterthought or exclamation point to the battle of November 13. And the sinking occurred just before the equally consequential contest of the night of November 14–15 and deflected attention from Hoover and his ailing ships. We have commonly come to call this chaos and disarray the "fog of war." Nonetheless, the reader should be aware of the various foul-ups and allegations of fault that punctuated the final act of this drama. Halsey himself, later in the war, barely escaped censure for his own misjudgments in other arenas of the conflict.

The navy did not exactly forget the men floating in the ocean, but at least for the moment they did not occupy anyone's attention. Time passed. The remains of *Juneau*'s crew hung on to the rafts, some cork netting strung out behind the rafts, and finally the inflatable boat that had been dropped near them. But fewer and fewer men—day after day in the blazing sun but exposed to cold at night and already hurt or debilitated—stayed alive. At first they had a little food, water, and cigarettes from the emergency rations on the rafts, but these were soon gone, consumed by the men, contaminated by the filthy sea, or lost. Weakened by the elements in the coming week, individuals came to blows with one another, drifted into madness, or left the rafts to be eaten by sharks—the common cause of death.

From what we can figure out, at least Frank, Red, and Matt died when the ship sank, apparently inside it, although we have one recollection that Red was alive in the early moments after the sinking. Two dead and probably three. Al may also have still been among the living, one of the 100-plus men who were catapulted into the ocean. In any event he did not last long. Four siblings gone. George, however, apparently lingered on the raft for several days, although all the testimony is suspect; only one report, which does not mention the Sullivans, antedates their transformation into American heroes. Of the small number who later told the tale, a couple remembered George first searching in the wreckage for his brothers. He used rolls of toilet paper floating in the water to wipe the oil from the faces of men in the ocean, trying to identify other Sullivans. From time to time, he would cry out for them. But after three or four days, hallucinating and with diminished strength, George lost his senses. By now sharks were orbiting the ever-diminishing population of men. One night, according to one of the few who did not die, George declared that he was going to take a bath. He took off his clothes and jumped into the water. A little way from his raft, "A shark came and grabbed him and that was the end of him. I never seen him again."[11]

After a week in the water, on November 19 and November 20, 10 men from a crew that numbered roughly between 660 and 690 made it to the comparative safety of Espiritu Santo. Five individuals were saved by air; a destroyer saved 2—1 at a time; a storm blew 3 in the rubber boat to an island where they were later rescued. Only 10.

The Sullivans were tossed into a kingdom of darkness and unrest. At work were fate and chance but not much free will. The brothers were young, certainly unknown to themselves. They took their secrets with them—of what they were and what they might have been. All five. By December 10 the highest naval authorities had a comprehensive account of what happened and had also carefully reviewed Hoover's obligations and how he had behaved. The admirals accepted Halsey's instant punishment of *Helena*'s captain and fretted about the advisability of having had the Sullivans on the same vessel.[12]

# CHAPTER FIVE

## NATIONAL HEROES

The mailman delivered the final letters from the boys to family and friends in Waterloo just before Christmas 1942. The brothers had dated them November 8, the day *Juneau* had left Noumea for the last time. The folks at home worried, but they also knew that war raged in the South Pacific and that conditions might prevent either the writing of letters or their dispatch. It did not help that, inevitably, the American government would not broadcast much news about deadly encounters until long after they had taken place. For the Sullivans in Waterloo, Christmas and New Year's did not pass easily. Then, on January 5, Alleta learned from a neighbor who had a son in combat that one of his letters had said: "Isn't it a shame about the Sullivan boys! I heard that their ship was sunk."[1] This could be hearsay or scuttlebutt, one of the many rumors that pervaded the daily lives of citizens in the United States ignorant of so many of the gory details of the war. But it also might be a failure of censorship.

Many anxious families asked their government directly about the status of their sons during World War II. This sort of inquiry frequently overwhelmed the War and Navy Departments and other agencies: "Dear Sir, Your High Excellency Secretary of War, Mr. Henry Stimson: Can you please tell me what has happened to my boy? I don't mean to disturb you but. . . . "

In January, after Alleta took in the neighbor's gossip, she wrote the Department of the Navy in her own hand:

Waterloo Ia, Jan 1943

Bureau Naval Personnel
Dear Sirs:
I am writing you in regards to a rumor going around that my five sons have been killed in action in November. A friend from here came and told me she got a letter from her son and he heard my five sons were killed.

It is all over town, and I am so worried. My five sons joined the Navy a year ago, Jan. 3, 1942. They are on the Cruiser, U.S.S. JU-NEAU. The last I heard from them was Nov. 8th. That is, it was dated Nov. 8th, U.S. Navy.

Their names are George T., Francis Henry, Joseph E., Madison A., and Albert L. If it is so, please let me know the truth. I am to christen the U.S.S. TAWASA Feb. 12th at Portland, Oregon. If anything has happened to my five sons, I will still christen the ship as it was their wish that I do so. I hated to bother you, but it has worried me so that I wanted to know if it was true. So please tell me. It was hard to give five sons all at once to the Navy, but I am proud of my boys that they can serve and help protect their country. George and Francis served four years on the U.S.S. HOVEY, and I had the pleasure to go aboard their ship in 1937.

I am so happy the Navy has bestowed the honor on me to christen the U.S.S. TAWASA. My husband and daughter are going to Portland with me. I remain,

> Sincerely,
> /s/ Mrs. Alleta Sullivan
> 98 Adams Street
> Waterloo, Iowa[2]

The well-known Sullivan brothers had given the navy some great publicity nine months earlier. On January 12, Alleta's letter was received and apparently at once reached some important military bureaucrats.

By coincidence, the navy had just decided to inform Americans of the mid-November fighting. The day before the service got the letter, it had taken on the forbidding chore of telling families that the *Juneau* had gone down. Although bureaucracy and ineptitude, and not malevolence, were at issue, almost two months had gone by since the destruction of the cruiser. In the case of the Sullivans, however, the navy found inadequate the usual telegram—"The Secretary of the Navy regrets to inform you. . . . "

On Monday morning, January 11, in the early hours while Tom was preparing to go off to the freight yard, a dark sedan pulled up in front of 98 Adams. Three navy men, dressed in black uniforms, got out of the car. Their leader, Lieutenant Commander Truman Jones, ran the recruiting center in Des Moines that had sworn in the brothers a year before. Now the navy had ordered him, with his delegation, personally to inform the Sullivan parents and Keena Rooff Sullivan that the five young men were missing in action.

As Jones and his deputies approached the house, Tom had to know something bad had occurred. After he invited the naval officers in but before they could speak, Tom roused the rest of the family. Gen, Keena, and Alleta (and probably May Abel) padded into the living room in bathrobes and slippers. Alleta, or more likely some writer who helped her compose the story, later wrote, "I think we all had a premonition of what the news was going to be."[3] Commander Jones said, "I'm afraid I'm bringing you very bad news." The way these things were ordinarily done, "you'd get a telegram right from the Navy Department, but because. . . . " Silence. In some accounts, someone asked "Which one?" and the answer was "All five." In any event Jones pronounced: "The Navy Department deeply regrets to inform you that your sons Albert, . . . Francis, . . . George, . . . Joseph, . . . and Madison Sullivan are missing in action in the South Pacific."

The navy men and the dismayed remnants of the Sullivan family stood around for some moments in grief and embarrassed silence. Then Tom said that he had to go to work and asked the commander to excuse him. He kissed his wife and left the house, and the discomfited visitors soon followed. The women collapsed in tears.

An unimaginable disaster had engulfed this family.

Sometime during the day of January 11, Tom got in touch with his brother in Harpers Ferry. That evening, Monday, Tom did not go home. The two older Sullivans met in Dubuque and got drunk at Huss House. Another story tells us that Tom continued this binge at a Waterloo bar when he returned to town on Tuesday.

Meanwhile, once Lieutenant Jones notified Washington that he had carried out his uncomfortable duty, the navy sent the family a formal telegram. Immediately thereafter officials issued a public statement about the successes America had achieved in the battles over the Solomon Islands, about the heavy losses in life, and about the trial that was befalling the Sullivan family. The military proclaimed the courage of

All Five. This is the publicity still from the crucial moment in the film (Everett Collection).

the five brothers, missing in action (and certainly believed dead). But the navy noted that the presence of the five on the *Juneau* was "at the insistence of the brothers themselves in contradiction to the repeated recommendations of the ship's executive officer." The statement concluded: "Serving together had been one condition of their enlistment." Although this was false, the untruth did not clear the navy of responsibility for having the Sullivans on one ship. If service together had been a condition of enlistment, the navy had merely to decline to enroll them if it wished to eliminate the risk of having five brothers dying together.

On Monday afternoon, with Tom still on his freight run, Waterloo's *Daily Courier* sent a reporter and a photographer to the Sullivan women on Adams Street. Other journalists soon descended on Waterloo, shameless in their craving for a human-interest story. In the next few days, pictures of the family—both before and after—appeared in newspapers across the country, and articles stressed the patriotism of the boys at the bottom of the Pacific and the fortitude of the family, especially Alleta.

In these initial numbing days Americans learned about the Sulli-vans through words that journalists probably put into Alleta's mouth, reported as her response to the deaths of five of her children:

> The boys always wrote at the end of their letters, "Keep your chin up," and now's a good time to do that. . . . They were good average American boys. . . . They all had gone to high school and they played basketball there and on the church team. . . . I am going to do ev-erything I can to win this war. . . . We got twenty-eight Jap planes, didn't we, and aren't the Russians doing well? . . . Everyone should work harder to turn out more ships, and to help win the war. Moth-ers should pray for their boys and, above all, be brave and keep their chins up. . . . My boys did not die in vain.[4]

Photographers from Chicago papers roamed Waterloo taking pic-tures of the boys' schools, the Sullivans' sometime church, and IC in-stallations, in addition to 98 Adams. Tom and Alleta allowed camera crews from the motion picture newsreel companies into their home. Sound equipment and thick electric cables ran through the house.[5] The brothers had mustered newsreel attention when they enlisted together the year before, and now their parents would also figure in movies, as Tom and Alleta talked to the world about this loss.

The movie-news interviews milked the horror for all it was worth. Producers had Alleta read the identical little speech over and over again to get the best on-screen delivery from her. She was not much of an ac-tress, even though she would learn. Her first interview was stilted, and the newsreel required many takes and cuts even to get the clumsy and disturbing shots that made it into theaters. She emphasized here, as she would everywhere, that the Sullivan siblings had perished to great purpose. Her sorrow was real—tears, a cracking voice, and a face swol-len and distorted. She also sounded as if her testimony was extorted, taken under duress: "I know now what my—my five boys meant when they said: Keep your chin up Mother. All I can say to you mothers here in America, England, Russia, and all our Allied nations, is keep your chin up too. Our boys did not die in vain. . . . Dad [turning to Tom], our boys did not die in vain."[6]

It took a little time for the films taken at the Sullivans' in the second week of January to make it to screens in Waterloo, but soon moviegoers who went to their neighborhood theaters could look close up at the misery in the Adams Street living room. By the last week in January two Waterloo movie houses were advertising that patrons could view the couple with photographs of their dead sons: WATERLOO'S 5 FIGHTING SULLIVAN BROTHERS; SEE THE NATION'S GREATEST WAR FAMILY; NEWS SCENES OF MRS. SULLIVAN AND SONS.[7]

Information and guests, expected and otherwise, now reached 98 Adams. In the mail of January 14, nearly two months after the ordeal on the open sea but just days after the announcement of the sinking of *Juneau*, a letter arrived from one of its few survivors, Lester Zook. Zook was furious about the navy's treatment of the *Juneau*'s men still alive after the sinking of the ship. His letter related that the four younger brothers had gone under with the cruiser and died at once. He wrote Tom and Alleta, however, that the torpedo strike had not killed George and that he had succumbed on the life raft, "looking for his brothers." Zook spared the family the details about the shark that had eaten George—Tom and Alleta would learn that later. Zook's communication came in the mail just as husband and wife were preparing for an interview with newsmen, and they read Zook's message to the assembled crowd. Immediately, the Associated Press wired from Waterloo that the boys were not just absent but dead, and that at least one death was protracted.[8]

In some measure the navy was simply careful in listing as unknown the whereabouts of the five brothers and many others. Yet for the Sullivan parents and the people of the United States, personnel classified as "Missing in Action" after a naval encounter were more than likely to be at the bottom of the ocean. Nonetheless, with the evidence from the one survivor it was clear that the service was at least obscuring what had happened after the ship sank. Zook was announcing that the Sullivans were dead. Even so, no one, least of all the Sullivan family, faced up to the foul-ups that led to the unnecessary demise of so many in the water. The letter only told the Sullivans what, in their hearts, they already knew. But maybe not. Alleta said to one reporter: "I haven't given up all hope. Maybe one . . . escaped death. Maybe he is floating on a raft somewhere."[9]

A notable early visitor was Margaret Jaros, the Pittsburgh woman whom Red had met through the mail. He had proposed to her after she spent time with him on two weekends. She had visited her in-laws-to-be the preceding October, and now she came to mourn with them. Janos got to Waterloo at midnight on January 14, and journalists wrote soon after that she had come to support the family: "Everything I ever hoped to have went down with that ship."

The agony of waiting was over for Mother and Dad Sullivan, as they were now quickly personified and humanized. But a new agony began as politicians and the public conspired with a bewildered and naïve Tom and Alleta to memorialize the family's fateful injury. Pearl Harbor had given the boys a virtuous way to reconfigure their lives. Then the five young men became victims, part of the cannon fodder of war. After January of 1942 opinion makers and the media rendered the brothers into heroes, finally taking the five to the superhuman. The lives of the children acquired a positive significance only after they had ended in calamity.

What is a hero? One mythological tradition intimates that mortals' lives have no cheerful outcomes. The bravery of chiefs who die in the service of the tribe or clan is the best that can be hoped for. Boldness in deadly combat makes for a hero—the Trojan Hector; the Scandinavian Beowulf; the Thracian Spartacus. Analysis took a new turn in the debates of the intelligentsia in the nineteenth and twentieth centuries. A hero was always a Great Man who changed the course of history, usually a political or military figure—Caesar, Martin Luther, Oliver Cromwell, Napoleon.[10] By the early part of the twentieth century in the democratic United States—in the 1910s, 1920s, 1930s, and 1940s—the definition had shifted dramatically, and a hero could be a celebrity, or an athlete, or ordinary people who had done something extraordinary. Douglas Fairbanks and Mary Pickford thrilled movie audiences. Heavyweight boxer Jack Dempsey commanded the world with his fists. Babe Ruth swung a mighty bat. In Salmon River, Idaho, cowboys were elevated to hero status in January 1929 for plunging through 10-foot snowdrifts to take an eleven-year-old girl to a surgeon. There were many people connected to aviation—the Wright brothers, Eddie Rickenbacker, Amelia

Earhart, and—second to none—Charles Lindbergh, who had flown the Atlantic alone.

By World War II, Americans had returned to the primordial tradition of sacrifice in battle, but with major differences. War gave the heroic a dark aspect, but heroes could be ordinary men, and also live. Alvin York, the most highly decorated American soldier of World War I, had put himself in danger, single-handedly killed a lot of Germans, and survived. The 1941 movie *Sergeant York* had recalled him to mind. Gary Cooper played York, a down-home and God-fearing boy from Tennessee. In World War II Audie Murphy, a much-decorated combat veteran, went on to a film career making war movies and westerns. Both York and Murphy showed courage as individuals in armed struggle.

The loss of the five Sullivans contributed to an even wider notion of the heroic than that exemplified by York and Murphy. The brothers had been under fire, but so far as we know they did not behave as York and Murphy, or did not have the opportunity to do so. The boys were fatalities and received the status of heroes not because of how they acted but because of the unique and unforgiveable injury done to their family, and because the navy and the Roosevelt administration wanted the public to be thinking about the necessity for collective sacrifice and not the incompetence of the admirals and officers.

An admiral, the Chief of Naval Personnel, had signed the formal telegram notifying Tom and Alleta that their sons had gone down with the *Juneau*. The condolences of a number of VIPs followed. Vice President Henry Wallace telegraphed Tom and Alleta about their "marvelous spirit." Eleanor Roosevelt, the president's wife, wrote "Mrs. Sullivan" that Alleta was teaching a lesson of "great courage." It was "heartening," wrote the First Lady, that the couple could "always find solace in your faith and your abiding love for our country." Secretary of the Navy Frank Knox, after earlier asking Alleta to christen a ship, now wrote offering personal sympathy. Iowa's Senator Guy Gillette and Congressman John Gwynne prepared remarks for the *Congressional Record*, in tribute to the boys' bravery and that of their family in adversity.[11]

The big Chicago newspapers most importantly carried forward the saga of the Sullivans. The *Chicago Herald-American*, a tabloid filled with pictures, ran a succession of essays. The author, Basil Talbott, had gone to Waterloo with a staff photographer in mid-January and stayed a week. Talbott concocted syrupy conversations with the Sullivans and told a sentimental tale of the boys growing up, a white-picket-fence re-working of their lives. Pages of images accompanied the reporting. We cannot know if Tom and Alleta even registered the inventions.

Many journalists produced accounts that molded the public under-standing of the five brothers and the remnants of the family. Nonethe-less, the syndicated work of Talbott had a great impact—and not just on the Sullivans. His serial romances suggested how leaders should and could comport themselves in respect to the deaths of the siblings. Talbott gave the world "the Fighting Sullivans" and made them "the na-tion's greatest war family" whose memory would be "enshrine[d] . . . in the hearts of all Americans." He paid particular attention to how "the Fighting Sullivans' brave mother" carried on, a "woman of great spiri-tual strength." He put these words in her mouth: "Someday this whole world will be free. Someday peace will again come to all countries and men and women and children will be free to live with the dignity that is the basis of all human existence. When that day comes we will realize that our sons will live forever in glorious memories."[12]

Talbott's articles nourished Alleta's evolving self-conception, and they later formed the sentiments from which came the script for the movie version of the life and death of the family. Overnight, the news-papers transformed the boys to Protestant respectability. We may never grasp the pain suffered by the parents, their daughter, their daughter-in-law, and May Abel—the only hope of the hopeless is to have no hope. Yet Alleta may have semiconsciously offered up a silent Hallelujah at this rejuvenation of her brood. Talbott's seven stories in the *Herald-American* in the last part of January blessed the family.

In the midst of all this terrible excitement a New York radio station offered Mother and Dad Sullivan an all-expense-paid trip to Manhat-tan to participate in the nationally aired show *We the People*. Across the United States, Americans listened to the parents on the evening of January 31. We don't know exactly what they sounded like on radio, but if their usual routines provided a clue, we can imagine a contrived, even ghoulish recital, designed to elicit the maximum emotional response from the audience.

The newspapers tell us that Alleta said:

> I want to thank the hundreds and hundreds of persons across the country who have sent expressions of sympathy. Our boys went into the Navy together and demanded to serve together. They wanted to stick together, that is the way they wanted it to be. The boys would have wanted us to keep our chins up, too. Dad and I are trying, no matter how hard it is. Other sons are fighting all over the world, to make it a better place. Our boys always felt, if you can fight you ought to. We all have to pitch in and speed up the victory.

Tom, usually taciturn, also spoke at greater length, perhaps because of the more careful scripting of a radio show:

> Mom and I will miss the boys, but my youngest son, Al, has left us a cute little grandson, who will be two years old. My own boys were in the fight to make sure this little kid and others like him all over the world will have a decent world to grow up in. We've all got to get into this fight, every one of us, and we feel we have a right to ask you: what have *you* given to this war.[13]

# CHAPTER SIX

## A NEW MRS. BIXBY

The historian again must look to the Civil War to find parallels to what Americans faced from 1942 to 1945. Among mid-nineteenth-century politicians, North and South, Democrat or Republican, only Abraham Lincoln had the stomach for the bloodletting that the Civil War came to entail. Although he had much backing in the North to pursue a war for the Union, Democrats in the North remained unenthusiastic, and some—called "Copperheads"—even sympathized with the Confederacy. After the immediate rush to fight when the war began in the spring of 1861, and after its carnage emerged, Lincoln had to manage public opinion or face a debacle. The president made statements that promulgated his views with unusual effectiveness. The 1858 debates between him and Illinois senator Stephen A. Douglas, and Lincoln's speech to top Republicans at New York City's Cooper Union in 1860, early exemplified his achievements at oral communication. But later the president even more profitably corralled the newspapers to print originally private letters so that the people could understand his positions. This early use of "spinning" to the mass media of the era shored up the people for the continued spilling of blood. In Lincoln's view, the president had to reassure the common folk of the Union that the injuries to their sons and husbands and brothers had some great purpose.[1]

At Gettysburg in November 1863, to commemorate the grisly fighting there the previous July, Lincoln delivered a speech that the newspapers circulated. The president reminded his listeners and then his readers that Americans were building a special kind of political regime and participating in a holy sort of experiment. They could not give up the fight. The great experiment of a republic of, by, and for the people, which Lincoln's speechifying pointed out, legitimated the losses at Gettysburg and, indeed, all the anguish of the ongoing war. We had "words that remade America," in the language of historian Garry Wills.[2]

The next year, Lincoln ran for reelection. While he handily won, for a time the result was in doubt, and the Republicans used every advantage a wartime presidency could marshal. Just after the election, Lincoln effectively wrote again to venerate patriotic commitment, when he learned that a Boston mother had lost five sons in the war.

The adjutant general of Massachusetts, that state's highest-ranking military official, reported directly to the governor of Massachusetts. In 1864, probably in the late summer, Mrs. Lydia Bixby had presented Adjutant William Schouler with evidence that her five sons had been killed serving in the Union Army. Schouler praised Mrs. Bixby to Governor John A. Andrew as a wonderful example of a loyalist mother, and the governor wrote the War Department in Washington, asking if the president would address her. When the White House received the request, Lincoln responded to Mrs. Bixby on November 21, 1864:

Dear Madam,

I have been shown in the files of the War Department a statement of the Adjutant General of Massachusetts that you are the mother of five sons who have died gloriously on the field of battle. I feel how weak and fruitless must be any word of mine which should attempt to beguile you from the grief of a loss so overwhelming. But I cannot refrain from tendering you the consolation that may be found in the thanks of the Republic they died to save. I pray that our Heavenly Father may assuage the anguish of your bereavement, and leave you only the cherished memory of the loved and lost, and the solemn pride that must be yours to have laid so costly a sacrifice upon the altar of freedom.

> Yours, very sincerely and respectfully,
> /s/ A. Lincoln

Soon thereafter, before Christmas 1864, the letter was appearing in newspapers across the North, and citizens might obtain a lithograph of the document, the nineteenth-century equivalent of a print or photographic reproduction. Events turned Mrs. Bixby into an icon of the mothers of the Republic. Commentators have favorably compared Lincoln's letter to his talk at Gettysburg and then to the Second Inaugural Address of March 1865, the last statement by the president on the need to put the country above all other considerations. Americans must make war "if God wills that it continue ... until every drop of blood drawn with the [slaver's] lash shall be paid by another drawn with the sword [of the war]." Lincoln communicated his vision to Mrs. Bixby and to American citizens. The United States was not Thomas Jefferson's contractual Enlightenment polity composed of separate federated republics but a new United States—national, religious, corporate. Lincoln persuaded the people he governed that, whatever the cost, they must sustain the goals of his administration.

Historians have not judged the Bixby letter or Mrs. Bixby gently. Her family had lost only two boys. Of the other three claimed as dead, one had deserted to the Confederacy, a second may have done so, and the Union Army discharged the third. Scholars have also reported on Mrs. Bixby's dubious patriotism. She apparently sympathized with the South, disliked Lincoln intensely, wanted to assist the Rebels, and desired to use her loss to get something out of the Massachusetts government. She may moreover have run a bawdy house in Boston and was evidently so annoyed with the missive from Lincoln—we know of its contents only from newspaper reproductions—that she destroyed it. Scrupulous exploration finally confirmed that the president did not even draft the letter. His secretary, John Hay, who often took on the burden of replying to many requests of his president, wrote it. Lincoln would sign such letters that Hay had written, or the secretary would imitate Lincoln's signature.

Nonetheless, in the long run who could deny the dignity of Mrs. Bixby? Two children or five? Did it make a difference? Carl Sandburg's huge and poetic life of Lincoln, completed just before World War II, evinced the conventional scholarly interpretation of the significance of the letter, no matter who wrote or signed it, no matter the character of Mrs. Bixby or the number of children dead. Sandburg noted that the president had not sent his own twenty-one-year-old son, Robert, off to war, and he reasoned that Lincoln bowed to the wishes of his mentally unsound and unstable wife, Mary Todd Lincoln. Sandburg also argued that when the government of a republic, through a military draft, reached into a home by force and took its sons during war, the mother should not be addressed as if she had voluntarily sacrificed her children to freedom. Of Mrs. Bixby, nonetheless, Sandburg wrote, "From her womb had gone blood to the altars of the Union cause," and the author found her exalted status justified.

Mrs. Bixby's paradigmatic hurt lay in giving up her offspring for a greater good. This truth resonated for those who wanted to justify wartime destruction, as well as for those servants of the state who looked for ways to forge a national loyalty as lives were cut down. Later scholars focused on the message and not the provenance of the letter; opinion makers ignored the scholarship and emphasized that five Bixby sons had died for the Union. Lincoln gave meaning to the war.[3]

As soon as the deaths of the five Sullivans received public attention, Lincoln's tribute was revivified. On January 12, 1943, the *Courier* first explicitly compared Mother Sullivan to Mrs. Bixby. Like Lydia Bixby during the Civil War, Alleta was "today a symbol as a transfigured American mother deserving enshrinement for loyalty and heroic service." A few days later, as national sympathy overwhelmed the Waterloo parents, a widely circulated Associated Press report also likened Alleta to Mrs. Bixby, and more references followed. Iowa's state legislature formally resolved that Alleta was another Mrs. Bixby. On the radio show from New York at the end of January, an announcer had introduced Alleta as "today's Mrs. Bixby."[4]

On February 3, a message from President Franklin Roosevelt to Alleta was released to the press. Roosevelt had been traveling during the second half of January, mainly to Casablanca for a conference with British leader Winston Churchill. In the middle of the month, someone in the navy had apparently drafted the condolence missive for FDR, although he signed it February 1. The letter was in the style of Lincoln or Hay:

Dear Mrs. Sullivan:

The knowledge that your five gallant sons are missing in action, against the enemy, inspired me to write you this personal message. I realize full well there is little I can say to assuage your grief.

As the Commander in Chief of the Army and the Navy, I want you

Alleta, 1943. Mother Sullivan reads the letter from President Roosevelt (AP).

to know that the entire nation shares your sorrow. I offer you the condolence and gratitude of our country. We, who remain to carry on the fight, must maintain the spirit in the knowledge that such sacrifice is not in vain. The Navy Department has informed me of the expressed desire of your sons; George Thomas, Francis Henry, Joseph Eugene, Madison Abel, and Albert Leo, to serve on the same ship. I am sure, that we all take pride in the knowledge that they fought side by side. As one of your sons wrote, "We will make a team together that can't be beat." It is this spirit which in the end must triumph.

Last March, you, Mrs. Sullivan, were designated to sponsor a ship of the Navy in recognition of your patriotism and that of your sons. I am to understand that you are, now, even more determined to carry on as sponsorer. This evidence of unselfishness and courage serves as a real inspiration for me, as I am sure it will for all Americans. Such acts of faith and fortitude in the face of tragedy convince me of the indomitable spirit and will of our people.

I send you my deepest sympathy in your hour of trial and pray that in Almighty God you will find a comfort and help that only He can bring.

Very sincerely yours,<br>
/s/ Franklin D. Roosevelt[5]

A less moving example of English prose than Lincoln's correspondence, Roosevelt's also had little impact on American culture. It rather became another example of the depiction of Alleta as a suffering but accepting and patriotic parent. She fell into this role, and Tom played a quieter, supporting position. Had the two denounced the government or displayed hysteria about the cruelty of the war, who knows how the Roosevelt administration would have responded? Instead, the state and this loyal family mutually embraced. Alleta, especially, learned to perform as an ideal Mrs. Bixby. She would get considerable practice as the navy, in a new turn to this story, sent her and Tom around the United States over the next four months to preach sacrifice on the home front for the common good.

# CHAPTER SEVEN

## THE NAVY TOUR AND AFTER

In attending to Tom and Alleta, Americans sympathized and showed solidarity and attempted to convert the deaths of the boys into an explicable national misfortune. The need for political luminaries and many ordinary people to share the pain of the remaining Sullivans had many motives and expressions. With the parents in New York in early February, naval authorities encouraged the pair to come to Washington. Admiral Clark Howell Woodward took charge of the official affairs of the bereaved Tom and Alleta. At the behest of the navy, Eleanor Roosevelt and Vice President Wallace now met with the parents.

Woodward arranged a further project. He headed the navy's Industrial Incentive Division, which coordinated the service's efforts in the United States to increase defense production, broadly defined as any manufacture of products used by the navy, not just weapons. Labor disputes and absenteeism plagued many of the companies involved in this war-work, especially because women who went off to jobs also had commitments to childrearing. The government pressed the companies, which in turn pushed their stressed employees to work harder and longer. To keep workers up to the mark, the Industrial Incentive Division sponsored programs—traveling displays of weapons, morale-boosting lectures, the appearance of war heroes, showcases of memorabilia, and anti-Japanese and anti-Nazi exhibitions. The most effective and popular of these shows may have been the talk and Q&A delivered by Seaman Basil Izzi. He had spent eighty-three days on a raft off the coast of Brazil in late 1942 and early 1943, after the Germans sank his ship. Nonetheless, the "Seaman Izzi" presentation was only one of hundreds repeatedly made to thousands of groups. Each patriotic display would allay labor-union issues and malingering only for a time, and then workers would have to be reminded again of their obligations.[1]

The Sullivan couple joined this endeavor and traveled around the

United States with a dutiful message for millions in defense employment. In coordinating visits to facilities by Tom and Alleta, the navy had goals in addition to having the two Sullivans testify to the importance of not shirking on the home front. If citizens, at the urging of Mother and Dad Sullivan, rededicated themselves to winning the war, the nation might justify the five deaths. Moreover, what had happened to the *Juneau* shocked navy officers, who wanted to mourn with the parents. The service would supply them with something to do, so that they would not focus on what could not be alleviated.

The service, finally, wanted to keep the nation's attention away from the details of the drownings. As early as January 13, 1943, a long Associated Press article, datelined Waterloo, appeared in the *New York Times* and gave an accurate account of the battle of November 12–13 at Guadalcanal and the torpedo strike that destroyed the *Juneau* on the morning of November 13. But the public had not really understood the human costs of the government's lack of preparedness for this ocean war, and officials continued to give varied accounts—some false, some obfuscating—to gloss over the days that the *Juneau*'s men spent on the open sea after the ship went down. No one in the navy let on that Admiral Halsey had relieved Hoover of his command for his negligence in not looking for survivors. As late as 1944 one relative of a *Juneau* victim wrote a "sorry-to-bother-you-but-what-happened?" letter to the navy. The department responded, "Efforts consistent with the paramount tactical necessity of the time were made to rescue as many survivors as possible. That these efforts were not successful in the case of many gallant officers and men is deeply regretted by the navy."[2] The tour would focus on the stalwart parents and not on navy mistakes.

The navy began to fashion a story about the Sullivan family in American folk history. Not just the navy but also filmmakers and Midwestern and national leaders would continuously renew this story for over eighty years. Varied authorities with a purchase on the mass media would convince Americans of the luster of the boys and ignore official shortcomings that might have contributed to their deaths. A larger pattern of meaning might make the wretched end of the Sullivans intelligible, and the United States would single out the remaining family members in admiration.

Tom and Alleta began their trips in the first week of February 1943. The Illinois Central donated Tom's salary, and navy officers chaperoned the couple, paid expenses, and managed interactions with their fellow Americans. The government put Tom and Alleta up at some of the fanciest hotels in the United States—the Statler in Washington, the Waldorf Astoria in New York, the Palmer House in Chicago.

The eastern swing that led off the itinerary took them to Baltimore, Philadelphia, New York, Newport in Rhode Island, Bridgeport and Hartford in Connecticut, Pittsburgh, and Chicago. In New York for a second visit, the couple went to Mass at the famous Saint Patrick's Cathedral, where so many Americans have visited in times of trouble and where Archbishop Francis Spellman furnished Tom and Alleta with comforting news. Spellman had learned that George, Frank, Red, Matt, and Al had all received Holy Communion three weeks before the sinking of the *Juneau*. "I have worried and worried about it," Alleta told the press. "Dad tried to make me stop fretting. So did our pastor back home. Now this lifts a weight right off me." "That gives me real consolation," said Mother Sullivan.[3]

A Lieutenant Kenneth Taylor, a former public-relations man from Philadelphia, accompanied the Sullivans and would give a brief and apparently effective presentation before he introduced the parents.[4] Alleta perfected a remarkable act during the first part of the expedition. Admitting that she was "kind of nervous" at the onset, she learned to give moving little talks about the higher morality of the effort, her personal heartache, and the need to recall a mutual purpose that made the deaths of five of her children meaningful.[5] Despite a grating voice, Alleta could be compelling:

I want to say a few words about my sons. They joined the navy a year ago. . . . My oldest boy, George, wrote to Washington for the boys to all stay together—they wanted to stay together. When the ship was sunk and they all lost their lives, Dad and I knew that was the way they wanted it. . . . I hope workers will turn out more and more of everything the navy needs, especially planes. I keep thinking that maybe if there had been more planes out that day the *Juneau* went down, maybe my boys would still be alive.

We have no regrets that our boys joined the navy. I'd want them to do it again; it made men of them. I have a little grandson, Jimmy, who is almost two, and when he gets old enough, I want him to join. . . . My boys did not die in vain.

The newspapers reported that for the most part Tom kept "shyly in the background" and said he let "the Mrs" do the speaking. But the stage-struck and sometimes uncomprehending husband could overcome his reticence and tell about his loss and about the special need for American workers in industrial unions to produce for the war:

I'm a working man, just like you, brothers. I work on the Illinois Central. I'm a freight conductor. . . . We're giving ten per-cent of our wages in war bonds. I want to ask you to think about doing that.

Maybe if the men and women in war plants realize what it has meant to mom and me—and to a lot of other mothers and fathers— that there weren't enough planes and ships, then they will work their level best to make sure there will be enough from now on.[6]

In mid-February the couple took the train back to Waterloo for a brief break. In their hometown a further whirl of activities overtook them as authorities memorialized the Sullivans. In one of the many twists in this surprising story, the *Courier* repeatedly reported that one Pearl Schroeder, an old girlfriend of Red's, accompanied Tom, Alleta, Gen, and Keena to all these events.[7] Who can know why Pearl upstaged distraught fiancée Marge Jaros, who had visited from Pittsburgh less than a month before?

Then Gen joined Tom and Alleta on a western swing. On February 22 in Portland, Oregon, Mother Sullivan commissioned the navy tugboat *Tawasa*, as she had agreed to do when the five brothers had first come to the attention of the navy just a year before. They traveled on to Seattle, then "back East" to Minneapolis and Chicago. Toward the end of March, the Sullivans and their entourage again returned to Waterloo on a flying visit before undertaking another West Coast circuit.

When the journeys had gotten under way in February, many people had suggested that the navy must do something better than have Alleta baptize a tugboat, and after the siblings had drowned the service

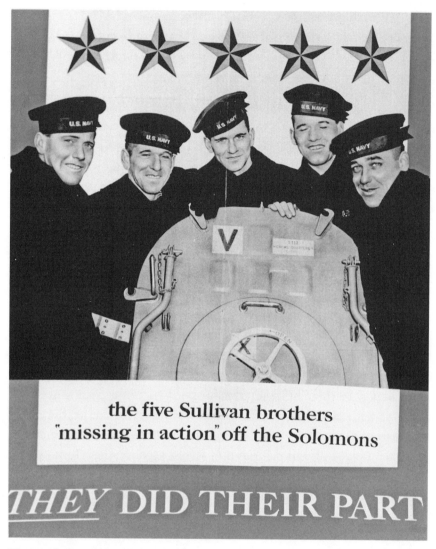

the five Sullivan brothers
"missing in action" off the Solomons

## THEY DID THEIR PART

They Did Their Part. This navy poster was released on March 22, 1943 (Naval History & Heritage Command).

decided to name a destroyer after them. The navy was to have called the chosen ship something else, but now the service would christen it the USS *The Sullivans*. Again President Roosevelt wrote Tom and Alleta. The ceremony would express "in a tangible way" the nation's appreciation of the family's "gallant spirit." In early April, in San Francisco, with Tom and Gen beside her, Alleta broke a bottle of champagne on the prow of *The Sullivans*. At the Bethlehem Steel Shipyard, where the event took place, she read from a statement the navy had helped prepare, and a national radio network relayed her words:

> I am proud today. I am proud to be here to christen this lovely ship in the name of my five boys. I only wish that my boys could be here to see this warship. . . . My boys have made their contribution. Your boys will make theirs too. But I hope their contribution will not be their lives. I hope your boys will soon be home, so you can be happy and so you won't suffer as I have. . . . I ask God to watch over the officers and crew. I hope that it will sail away and do the job my boys intended to do.

A few minutes later, she repeated her speech for the newsreel journalists.[8]

Alleta had some kind of minor collapse in San Francisco toward the end of the couple's appearances—"sobbing," "heart-broken and emotion-wracked, the Iowa housewife who has become a nation's heroine could stand no more."[9] Nonetheless, soon back on her feet, Alleta went to Los Angeles, where she named five navy dive-bombers for each one of her sons; to San Diego; to defense installations in Texas; and to Memphis, Saint Louis, and, by the third week in May, Cincinnati. But the parents left the trek to tend to Keena, ill in Waterloo, and in late May 1943 the navy officially ended the tour.

The military regularly queried executives at the businesses that participated in order to evaluate the success of these events. The reports on the Sullivans were complimentary, especially in respect to declines in absenteeism and an increase in productivity after employees saw Tom and Alleta. The Sullivans "are just plain common Americans," but just that fact "stirred our workers . . . deeply." "How proud we feel that we were selected to be honored with a visit from these brave and generous parents." "The most noticeable reaction that we have experienced" was "in the deportment of younger employees" and in "a more serious atmosphere in the Plant." The presentations "bring home to each individual" "the grim reality of conditions created by war."[10]

With the backing of the service, Tom and Alleta had gone to scores of industries and had tapped their dreadful celebrity to arouse American workers to their duties on the home front. After the first part of the trip, Undersecretary of the Navy James Forrestal wrote to Secretary Knox that the Iowa couple had been a "remarkable success" and hoped that the navy could "use them to the maximum degree."[11] At the finish of the speaking engagements, Tom and Alleta had seen more than a million people.

The navy had thrust the couple into new positions that helped the nation to make sense of the five fatalities. In death the Sullivan sons were transformed from marginal youths to heroic men. In many ways the parents remained insecure and out of their depth. Nevertheless, in the end Alleta displayed intelligence and gravity. She exemplified patriotic motherhood and had lifted the boys from a watery grave to a station they had never attained when they walked the earth.

While the trip of the Sullivan parents lodged the sons in the nation's consciousness, the country showered other tokens of esteem on the family. A Mother's Day "oration" focused on the family's patriotism. Knowledge of the fate of the brothers registered as an item on a current events quiz. Recruiters in Dubuque inducted thirty "Sullivan Avengers" from Iowa into the navy. The famous newspaper feature "Ripley's Believe It or Not" requested a picture to make the Sullivans a subject of the syndication. The Golden Rule Foundation in New York nominated Alleta for America's Foremost Mother. More organizations called attention to her similarity to Mrs. Bixby. A company building emergency landing strips asked Secretary of War Stimson to designate a Sullivan Airfield somewhere in the Pacific.[12]

Even after the appearances for the navy ended, Alleta accepted invitations to varied civic forums in Iowa and other states. She always spoke briefly and to the same point of renunciation for the shared defense. At a June Flag Day rally in Dubuque, Tom and Alleta addressed an audience of over 2,500 while a nationwide radio hookup carried their words across America. On a trip to Boston in August to raise funds for that city's memorial to deaths in all families named Sullivan, the couple participated in ceremonies at Fenway Park for a Boston "Sullivan Fund." The parents met luminaries and visited Mrs. Bixby's house.[13] Back in

Waterloo, they sifted through gifts and mementoes and condolences from all over the Western world. More than forty voluntary groups designated Alleta Mother of the Year. The Associated Press named the five Sullivans the most important Iowa story of 1943.[14]

As national recognition and accolades showered on Tom and Alleta, the *Courier* canvassed for a suitable memorial to the boys in their hometown. This began a crusade for the Sullivans that would last for over seventy years. Like many newspapers in modest-sized cities in the middle of the twentieth century, the *Courier*—a serious enterprise—covered local news, international affairs, and national arts and culture. But the paper also functioned as an instrument of unsophisticated provincial boosterism. The paper published a lot of doggerel poetry about the family. The day the navy announced the deaths of the five brothers—January 12, 1943—the *Courier* speculated that after the war the town would venerate Waterloo's courageous five. "The Sullivan saga had made Waterloo known thruout the country," and "customar[il]y" war heroes afforded names for buildings, parks, and monuments.[15]

In February, as Tom and Alleta began their tour, a page-one headline publicized a Sullivan Brothers Memorial Fund, and articles explained it as the right thing to do. Civic leaders quickly came on board. "Done is their battle, but imperishable is their name," said the Roman Catholic archbishop of Iowa on the radio. A *Courier* editorial called for a memorial "strong enough to last a thousand years." While letters to the editor deliberated on the kind of monument to put up, the city's leaders pressed for a huge statue. The governor of Iowa and every other official who could claim someone's notice offered assistance, and soon the paper set up a monetary account. A committee of opinion makers volunteered to oversee the financial arrangements of "The Fighting Sullivans Memorial Fund." The newspaper quoted Alleta: "The boys would think it was swell of Waterloo and people all over the country to think of paying them such a tribute."[16]

Every day for over two months, the details of the fund garnered front-page attention in Waterloo. In headlines that competed with the world-shaking details of the global war against Japan and Germany, the *Courier* told readers the details of Tom and Alleta's heartbreaking trip around the United States. The paper ballyhooed contributions for some sort of a cenotaph, although no one seemed to know what that word meant. The fund got under way with substantial cash from Waterloo-based businesses, with the IC and Rath Packing in the lead. Rath gave $1,000. Donations large and small also arrived from across the country—New York City war workers gave almost $500; and smaller gifts were posted from private individuals in other countries, notably Ireland; and finally from Sullivans across the globe. Friends of the boys also donated—$24 from the motorcycle club; $5 from the Tic Toc Tap; and $2 from Schulz's Sunoco.[17] But precious little more came in, and certainly very little more from Waterloo itself.

After the Navy Mothers of Des Moines gave $5, the Waterloo chapter gave $10 but wrote to the newspaper that the fund should note "all the men and women of Waterloo and vicinity who give their lives in World War II."[18] The cinema palace of Waterloo, the Paramount Theatre, seated 1,800. A special movie show one evening in early March 1943 put all the money from admissions into the fund. Joan Crawford and John Wayne starred in *Reunion in France,* at fifty cents a head. Only 346 people paid, which yielded a check for $152.24; the Paramount was more than four-fifths empty. A week later, the disabled veterans had a well-advertised—screamingly advertised—fund-raiser; it netted $21.78. The newspaper tells us that the Waterloo Red Cross had raised over $50,000 in 1943; and a Sunshine Fund to provide summer fun for underprivileged kids had over $1,500. People also had money in their pockets—six of Tom's fellow employees of the IC had just won among themselves $190 for their zealous work efforts, and historians have noted for decades that World War II brought a full-employment economy and few consumer goods to purchase. By mid-April the fund had stuck at $5,500.[19]

Something had gone shockingly awry with the response in Waterloo to the Sullivan Fund, although a little-noted slight three months before had anticipated the rebuff to the money-raising. When the navy had first announced the five as missing in action, Waterloo's ordinary people had ignored their mayor's call for a Sunday of prayer that might ensure the recovery of the brothers alive.[20] This snub signaled the first public reaction by Tom and Alleta's neighbors. Now the state of the fund confirmed that inhabitants had trouble swallowing the acclaim for the Sullivans. Even the ferocious injury that had resulted from the sinking of the *Juneau* did not put to rest what must have been antagonism toward the boys and the family. The merciless voting-with-your-feet response evidences that the Sullivans had a doubtful repute in the town before December 7, 1941. Residents of Waterloo were unforgiving even after the slaughter of "all five." The after-death rejection had to have added to the hurt of the living Sullivans.

The newspaper—and all public functionaries—had no interest in joining even the silent detractors and initiated a long-lasting effort of damage control. Public "political" judgment diverged from private moral critique. The *Courier* reacted by noting that any memorial in the city would commemorate all those who would give their lives in World War II. The committee that the newspaper had charged with administering the fund sent 1,000 letters to people all over the United States asking for "suggestions on the raising of the Fund." Editorials sought new justifications for the memorial.[21] By July 1943, however, the *Courier* had retreated. Stories about the fund ceased to appear. When they did, the newspaper talked about "Courier Funds" that blended the Sunshine Fund and a renamed "War Heroes' Fund" that would celebrate the Sullivans and others.

The famous American bomber *Memphis Belle* had safely completed its requisite twenty-five missions, and by midsummer 1943 its crew had a Sullivans-like travel plan to energize war workers on behalf of the Army Air Forces. Throughout the United States, where citizens certainly did not discredit the Sullivans, the boys were even so becoming old news, and messages of sacrifice began to give way to tales of triumphal advance across the Pacific and in Europe. It looked as if Tom and Alleta would be thrown back on their own resources to deal with their irrevocable loss. This hit the parents like a body blow. As Alleta told a reporter in April, "The trip has kept me from thinking. . . . It's bad to think too much."[22]

Hollywood rescued the Sullivan parents—and the leadership of Waterloo. On January 17, 1943, less than a week after the navy had informed Tom and Alleta that the boys were missing, the first call had come from the movie capital.[23] As schemes for a picture ripened, official Waterloo and its newspaper did everything possible to advertise what would be a major event for the city. A feature film would situate the town on a world map and give the fund a positive jolt. It would also distract Mother and Dad Sullivan from the reality of their circumstances.

# CHAPTER EIGHT

# HOLLYWOOD IN WAITING FOR
# THE SULLIVANS

World War I did not traumatize the United States as had the Civil War, but from early 1917 until late 1918 Democratic president Woodrow Wilson did worry about the dangers of war for leaders of democracies, just as Lincoln had worried. Wilson needed the approval of the governed, for American politicians could not rely on an expert military that operated independently of public support. The people had simple and uncomplicated requirements—they had to see the righteousness of battle and the inevitability of triumph. The president worried that a war fever might sweep up citizens but that they might also just as quickly tire of a conflict. At first Wilson seemed just the man for such a fickle mass, for he proved an inspirational leader and introduced his "idealism" into American foreign policy. Although opposition arose, and although the government manipulated public opinion, Wilson's soaring rhetoric conveyed Americans into and out of the war. He defined the conflict as "the war to end all wars." The peace would realize Wilson's new League of Nations and usher in cooperative politics around the world.

In the end, however, events verified Wilson's beliefs about the perils of taking a democracy into battle. The peaceful planet promised by Wilson bumped up against the actuality of World War I and its consequences. Americans wearied of prolonged fighting and turned their backs on his brand of interventionism. Wilson's Republican opponents led the country to reject his League of Nations. The United States did not join and drifted into what some called the foreign-policy isolationism of the 1920s.

Politicians in the 1930s absorbed different lessons from the experience of 1917–1919, and the different notions about Wilson and the earlier war accompanied the bitter public clashes of opinion during the period leading up to the Japanese attack on Pearl Harbor. Once the

United States was in World War II, however, both Democratic and Republican leaders rallied to the flag but still distrusted a wavering public. The surprise attack had generated a wealth of patriotic devotion. How long would it last?

To be effective America needed a committed people who could anticipate a justifiable, straightforward, and uncostly triumph. A leader must generate an idealistic outlook, yet the electorate had a brief attention span. Politicians could not expect zeal for justice abroad to keep the nation focused if they did not offer repeated victories and final success. FDR's administration fretted that the people would abandon the fight just as they had abandoned Wilson. As we have seen, this apprehension partly generated the Sullivan tour.

Up until after Wilson left office, newspapers and magazines were the chief disseminators of information, as they had been during the Civil War. The radio, common by the 1920s, brought changes. But even in the 1930s, most politicians were not adept at the public speaking that the radio required, although FDR mastered the medium. More significant than the radio, the Hollywood film emerged as the most popular form of entertainment in the United States and as an intoxicating and even uncontrollable form of mass communication. Movies did more than communicate; they shaped morality, politics, and attitudes toward social problems, and through the film Americans understood dating, accounting procedures, housekeeping, churchgoing, and everything else. Movies afforded many people the only apprehension of a wider world they had, even if the apprehension was distorted. Cinema allowed ordinary viewers to glimpse otherwise inaccessible spaces and times and to gain entrée into, say, a newspaper office; a business deal; a remote island; or a diplomatic negotiation. Moviegoers got a fanciful sense of participating in many unique or private or momentous activities.[1]

Navy movies in the 1930s may have influenced the Sullivans, and the newsreels later informed neighbors in Waterloo and people across the country that the boys were dead. Academics today might worry about the impact of cinema on culture, and vice versa. In the 1930s, 1940s, and 1950s, however, politicians, Hollywood grandees, various censors, and writers on film—buttressed by social scientists of the middle third of the century—supposed that moviemakers in some measure dictated to America. Progressives would harness the movies to promote positive change. On the other side, stand-patters dreaded that adventurous or frivolous or radical moviemakers could bring down the entire cultural order and lead an anarchical population amok.

By the late 1930s, with war on the horizon, everyone believed that films could indoctrinate or, if you will, serve as a vehicle for transmitting coded facts.[2] Newspapers and the radio crucially circulated news, but the movies could deliver a message more intense than a widely distributed letter to a latter-day Mrs. Bixby.

The businesses with a studio system that produced movies had grown up in the 1920s, and while the organizations evolved and changed, they remained basically intact into the 1950s. In Los Angeles eight companies with facilities that functioned as self-enclosed villages manufactured films, although corporate headquarters in New York City decided finances. The "movies" occupied a broad spectrum: newsreels, like those that had presented the Sullivan boys in 1942 and Tom and Alleta in 1943; cartoons; short subjects running ten minutes or so—travelogues or abbreviated comic topics and, in rare instances, something substantive like John Ford's *The Battle of Midway*; serials—full-length items of a very low quality shown a chapter at a time over many weeks; and "feature length" movies like those about the navy that we have noted. Finally, there were coming attractions—brief clips from future movies telling us why we must see them.

The perspective of the New York managers of the separate businesses differed from that of their better-known employees in California. New York set the budgets, sometimes specifying for a year an estimated number of modestly priced feature films with run-of-the-mill players, or so many films in which stars performed. The calendar would tell filmmakers when, throughout the year, they should have one or another of various sorts of movies ready for exhibition. The New Yorkers built and leased theaters; hired and trained staff to run them; scheduled releases for propitious times; and planned daily and weekly programs. Manhattan financiers oversaw a complex distribution to chains of theaters that they owned, orchestrated advertising and publicity, and rented films to movie houses they did not own. During World War II the delivery of movies to the public required no mean effort, for theaters often operated around the clock to accommodate men and women working on shifts in defense industries. Sometimes the movie houses, in addition to "the show," had live entertainment, sold war bonds, collected for war charities, or sponsored patriotic events—as the Paramount had done for the Sullivan Fund. Businessmen in New York believed that California assisted with the main job of supplying a chain of stores with merchandise.[3] Yet focusing on the economics overlooks the unique product the New Yorkers were selling. As one cinema critic has written, movies "are more than a business. . . . Hollywood . . . constitute[s] the world's primary tradition of visual storytelling."[4]

At the Hollywood studio, but sometimes elsewhere, called "on location," individual movies appeared as if off an assembly line in a predictable but extraordinary fashion. A finished film blended the talents of a capable group of technicians—cameramen, set designers, costumers, makeup artists, lighting experts, and film editors—and the gifts of actors and actresses often with distinctive screen personalities. The success of the effort also depended on a film's being tailored to fit into a recognizable genre like the western, about which even a global audience had certain expectations. Moreover, the approach of a particular director, the person who actively guided the movie to completion, might stamp it.

More usually, the director had only a part in a management unit that oversaw each studio's creations. This unit consisted of the director, as well as a changing group of writers and a producer who was more or less responsible for organizing the finances, assembling a cast, and piecing together various nuts-and-bolts. For a time, an executive in charge of production supervised all of a company's movies and ran herd over a studio's output, men such as Irving Thalberg, Darryl F. Zanuck, David O. Selznick, and Hal Wallis. These autocratic and feared decision-makers found scripts, issued commands to writers, conveyed orders to directors and individual producers, and monitored films as they came into being. Enormous egos pandered to middle-brow national tastes, for which Hollywood leaders had an instinctive sense. Ever mindful of profits, they also often wanted to educate or inform their audiences, or to subvert homilies, or to experiment through their medium with social mores—all the while turning out an impressive professional piece of goods.

The movie industry contained more than its fair share of prima donnas, lunatics, and incompetents, yet films possessed an enchantment that transcended the limitations of the individuals involved. Joseph Goebbels, Nazi Germany's minister of propaganda and a barbarous enemy of the United States and the Jews so prominent in Hollywood, over and over again delighted in the skill of American pictures. He wanted German filmmakers to learn from cinema czars in the United States.[5] By World War II, when Hollywood had thoroughly seduced Goebbels, decentralization in the US movie industry had diminished the power of these kingpins. They might relocate from film company to film company, while independent entrepreneurs sold package deals to the studios, which would in exchange provide facilities and channels of distribution. The early Hollywood managers left in their wake commitments to the rigorous development of scripts, meticulous scheduling, collaboration with the "technical" departments, and careful supervision of each picture.[6]

The studios operated within a peculiar web of censorship. Movie businessmen had first to deal with their own regulators. In 1930 the Motion Pictures Producers and Distributors Association adopted a Production Code. It set ethical standards to guide an industry that many thought displayed a wild unconventionality. Hollywood ignored the Code until 1934, when vigorous enforcement began. Applied by conservative Roman Catholics, the Code promulgated narrow, prudish, and racist ideals. It affirmed middle-class decency, eschewed violence, and avoided bodily functions, especially in regard to sex. Commentators have persuasively argued that before 1934 Hollywood toyed with many debased notions and put some morally insensitive material on the big screen but that after 1934 it was foolishly conventional. The effective head of the Production Code Administration—the PCA—was Joseph Breen, a Roman Catholic connected to influential churchmen who had become outraged at how Hollywood had overlooked the Code. To make Hollywood's vision of sex, violence, and political commitments acceptable, film executives negotiated with what they called "the Breen Office."

Moreover, in the 1930s the movie town had strident arguments over politics, but supporters of Franklin Roosevelt were most numerous; Hollywood tilted toward internationalism. Until the end of 1941, however, both the PCA and politicians hostile to Roosevelt restrained his movie partisans. Breen did not want Hollywood to insult the Germans and made trouble for filmmakers who wanted to exhibit anti-Nazi films.[7] Then, in the fall of 1941, congressional opponents of the Roosevelt administration convened hearings, interrogating filmmakers about Hollywood's bias in favor of the anti-German Allies—at this alarming time mainly the English and the Russians. First Amendment court decisions about the right to free expression would later protect Hollywood, but in 1941 Congress could threaten the movies with the law. If legislators thought that the Hollywood product, its making, or its distribution stepped over some boundary, they might police the film business like any other. Although the initial hearings embarrassed the isolationists and had petered out well before the end of 1941, the Pearl Harbor attacks confirmed the movie capital's allegiance and possibly saved Hollywood from further investigation.[8]

The Japanese strike and Hitler's declaration of war on the United States destroyed the opponents of internationalism. All Americans conceded that the Nazi decision and the raid without warning required the United States to fight the Axis, and even to partner with the Soviet Union, which was killing Germans. Hollywood was cleared for its own approach to mobilizing the United States to its new responsibilities, and the movie interventionists got no more complaints. For the duration, film people additionally put aside their own divisions, and a united-front mentality even became acceptable in much of Hollywood: some of the politically committed saw the war against fascism as the best way to raise up the Soviet Union. Nonetheless, the conflict made censorship issues more complex, for in addition to the Breen Office the government established various agencies to influence Hollywood's output.

The PCA quickly did an about-face, promoting animosity toward the Japanese and Germans and nodding to an embrace of the Russians. Breen had briefly left his job in 1941, but when he returned to it in 1942 he wanted to arouse loyalty, and he even allowed greater violence on the screen to depict the stakes of World War II for American servicemen.[9] During the war, when Hollywood profited from heartwarming films that portrayed the American way, the studios had an effective and pragmatic rapport with Breen—less adversarial than had existed previously.

Despite Pearl Harbor, from December 1941 onward, Roosevelt, his war cabinet, and the military worried about how the populace would respond to the nation's needs. The elite could not coerce citizens; people were inconstant and might prove fainthearted. The Sullivan tour was one of many, many efforts to shore up the country's loyalties. Among the councils of the mighty, misgivings about the masses continued until late 1943, when it became apparent that the United States would defeat Germany and Japan. Up until that time, and even later, authorities presented the restrictions and obligations that war brought to America as more pleasant than they were.[10] In its efforts at home the administration encouraged the movies to instill beliefs through entertainment. In due course, Hollywood would point out the higher purposes of the war in a film about the Sullivans.

In mid-1942 FDR created a propaganda agency that enlisted the film world. The Office of War Information (OWI), with a Bureau of Motion Pictures, came into being at a time when the government worried about a falloff in public morale in the aftermath of Pearl Harbor. The OWI reviewed movies and gave helpful proposals about how films might ensure the widespread espousal of Allied aims. Washington eschewed censorship, so it said, and its hints about making appropriate movies were not mandatory. Nevertheless, Hollywood ignored the OWI and its associated Office of Censorship at its peril. The government could refuse to give a film an export license during the war if the OWI thought the movie would insult fellow Allies or offend other countries and cultures. Because Hollywood's profits even in this period often depended on money made overseas, respect for the OWI influenced producers and directors.[11]

The liberals in this bureaucracy were pledged to the opinions that the president's wife, Eleanor Roosevelt, championed. The film censors had advanced, if still paternalistic, ideas about race; they believed in a global amelioration that a new League of Nations would shape; they saw in the Soviet Union a budding democracy; and they allotted time to "women's issues." Following the line of the popular front, the OWI defined the war as fascism versus democracy and might censor depictions on the screen that did not forward its views. The gentle instruments of repression in the OWI made the free expression of ideas secondary, although we should remember that the United States had joined a dire struggle. Failure to win the war could have meant the death of American civilization, and the First Amendment was not at the top of the list of things liberals were guarding.

Of course, the First Amendment did not interest Hollywood on account of principle. Support of the war certainly animated moviedom, but the business also had to offer a diverting and profitable article. If people did not like watching a movie, it could not make an impact. Stars, directors, producers, and financiers had their own civic preferences but nonetheless worked in sync with the OWI. They usually followed whatever lead the government gave. Additionally, Washington needed the film industry's cooperation because blue-pencillers believed—probably rightly—that audiences distrusted an amateurish officially sponsored article more than a Hollywood film. Censors knew that Hollywood, adroitly co-opted, could disguise didactic intent, although moviemakers, on their side, might turn censorship to their own purposes. Moreover, Hollywood had another way to moderate the politicians' power. When it came to movies, or parts of movies, that were military in nature, the army and navy provided technical help and favorable publicity; they gave authoritative advice to Hollywood. The military could throw up roadblocks but also could be set against the civilian propagandist-censors in Washington.

The number of agencies seeking to regulate the movies gave Hollywood headaches and reflected everyone's conviction—as we have already noted—that this amusement had the might of TNT. Competing agencies, nonetheless, often gave movie entrepreneurs the space to do what they wanted. And by early 1943 they wanted to screen a drama about the Sullivans.

Hollywood had produced many ostensibly true stories about the past. They were mainly film biographies—"biopics"—a successful genre that insiders poked fun at because of the hokum that circulated as history.[12] Examples abound. *Young Mr. Lincoln* (1939) starred Henry Fonda and obsessed 20th Century-Fox executive Darryl Zanuck. Other films with claims to be serious dramatized the story of Paul Julius von Reuter's first European news service—*A Dispatch from Reuters* (1940); of Paul Ehrlich's struggle to find a cure for syphilis—*Dr. Ehrlich's Magic Bullet* (1940); and of President Andrew Johnson's plans for Reconstruction after the Civil War—*Tennessee Johnson* (1942). Gary Cooper followed up his 1941 performance in *Sergeant York* with *Pride of the Yankees* (1942) about baseball great Lou Gehrig.

The Fighting Sullivans* would push the boundaries of Hollywood's genres by going a bit beyond the biopic to what amounted to family history. Filmmakers had stretched the edges of the biopic in *The Barretts of Wimpole Street* (1934) and *The House of Rothschild* (1934). 20th Century-Fox had produced a film about the Dionne quintuplets in the 1930s (*Five of a Kind*, 1938) and, after *The Fighting Sullivans*, about the Brontë sisters (*Devotion*, 1946); the Dorsey brothers (*The Fabulous Dorseys*, 1947); and the Gilbreths (*Cheaper by the Dozen*, 1950).

In all of these films moviemakers blurred the line between truth and something else, and they regularly provided a loose historical environment for many of their confections, especially when dealing with the contemporary history of World War II, where we have many further illustrations. In *The Story of GI Joe* (1945), Burgess Meredith played celebrated wartime correspondent Ernie Pyle, who reported the fighting of typical American infantrymen. Critics applauded the film for its authenticity in part because it lacked Hollywood-style heroism, in part because it took narration and dialogue from Pyle's columns, and in part because Pyle was killed covering the invasion of Okinawa in the Pacific two months before Hollywood released the movie. Then Hollywood produced movies such as *Wake Island* (1942) and *Bataan* (1943), based on key events in the Pacific War but not on real people.

The Fighting Sullivans* would also trade on and participate in Hollywood's Americanization of the previously questionable faith of Roman Catholicism, or at least its Irish American ethnic variant. In 1927 Hollywood had issued *The Callahans and the Murphys*, a light silent comedy that, in its clichéd portrayals, enraged Irish Americans and the Church in the United States.[13] In 1931 James Cagney became famous performing as the Irish hoodlum Tom Powers in *The Public Enemy*, although the movie did not revile all Irish in America. Into the early 1930s a number of movies fostered stereotypes of Italian Americans whom Americans saw as criminals, peddlers, or barbers speaking broken English. Nonetheless, by the late 1930s and early 1940s, with cheerful stories, Hollywood welcomed the Irish American adherents of the Church of Rome. Producers and directors were placating Joseph Breen, his Production Code Administration, and the high-up Irish Catholics with an interest in controlling movies. Breen had a cramped and reactionary view of the moral life, however, and the generous and open-minded Irish Catholics he saw on the screen little resembled him.[14]

Some of these movies featured Roman Catholic actors playing real-life priests, whom Hollywood saw as ecumenical, and regular guys—Spencer Tracy as Father Edward Flanagan in *Boys Town* (1938) and Pat O'Brien as Father Francis Duffy in *The Fighting 69th* of World War I (1940). In the most successful of these religiously oriented films—the hit *Going My Way* (1944) and its sequel, *The Bells of St. Mary's* (1945)—the movie capital had invented the priest. In these two films Bing Crosby starred as Father Chuck O'Malley, a mild and generous regular Irishman. Not all the Catholic protagonists were priests. The outstanding movie, a family biopic, came in 1942. In *Yankee Doodle Dandy*, the now well-established Jimmy Cagney, instead of acting a murderous thug, performed as the Irish Catholic song-and-dance man and songwriter George M. Cohan.[15] Cagney won a Best Actor award for his role.

# CHAPTER NINE

## THE FILM IS BORN

For over eighty years Iowa has attracted American filmmakers who have used the state to stand for middle-America values. *State Fair* had incarnations in 1933, 1945, and 1962; *The Music Man* appeared in 1962; *Field of Dreams* in 1989; and *The Bridges of Madison County* in 1995.

More important, during World War II, Hollywood could not resist Guadalcanal. By 1943 Americans had heard of the island and the crucial battles against the Japanese that had occurred, or were occurring, there. Soon art, books, and movies enshrined the battles in popular culture. In addition to the productions of the Japanese, we have ever so many American depictions of battle scenes on land and sea in the Solomons, beginning with those of Marine Lieutenant Dwight Shepler, who sketched at Henderson Field in August 1942.[1] Richard Tregaskis's book *Guadalcanal Diary*, a reporter's story of fighting on the island in 1942, became a best-seller in 1943. Another correspondent, John Hersey, at the beginning of a brilliant career in 1943, published *Into the Valley*, also about the 1942 fighting. James Jones's *The Thin Red Line* came later, in 1962. Accounts by historians were legion, first among them Samuel Eliot Morison's *The Struggle of Guadalcanal* (1949), which turned history into literature.

Hollywood made Tregaskis's book *Guadalcanal Diary* into an important "true" film of the same name that came out at the end of 1943 and that was better known than the book. Film buffs still widely praise *Pride of the Marines* (1945) as the real-life story of Al Schmid, who was blinded at Guadalcanal. Also about the Solomons, *Flying Leathernecks* starred John Wayne and appeared in 1951. *The Gallant Hours*, with Jimmy Cagney as Admiral Bull Halsey in October and November 1942, came in 1960.

Each of these productions, and many more, had its own perspective on the South Pacific war making, but the conflict was ever enticing to

Hollywood. Within days of the announcement of the sickening destruction of the Sullivans, moviemakers were considering how to put the catastrophe on the screen. We don't know who in Hollywood first contacted Tom and Alleta in mid-January 1943. United Artists and Warner Brothers intimated an interest in a film. The gossip columnist Louella Parsons recounted that David O. Selznick, who had created his own enormously successful independent production company and had triumphed with *Gone with the Wind* (1939), had the lead.[2]

This ripple of notice began Hollywood's shaping of the story about the Sullivans, which would survive in American beliefs. Idiosyncratic in leaning more heavily in the direction of Iowa than the South Pacific, *The Fighting Sullivans* would eventually leave a permanent residue on Waterloo as well as on the United States.

In their dismaying but exotic position, Tom and Alleta at once signed an agreement with the William Morris Agency. The agency represented people not under contract who had something to sell to Hollywood. William Morris would speak for the rights the couple had over the family's history. Here again we do not know exactly how the couple executed this bargain. More than likely, naval authorities who held the hands of Tom and Alleta designed it. The arrangement expired on March 10, 1943, and was probably drafted to keep everyone at bay until the poor parents could make at least a minimally measured decision.[3] Moreover, one of the naval officers piloting the husband and wife around had a connection to Jules Schermer, a Hollywood writer and critic. Schermer was developing the outlines of a story and working with Edward Doherty, a reporter on the *Chicago Sun* known for his sentimental but straightforward human-interest stories. Doherty was writing up a Sullivan tale using the seven articles from the *Chicago Herald-American* that Basil Talbott had written. These weepies had reimagined the Sullivans for people across the United States as soon as the sinking of the *Juneau* got into the papers. With his own trips to Waterloo Doherty supplemented the inquiries of his colleague Talbott.[4]

Naval authorities saw the possibilities of a film and pushed the living Sullivans to mull over how Hollywood might put the five brothers on the screen. Then the service encouraged Hollywood to tell the family story and introduced Tom and Alleta to the right people. The navy's

Industrial Incentive Division wanted to enlarge its connection to the Sullivans, and again its commanding officer, Clark Woodward, hoped that a movie would continue to energize war workers, certainly those building ships.[5]

The prize went to Sam Jaffe, a successful agent and an imposing jack-of-all-trades. He led production at Paramount and Columbia Pictures before expanding his career as the head of an effective talent agency, breeding stars and linking players and studios. He represented actors and actresses, but he also had skills in amassing the elements necessary for a picture—a script, suggestions for casting, a production team, and some capital. He could sell such a package to a company. Schermer initially went to Jaffe with ideas for a movie and some of Doherty's written work, but as Schermer and Doherty roughed out a story, Jaffe moved ahead on his own.

He embarked on a partnership with Lloyd Bacon, an experienced Hollywood director. Bacon had begun his working life as an actor in silent films. But he soon graduated to the role of director by the late 1920s. By the time his career ended in the mid-1950s, he had directed about 100 mainly nondescript movies, although he reliably and efficiently turned out acceptable commodities. His *42nd Street* in 1933 was exceptional. Perhaps his most famous movie was the biopic of Notre Dame's illustrious football coach, *Knute Rockne: All American* (1940). Among many other things in this picture about South Bend, Indiana, Rockne inspired his Fighting Irish to win a game for their dead teammate George Gipp, played by Ronald Reagan. A longtime director with Warner Brothers, Bacon had authority over many of Jimmy Cagney's films with that studio.[6] In the spring of 1943, for Warners, Bacon had finished *Action in the North Atlantic* with Humphrey Bogart. But Bacon was looking for new venues, and a Sullivans' film intrigued him. He bought himself out of his Warner's contract to collaborate with Jaffe.[7]

Bacon had clout with the navy, a major asset. He had served in World War I and in 1943 was in the naval reserve. Bacon also had experience in making films about the navy that required its cooperation: *Here Comes the Navy* in 1934 and *Devil Dogs of the Air* in 1935, both with Cagney, and *Wings of the Navy* in 1939.[8] Again and again Bacon used his naval contacts to ensure that the Sullivans would sign on with him and

Jaffe. Over and over the naval officers who were squiring the Sullivans around the country recommended Bacon as the man who would treat the family with the appropriate thoughtfulness.

Jaffe orchestrated a visit with the Sullivans while they were on the navy tour through the Midwest in March 1943 and brought Bacon with him to Minneapolis to arrange a deal. Jaffe slathered the parents with patriotic talk. In addition to telling Tom and Alleta about Bacon's navy service and his role in navy pictures, Jaffe introduced Bacon as the famous director of *Knute Rockne*, because "it had captured some of the motive and sentiment" that a film about the Sullivans would express.

Stimulated by the announcement that Alleta would baptize a destroyer named after her boys, Bacon and Jaffe initially titled the movie *The USS* The Sullivans. It would begin with the actual christening of the ship and then tell the "wonderful story" of how the destroyer received its name and pay tribute to "an American family and their devotion and loyalty." Hollywood would show Tom and Alleta, honest and hardworking, raising their five boys and a daughter in an ordinary American community. Always kept in line by strict but caring parents, the children would grow up. Little adventures, minor scrapes, and a growing fraternal bond would define their lives. Nonetheless, as Jaffe and Bacon realized, every happy moment in the movie would foreshadow what must happen after the boys joined the navy. A movie about wholesome familial life would have a stunning turnaround when *all five* in one family would die at the hands of the brutal Japanese.

But in Minneapolis, Jaffe and Bacon were negotiating with Tom and Alleta while the couple was still obligated to the Morris Agency. Apparently the parents, or more likely the navy, found reason not to work with William Morris, but a deal could not be consummated with anyone else for a few days. Thus, when the parents (and Gen and Keena) went to Chicago, the next stop on their trip, Jaffe and Bacon tagged along waiting for the expiration of the William Morris option. A lawyer accompanied them for this last round of consultations. With the goodwill of the navy men surrounding the family, the two entrepreneurs secured the film rights to the family's story. The Sullivans' world had collapsed just two months before. Tom and Alleta dealt with a business, The U. S. S. The Sullivans, Inc., that Jaffe and Bacon incorporated and that would make the film. Jaffe also signed on Tom, Alleta, and Gen as technical advisers. In her latest unaccustomed job, Alleta suggested that Cagney play the lead role of her firstborn, son George.[9] Jaffe recalled that "at the end of . . . [each] day [Tom] was drinking a lot, boilermakers"—a shot of whiskey followed by a beer chaser. "He was . . . so drunk at night."[10]

In Chicago, sister Gen announced that she was joining the WAVES (Women Accepted for Volunteer Emergency Service); she wanted to contribute to the war effort in this women's naval reserve. Tom and Alleta then visited one of the *Juneau*'s ten survivors, now recovering in a nearby hospital from his week in the ocean after the sinking of the light cruiser months before. Allen Heyn told Mother and Dad Sullivan that a shark had eaten their oldest child. "They didn't take it well, of course."[11] Who would not have been drunk as much as possible?

Jaffe recalled years later that he had borrowed $450,000—about half the cost of the film—to make it viable. Tom and Alleta, along with Gen and Keena, according to Jaffe's recollections, required only that the two moviemen contribute to a navy charity and give the family money for a chicken farm, estimated to cost between $25,000 and $35,000; other sources say that the family wanted money for grandson Jimmy's education. The extant official records indicate that $5,000 went into the estates of each of the boys—a total of $25,000.[12] Because of the tax laws, this procedure ultimately gave Tom and Alleta (and Al's son Jimmy, who received his father's share) more cash from the deal.

In California in early April at the christening of the destroyer the USS *The Sullivans*, Bacon, Jaffe, and Schermer discussed their production with Admiral Woodward, then in charge of the Sullivan parents. Nonetheless, the navy's Industrial Incentive Division would not permit the Hollywood people to film the actual ceremony, which they had wanted to use in the movie. This eventually prompted a name change—to *The Sullivans*—for the proposed film.[13]

Following the christening, Tom and Alleta went south to Los Angeles and Hollywood, under the wing of Bacon and his wife. Bacon and Jaffe had matters in hand, but part of the reason for this trip was to shop the Sullivans around and to look for a studio that would underwrite the so-far independent production. Bacon wined and dined the Waterloo parents and showed them the town. "He sure is wonderful," wrote

Alleta to her friend Nell Turner in Waterloo. During this traveling, Alleta fussed via the mails about Tom's opportunities to drink. Her anxieties peaked when they toured Hollywood. She might have to "Hog tie" her husband.[14]

According to the *Courier*, Bacon declared in mid-April that Doherty would write the story. In the early spring, Doherty had traveled to Waterloo to interview people and, after a break, returned to the town for more information. At the end of April and in early May, he was still investigating, seeing people in the city, and reporting daily by phone to Bacon in Hollywood. By the middle of May Doherty was in Hollywood to do the writing. But Bacon himself was also putting on paper notions that had occurred to him after his several deliberations with the parents about their children.[15] Then, in the late spring of 1943, Jaffe spent $25,000 to buy Doherty and his friend Schermer out of the project. For some reason, Jaffe did not want the two involved, and the money avoided a possible lawsuit. The newspaper man and the writer did receive screen credit for the story (and later an Oscar nomination for a now-defunct award, Best Original Script). Toward the end of May, Jaffe and Bacon turned over the material from Doherty, as well as their own ideas, to Mary McCall Jr. McCall was an independent and educated New York feminist. More important, she was a popular author of short stories and, especially, a fluent and talented writer of movie dialogue. The screenplay was hers, and the Jaffe-Bacon corporation paid her $25,000. Among themselves Schermer, Doherty, Bacon, Jaffe, and McCall had acquired a lot of facts and opinions about the Sullivans, and they were assimilated into the script (and ultimately the movie) that was being put together.[16]

Jaffe and Bacon had rushed to get Tom and Alleta's signatures. In return, as perhaps Alleta dimly realized, Hollywood offered a valuable prize and would give the family the burnished reputation that she aimed for but that had eluded the Sullivans before the war.

Bacon and Jaffe, independent entrepreneurs, had been looking for a film studio with which they could do business and, in July, made arrangements with 20th Century-Fox and its famed head of production, Darryl F. Zanuck.[17] Often impossible to deal with and sometimes enigmatic, Zanuck was instrumental in forming the Fox studio in the mid-1930s. He toiled prodigiously at this trade and had a brilliant sense of how to make entertaining and sometimes thought-provoking movies that would appeal to a wide range of Americans.[18]

For two years, from age fourteen through sixteen, Zanuck had served in World War I, and in 1942 at age forty he had gone back to the army to make films for the service and had even gotten himself in combat before he was mustered out. At his old job in the summer of 1943, Zanuck was looking for new ventures, and one of his first decisions in mid-July was to buy into the Sullivans' project.[19] Indeed, some of his people had earlier been in the running to deal with the Sullivan family through the William Morris Agency. Zanuck now put his stamp on the movie-to-be, which would serve Zanuck's core values.

Keenly patriotic, especially when it came to war, Zanuck liked romanticized American history and film biographies. Back in Hollywood in 1943, he wanted to make a movie of Wendell Willkie's internationalist book *One World* (1943). In 1940 FDR had defeated the popular Willkie for the presidency, and then Roosevelt employed him as a roving ambassador as World War II drew America in. *One World* had reported on Willkie's travels. When Zanuck could not bring off a movie about Willkie, he passionately took up a connected gamble—the story of Woodrow Wilson and the League of Nations at the end of World War I. He oversaw *Wilson*, a box-office loser, soon after he finished *The Sullivans*. Zanuck participated in Hollywood's determination to display all Americans as members of a perfect middle class and was imbued with nostalgia for the Midwest of the late nineteenth and early twentieth centuries. He had grown up himself in Wahoo, Nebraska, and the lot of common families attracted him—he had made Fox's *The Grapes of Wrath* just before the war.[20] This famous film was thought authentically to portray the experience of migrant workers—in this case the Joad family—during the Depression. There were the impoverished, like the Joads, whom Hollywood in the 1930s endowed with a certain seemliness; and the rich, whom it often spoofed; and finally the overwhelming majority of the rest of us. Zanuck thought of himself as a writer who knew ordinary citizens. Stars did not tempt him so much as scripts about real lives, and we can see these priorities in *The Sullivans*.[21] "The people" was a trope of the era.

Most of the film fit neatly into the formulas that two famous runs of movies had perfected. From the 1920s to the 1940s, a large number of short *Our Gang* comedies, mainly released by MGM, had entertained audiences. *Our Gang* highlighted poor kids who fought with the pompously wealthy, mean cops, and overbearing adults. Hollywood showed the exploits of regular children. In the late 1930s and early 1940s MGM also had a collection of hits in its *Andy Hardy* movies that cast Mickey Rooney as a well-off but supposedly typical American teenager. In *The Sullivans* Zanuck brought together elements of *Our Gang* and *Andy Hardy*. He was moreover sharing in Hollywood's Americanization of the Irish. In November 1944, Fox came out with *Irish Eyes Are Smiling*, a biopic of Ernest R. Ball, a famous singer and composer of sentimental ballads with Irish subjects. Zanuck wrote in early 1944 that *The Sullivans* was "a typical Irish Catholic story."[22]

Zanuck, finally, wanted *The Sullivans* to look like *How Green Was My Valley*, perhaps the finest film 20th Century-Fox had produced. From Richard Llewellyn's book of the same name, *How Green Was My Valley* had won the Academy Award for Best Picture of 1941, just as Zanuck left for the battlefields. The picture charts the destruction of the Morgans, a Welsh coalmining family of six sons and a daughter. *How Green Was My Valley* combined scenes of saccharine familial bliss and unspeakable heartbreak in depicting the woes that come upon the Morgans and their small community. The film made the career of Roddy McDowall. He became a household name after he played Huy Morgan, the youngest son, who told his family's story in flashback.

Now Zanuck planned to do the same thing with a similarly situated family in the United States. Fox would put up some of the costs, contribute its facilities, distribute the film, and collect part of the profits. Zanuck himself would oversee *The Sullivans*, and at various times he intervened with forceful orders on what had to be done to satisfy his ideas about the product.[23]

Mary McCall Jr. had readied her script by the end of the summer of 1943, and it presented few problems for 20th Century-Fox in dealing with governmental and nongovernmental regulators. The Sullivans' travails in 1943 had captured the attention of everyone, and McCall showed a modicum of respect for the family. Fox also sought and got official advice from the military for the scenes leading up to the attack on the *Juneau* and a brief battle scene itself. The film required only "limited cooperation." Bacon received stock footage from the navy—footage of battle at sea—and earned praise from the service.[24]

McCall's story did occur in many different time periods spanning over twenty-five years. In the first very brief part of the film, from 1914 to 1922, we witness the baptisms of the boys. We know nothing about this first set of players, babies or very small children, who had the roles. In the second and more substantial part of the film, which takes place in 1928–1929, the five boys are children, aged six to fourteen, and we learn how they are being raised. In the last part of the movie, we see a family of young adults in 1939–1943. There were thus several different Sullivan casts, but the making of the movie itself split up differently. Bacon shot the *exterior* scenes of Waterloo, both from 1928–1929 and 1939–1943, in September and early October on location in Santa Rosa, California, north of San Francisco.[25] The *interior* scenes ran from 1914 to 1943 and took place mainly though not exclusively in the Sullivan home. Bacon created them in Fox's studios in November.

In Hollywood, in mid-September, Jaffe was still auditioning young men to play the grown-up Sullivan boys while Bacon, in Santa Rosa, had kicked off the outdoor story. That is, the preteen and early teenage actors playing the Sullivan children of 1928–1929 were already working outside in the late summer, most notably on winter scenes in the (fake) snow when the temperature was 104 degrees. Only later did the young adults selected to play the grown-up Sullivans get up to Santa Rosa to shoot the outside portions of the period from 1939 to 1943. Although the moviemakers auditioned some experienced actors to play the five young men, Bacon and Jaffe finally settled on novices.[26] Then, in October, children and grown-up performers trouped south for the inside work, which also involved filming the christenings of 1914–1922 and putting to work the extras taking part in these rituals. McCall was rewriting in September and October but added only indoor scenes. While Bacon did not include all of these scenes in the finished product, he filmed them in November in the Fox studios.

This interior effort occupied only a few weeks, and war scenes that were to have been filmed at the San Diego Naval Base and other scenes of the boys in uniform were scrapped. These were cuts that Zanuck required: he wanted the focus on the Sullivans' life in Waterloo. This was a tragedy on the home front, he said, not a war movie. In mid-November, in their guise as technical advisers, Tom and Alleta, with Gen, briefly went again to Hollywood to observe how Bacon was shooting the story. The three remaining family members basically provided some positive publicity. Alleta wrote that the people at 20th Century-Fox were "a swell bunch" and that "the picture is going to be wonderful." According to *The Courier*, 20th Century-Fox told the Sullivans that "the film will be one of the greatest ever produced."[27]

By the end of November shooting was complete, and by early 1944, 20th Century-Fox had edited *The Sullivans*. In New York at the end of January, the studio privately showed the parents the "grand picture," as Alleta called it.[28] In February, for premieres on each coast, all eyes were on Tom and Alleta yet once more, although Jaffe and Bacon delayed the Waterloo opening until March.

# CHAPTER TEN

## *THE SULLIVANS* AND

## *THE FIGHTING SULLIVANS*

The reviews of the movie published in the wake of sold-out New York and California premiers were mainly admiring. The sentimentality of a movie that ended in tragedy did not seem to trouble sophisticated audiences or serious and urbane critics. They all noted what could not be missed: the evil that the war could do to an upstanding family. *The Sullivans* was "a distillation of Americanism, of American family life and American boyhood." Exhibitors were told, "You can stand in your lobby with your head up while you're playing [this] one."[1] But 20th Century-Fox looked to the Midwest, and particularly to Waterloo, for what your next-store-neighbor American would make of the movie. The film and its reception demand sustained attention. *The Sullivans* delivered the earliest and most influential history of the family; it is also the most important single piece of *evidence* we have today about the Sullivan family.

In Waterloo, as patrons settled into their seats in early March 1944 to see *The Sullivans*, they would first notice an absence of star-quality names—no Jimmy Cagney. Zanuck and Jaffe were content with many new faces.[2] The lead credit went to Anne Baxter, who had earned a reputation for a role in *The Magnificent Ambersons* (1942) and in 1946 would go on to win an Oscar for Best Supporting Actress in *The Razor's Edge*. In *The Sullivans* she did an indifferent job in her modest performance as Al's girlfriend and young wife and mother, Keena Rooff, always called in the film by her Catholic given name, Katherine Mary. A group that never reached stardom adequately played the other young adults of her age, the six Sullivan siblings. But the film also required real performers for that part of the movie that depicted the childhood of the boys in 1928–1929. These underage actors and actress cast in the earlier scenes did not receive screen credits. This group too never had much of a career except—as commentators often note—Bobby Driscoll, who played the six-year-old Al and graduated to notable performances in some Walt Disney movies including Jim Hawkins in *Treasure Island* (1950). His part resembled that of Roddy McDowall as Huy Morgan in *How Green Was My Valley*.[3]

Three character actors carry *The Sullivans*. Thomas Mitchell and Selena Royle play Tom and Alleta. An outstanding talent, Mitchell had, in 1939, made key appearances in *Gone with the Wind* and *Stagecoach* and won a Best Supporting Actor award for the latter. He was billed under Anne Baxter. Selena Royle, Alleta, had a career on the New York stage, but *The Sullivans* began for her a decade in Hollywood in a series of motherly parts. Tall, attractive, and decorous, she had a knack for being "maternal," despite a shapely hint of sexuality. In *The Sullivans* she received the lead billing among the supporting cast but made the greatest imprint on the movie. Mitchell and Royle gave exceptional performances that expressed the undercurrents of a sort of patriarchal marriage. Tom Sullivan hovers on the authoritarian, but love for his children, a competent woman, and a keenness for family life rescue him. Alleta Sullivan knows exactly how to handle her man, to defer to him when appropriate and to intercede with him for the sake of the children when necessary. This dynamic ran through the picture.

Ward Bond, the third character actor, had a small role. He played a Lieutenant Commander Robinson, who enlisted the Sullivans in the navy. Bond showed his acting prowess later when, as Robinson, he took on the ugly job of informing Tom and Alleta that their sons were dead. This gripping scene at the end of the film lasted only a few minutes, but it will receive close attention here. We must note at once, however, that Bond along with Mitchell and Royle made it work. The peerless acting of the three vividly showed the shattering of the lives of Tom and Alleta. The credits also tell us that Alfred Newman, who composed the at-times-similar music for *How Green Was My Valley*, was the music director for the movie. After the credits, we see (in quotes) THIS IS A TRUE STORY, and the story that follows evolves in flashback, as did the story of the Morgans in *How Green Was My Valley*. During a movie admiral's speech at the christening of the destroyer the USS *The Sullivans* in 1943, after the boys' deaths, Tom and Alleta think back to the christenings of the five. The admiral eulogizes the brothers, as the parents remember the Catholic baptism of each of the boys from 1914 to 1922. These sequences foreshadow the many happenings throughout the movie that show friendly and benign Roman Catholic ceremonies. But after quickly introducing us to an upright religiosity through the baptisms, the film has Tom and Alleta next remember events some years later, in 1928–1929, when the Sullivan children range from age six through fourteen.[4] This part of the film recalls the *Our Gang* comedies.

On a summer morning we meet the boys as they get up and greet their father while he is shaving. A nice touch tells us that these Iowans follow the Philadelphia Phillies and their pitcher Clarence Mitchell. The family breakfasts—the first of many times the Sullivans eat together—and Dad goes off to his trainman's job after tricking his sons into gardening while they dig for fishing worms. The boys run through the fields and alleys, climb a water tower overlooking the tracks, and wave good-bye to their father. In the next scenes they return from fishing, get a dog, and have a fight, which jeopardizes Al's first communion for which the boy is preparing. After the brothers discuss the fight with Father Francis, he clears Al for his communion. The Sullivans find an old boat and take it for a sail, only to have it sink. George rescues Al, who can't swim. This scene derived from a real incident. That same summer, Tom catches the boys smoking in the woodshed but cures them of early smoking by plying them with cigars, which make them sick. Real life also formed the basis of this scene.[5]

After another breakfast, Tom tries to pull out one of Al's loose baby teeth with a string but loses his own gold tooth. Winter arrives, and the boys—minus George and led by Frank—decide to build a wood box on the porch. They cut out a portion of the outside wall that abuts the box to get wood inside expeditiously, but in doing so they saw through a water pipe. This scene also originated from the recollections of family and friends, but it got elaboration. Tom and Alleta come back to the house, and Tom mistakenly blames George as the brains of the operation. An unpleasant argument ensues, and Tom slaps George, who runs away from home. Outstanding in conveying Tom's pugnacious streak, this scene shows a capable Alleta shrewdly deferring to paternal right. The contretemps skillfully carried forward this recurring theme. That night everyone goes out to look for George, who returns the next morning for breakfast. With Alleta's prompting, the boy apologizes to Tom for challenging his authority, but Tom also says he is sorry. George sits down at breakfast, and Tom beams down the table at his family. Fade to black, as we hear the admiral continuing his eulogy, and listen to up-to-date late 1930s popular music, as the recollections continue, ten years on.

This second part of the movie takes us from 1939 to early 1943, and we transition from *Our Gang* to an *Andy Hardy*—style movie, with the grownup Sullivan boys facing the challenges of young manhood in small-town America. Tom and Alleta remind themselves of the distinctive personalities of their sons in July 1939: George likes motorcycles; Frank, fishing; Joe, baseball; Matt, girls; and Al is the baby. As the film introduces the grown-up children at breakfast, it again introduces the Philadelphia Phillies, now minus pitcher Clarence Mitchell. Al, a junior at Waterloo East High, has won a varsity letter, but the rest of the boys are working. All five and Gen attend a sociable motorcycle race, where popcorn and cold drinks are for sale. With his passion for the cycle, George wins. There, love at first sight occurs when Al meets Katherine Mary Rooff. At a dance after the race, they become an item. Some months later, in March 1940, Al gives Katherine Mary a ring, with his sister's approval, and asks his mother if he can bring Katherine Mary to Sunday dinner. His brothers learn of the romance, and at dinner they make things hot for Al. They have discovered a draft of a love letter to Katherine Mary, and at the meal they exploit its sentiments to let on that Al has a "line" used on many women. Katherine Mary runs from the house, and Al chases after her, though his attempt to make up fails.

This story too had a place in family lore, but Hollywood artfully spun it out. A couple of scenes show Al, in his high-school sweater, depressed. The rest of the Sullivans, especially his four brothers, feel terrible, and the whole family troops off to Katherine Mary's house—Tom with a bouquet of flowers in his hands—to explain and apologize. Katherine Mary is appeased, and shortly after she and Al get back together a Catholic ceremony marries them in the spring of 1940. We next see them on their ten-month anniversary coming home from the doctor, who has informed Katharine Mary of a pregnancy. Al's brothers and sister come to hear the good news. Because Al took off work to accompany his wife to the doctor's, his boss has fired him. His brothers pledge to ante up some immediate cash and promise to find him other employment. In the next scene, they are all waiting to hear how Katherine Mary's labor is going. The couple has a son, James, or Jimmy, and the nurses present the baby to the happy pair. Fade out.

Now it is the morning of December 7, 1941. Hollywood had great expertise in depicting how Americans would recall the date. Filmmakers showed it on calendars, desk pads, invitations, and bulletin boards. In *Bombardier* (1943), a trainee airman tells men of the attack at prayer in a military chapel. The movies also proclaimed the evil tidings on intercoms and loudspeakers, but mostly on the radio.[6] In *Texas to Bataan* (1942), on Sunday just before church, a radio announcer breaks into the Christmas music with news of the airstrike. *Pride of the Marines* interrupts normal fare during Sunday dinner. In *The War Against Mrs. Hadley* (1942), she is annoyed that the broadcast spoils her birthday. *They Were Expendable* (1945) has a John Wayne character learning of Pearl Harbor as he writes a request for transfer away from ignorant military superiors. In *The Enchanted Cottage* (1945) the announcement foreshadows the disfigurement of the protagonist after he joins up.[7]

In *The Sullivans* the family, including Al, Katherine Mary, and little Jimmy, nine months old according to the script, has gathered at Adams Street on a Sunday day of rest. No one is going to Mass, but while reading the "funny papers," lounging around the living room, and listening to music on the radio, the Sullivans hear of the treachery. The boys decide at once to join the navy—that is, all except Al, who has a wife and child. The decision animates Tom, although of course it worries Alleta.

In a following scene the older brothers drop in at Al and Katherine Mary's before setting off to the naval recruiting office. Katherine Mary tells Al he must go with the others. He does, and the five march to the recruiter's. When the officer in charge, Lieutenant Commander Robinson, cannot guarantee that they will serve together, they spurn an enlistment. But in a letter delivered to 98 Adams the navy gives its permission; it accedes to the request of the Sullivans that they sign on as a unit. They enroll with Robinson. The boys meet with Tom, who tallies up their debts and proposes to pay them with a mortgage on the house. Katherine Mary and Jimmy will live at the Sullivan home. The boys leave Waterloo as a group. Fade out.

The Sullivans put five stars in their window. While the movie is in black and white, we can imagine that they are blue. But now the mailman is coming and Alleta, waiting at a gate, receives two letters. She and Katherine Mary read them over the breakfast table. Fade to black.

A sign says "NAVY DEPARTMENT," and a big military bureaucracy toils. Then a newspaper headline reads: NAVAL BATTLE RAGING IN THE SOLOMONS. Cut to ship's gunners firing at Japanese airplanes. George is wounded and taken below. The ship is hit and must be abandoned. The four brothers meet up, rush to sickbay, and take George off his bed. "We can't go swimming without you." The screen goes black as we hear an explosion. Although the screenplay had longer battle scenes, the film only briefly shows men at war. Additionally, although the movie battle bore little relation to how the *Juneau* actually went down, the screenplay had a long, sweeping shot of ocean water with a few specks in it—men. This scene from the screenplay did accurately represent what happened to George at the end of his life. Bacon and Jaffe seem to have deleted it on their own, and they must have had some idea that the navy would not want to see such a wartime truth in *The Sullivans*.[8]

Audiences at the movies in 1944 and 1945 knew how this film would end. How should Hollywood reveal that all the Sullivans were killed? In a sanitized way, standard war movies often had American soldiers die in combat. Hollywood had also shown families at home dealing with the death of their nearest and dearest.

In 1943 a number of films took up this kind of loss. In *Tender Comrade*, a new husband went off to fight, leaving his pregnant wife, and never came back. But she later affirmed to their baby that dad died to give the son a better chance in life. In *Air Force* the crusty sergeant of an air crew learned soon after Pearl Harbor that the Japanese attack had killed his pilot son. The father received the son's personal effects in a handkerchief, asked if that was all, and shed perhaps one tear before returning to his job. *A Guy Named Joe* had scenes in paradise, although this fantasy did not show the trauma of a family learning of death, but of a fiancée. Spencer Tracy played an aviator killed in action, and Irene Dunne his bereft beloved. His otherworldly superior, Lionel Barrymore, then ordered Tracy to help out novice flyer Van Johnson, and Tracy accomplished his mission with the advice of another, longer-dead sidekick, Barry Nelson. In the process Tracy also witnessed Johnson's successful romance with Dunne—or did Tracy somehow intrude in the proceedings? Steven Spielberg remade this effective bit of fluff in 1989 as *Always* with Richard Dreyfuss. *Happy Land*, released at the end of 1943, was set in the make-believe town of Heartfield, Iowa. The movie was filmed in Santa Rosa, where almost at that moment Bacon and Jaffe were putting together the outside scenes of *The Sullivans*.[9] In *Happy Land* the family lost its only child, Rusty, when his ship was torpedoed. Then his great-grandfather came down from heaven to help Rusty's dad face the news. Dad was accepting when he understood that Rusty had a full life, gave himself to a large and important cause, and had a good surviving army buddy who would substitute as a son. *Since You Went Away* (1944), distributed after *The Sullivans*, had the most complex plot. Dad came home in one piece, but the war took the fiancé of one of his two daughters. Critics praised the film for its mature treatment of the home front, particularly its concern for women.[10]

Hollywood had an impressive self-consciousness about its own role in conveying communal emotions. In *Wake Island* (1942), star William Bendix played a Marine shaving in front of a pinup picture of movie glamour-girl Betty Grable. In *A Wing and a Prayer* (1944), leading man Dana Andrews reprimanded a glory-seeking pilot by telling him, "This isn't Hollywood." *Since You Went Away* had an arresting scene in a movie house where a newsreel celebrated a returning veteran. A man in the audience got up and exited the theater. Anguished, he had on his arm a black mourning band.

If Americans did not know how Washington conveyed the distasteful tidings of death, they could have learned by watching MGM's film *The Human Comedy*, released in 1943. A sentimental but sometimes engrossing movie about small-town life during the war, the film focused on Homer Macauley, a boy working part time delivering telegrams. Mickey Rooney brilliantly played this sympathetic character, who rode up to homes on his bicycle with the fearful Western Union messages that would, in accord with the wartime convention, turn a blue star to gold. In one scene Rooney broke down as he informed a mother that her son had been killed. Indeed, Darryl F. Zanuck, the head of 20th Century-Fox, had ordered his employees making *The Sullivans* to attend *The Human Comedy*.[11]

After the screen went explosively black in *The Sullivans*, the next scenes in which the family (and the audience) are informed of the deaths of the boys are absorbing and flawless. The movie here relied on *The Human Comedy* and Alleta's recollections of the awful moment. *Our Gang* and *Andy Hardy* sentiments gave way to instruction in a common and sacrificial American civil religion. Tom and Alleta, Gen, Katherine Mary, and Jimmy are at breakfast. Tom prepares for work, even though the Sullivans in Waterloo are expecting Lieutenant Commander Robinson, who has called and said that he wants to see them. They don't seem nervous, though we cannot know what fears they may be disguising from each other. Robinson arrives, and the family greets him. He says he has very bad news. Gen screams, but Tom beckons her to be quiet. Robinson says usually the navy would send a telegram. Alleta asks: Which one? Katherine Mary asks: Is it Al? Lieutenant Commander Robinson says: "All five." Tom exclaims: "All five!" Closeups follow of Alleta, then of Katherine Mary, and last of the five stars in the window. Every member of the wartime audience would know that they will turn from blue to gold. Commander Robinson reads the telegram: "The navy regrets that Albert, George, Francis, Joseph, and Madison have been killed in action."

Tom hears the whistle of the train and tells the commander that he has not missed a day of work in thirty-three years and must go. In a remarkable shot that encapsulates a male expression of pain and comfort, he awkwardly pats his wife on the shoulder, then leaves the house. Again the camera focuses on Alleta as she says, "All five." Commander Robinson breaks the tension by saying that, on second thought, he will have the cup of coffee he initially refused. Alleta straightens up, gives him a determined smile, and goes to fetch the drink. Meanwhile, we trail Tom to his job. He climbs up on the train, and as it passes the water tower where the boys had waved him off to work fifteen years before, he gives a poignant, heartbreaking salute before he enters the caboose.

This set of shots, from Robinson's proclaiming of bad news to Tom's farewell, is a cinematic triumph. The sentiment in theaters sometimes was palpable, and later viewers from the late twentieth and early twenty-first century regularly report that they are reduced to tears—I certainly have been, and repeatedly. One film historian has written that "no other scene" in World War II movies produced "such deep emotion over the loss of American servicemen."[12]

The "highlight" of the film, Darryl Zanuck dictated, occurs when "the old man . . . gives his little salute." The executive producer was firm to his people: the movie was to wrap up quickly after Tom says good-bye. "Mr. Zanuck" ruled that many subsequent scenes were to be thrown out. Thus, we immediately hear the admiral concluding his eulogy, as the transition takes us to the present of the film, the christening of the USS *The Sullivans* in April 1943. Alleta baptizes the vessel and tells Tom that the boys are "afloat again." In the final few seconds we see the five Sullivan boys together in their navy uniforms—they will live in memory. Zanuck had said more than once that the end would be "a vision," "a shot of the five boys, in uniform, marching along . . . taken from the waist up."[13] Pictures of the five young actors posing as the Sullivan brothers when the *Juneau* was commissioned can be found. In our mind's eye we witness, as members of a screen audience, the brothers leaving our field of vision. The scene mimics the end of *How Green Was My Valley*, in which that film recalled, in retrospect, early happy days of the Morgan family in Wales. That Best Picture winner ended with an earlier shot of the five older Morgan brothers, who later in the film have died or left their village.

That is *The Sullivans*. At theaters less than two months later, however, picture-goers saw something different. The draw of the film in early 1944, despite the reviews, had been less than expected. The movie was renamed *The Fighting Sullivans* to intimate falsely that moviegoers were going to get a war story.[14] There may have been an argument with Zanuck, who expressly wanted a tale of trials at home, but we have little information about the decision to change the title. Bacon and Jaffe also wanted to simplify the complex flashback narration. *The Fighting Sullivans* soon became the familiar (and only accessible) version of the film, and we must describe how it differs from the unavailable original.[15]

From the time Bacon and Jaffe had joined forces as The U.S.S. The

*The Sullivans.* This movie poster dated from early 1944 (Everett Collection).

*The Fighting Sullivans.* This poster changed a domestic melodrama into a war movie (Everett Collection).

Sullivans, Inc., the symbol of the destroyer named after the family had intrigued Bacon. As we have seen, he had first wanted to call the movie *The USS The Sullivans*. When planning the picture in April 1943, Bacon prepared to shoot the christening of the ship the USS *The Sullivans* in which Tom and Alleta participated; as we have noted, he proposed to use the footage at the beginning of his movie.[16] But the navy forbade the filming, and all of McCall's scripts began as an actor-admiral extolled the virtues of the five dead sons at a made-in-Hollywood launch. The various versions of the script then all told the story by way of Tom and Alleta's reminiscences during the April 1943 baptism of the ship. That is, the original picture followed McCall's scripts and the flashback mode of storytelling.

*The Fighting Sullivans* differs from *The Sullivans* in that the story is not told in flashback. In *The Fighting Sullivans* the admiral's speech at the onset and its continuation at the inception of the second part vanish. The movie begins with the christenings of the boys. The careful viewer of *The Fighting Sullivans* can see that the priest's little spoken formula for each of the boys—"I christen thee . . ."—has been dubbed into this second version of the film. The original version did not have a priest talking, but rather an admiral at the ship's christening extolling the virtues of the boys, and the parents recollecting the baptisms of the boys themselves. In *The Fighting Sullivans* no voiceover accompanies the introduction to the scenes from 1928 and 1929, and a simple fade to black takes us from 1929 to 1939. In the later edition of the movie, at its end—after the upsetting declaration of their deaths in the Sullivan home, and Tom's good-bye in the train yard—the admiral makes a first appearance.

Tom, Alleta, Gen in a WAVES uniform, and Katherine Mary with Jimmy in a sailor suit are dedicating the USS *The Sullivans*. The admiral gives a continuous discourse about the boys. Alleta breaks a champagne bottle over the hull as the destroyer slips into the water carrying a deck full of cheering sailors. Alleta looks at her husband: "Tom, our boys are afloat again."

These alterations, I believe, strengthen the film by making the story easier to follow. Another alteration, which ends the film, is more problematic. The last shot of the boys marching together in *The Sul-*

*livans* does not appear. At the finish of a 1929 movie, *The Iron Mask*, the famed three musketeers, at the pearly gates, pull d'Artagnan up to them, and the four go skipping off to eternity. Now post–March 1944, in the last shot in *The Fighting Sullivans*, the four older boys are waving from heaven. Al runs up, and the five run in the direction of the musketeers. This scene replaces the shot of the boys marching, copied from the conclusion to *How Green Was My Valley*. THE END.

So we have a trio of climaxes in *The Fighting Sullivans*. First, the navy declares the deaths, and Dad Sullivan says good-bye. Second, not exactly an afterthought but a kind of rethinking of how the movie should end—the navy christens the USS *The Sullivans* in a longer continuous scene than in *The Sullivans*. Finally, we see a clear add-on—a scene in paradise in *The Fighting Sullivans* that does not appear in the original.

The scene depicting the christening of the USS *The Sullivans* dilutes one potent end to this film. If Alleta only offers Commander Robinson some coffee and Tom climbs into his caboose, we may have a dark film that hints at the meaninglessness of the deaths. Movies might represent death and trauma at home *if* Hollywood demonstrated the death as redemptive—*if* the film gave positive meaning to the loss. Hollywood had to make the deaths a renunciation for a greater good. So we have the ship-christening scene. However, I believe, someone thought even that inadequate. Bacon and Jaffe, or Zanuck, were looking to shape their own narrative of heroic salvation.

The Production Code Administration did not raise a question. Jaffe and Bacon submitted their script and rewrote bits of it a number of times to satisfy the PCA's Joe Breen. He asked that "Jeez" not be used; found unacceptable the phrase "before he was a gleam in his father's eye"; and worried about showing the toilet in scenes such as the opening one, when Tom shaves in the bathroom.[17] From the perspective of the twenty-first century, Breen made curious, even ridiculous, requests, but he did not complain about ending with the baptism of a ship; and neither did the navy or the government.

The moviemakers saw a problem and solved it their own way. The deck full of young men, and Alleta's remark that her sons were once more sailing, intimated that it might happen again; the immense family loss might serve no purpose. We did not discover salvation if the navy, with the *Juneau* as an example, filled a destroyer named *The Sullivans* with young men. The film insinuated that the bottom of the Pacific might soon claim this new ship of cheering sailors. What was achieved by recalling the boys to memory as the last scene in the original *The Sullivans* film had done?

These shots in *The Sullivans* bear comparison with the description of men off to war aboard ship in Willa Cather's 1922 novel, *One of Ours*, about the Great War: "The howling swarm of . . . arms and hats and faces looked like nothing but a crowd of American boys going to a football game somewhere. But the scene was ageless; youths were sailing away to die for an idea, a sentiment, for the mere sound of a phrase."[18] One could argue that the original *The Sullivans* was making a less than patriotic statement. What should the inventors of movie magic do? They provided a concluding scene of the Sullivans in another realm. Although Jaffe and Bacon (or Zanuck) borrowed this idea from the earlier *The Iron Mask*, they also worked with the actual ship-christening. There, a wooden Alleta had read from her own script that "the boys are looking down from heaven . . . happy."

Every Hollywood death implied salvation in the sense that, in the Christian framework in which the film industry operated, the evildoers received their just deserts at the Second Coming, and the good entered everlasting life. Hollywood sometimes explicitly showed this with the resurrection of the body (the musketeers and d'Artagnan in *The Iron Mask*); with benign ghost stories (the return of the great-grandfather in *Happy Land*); or with depictions of the ordered world of those who had passed over (the holy cosmos of *A Guy Named Joe*).[19] But *The Fighting Sullivans* grotesquely appropriated the spirit life from *The Iron Mask*.

The *Courier* made much of the New York and Hollywood openings in early February and, perhaps, gilded the lily in interpreting good reviews of the film as stellar. A headline bemoaned that Eager Audiences in Waterloo would have to wait until the Midwest premiere, although the largest cities in nearby states got the movie a few days before Waterloo. 20th Century-Fox set the date for March 9 at the East-Side Paramount with its 1,800 seats. During the period of waiting the local news attended to the remaining Sullivans—in January Tom and Alleta had gone to Washington to receive five Purple Hearts from the military.

Gen, who had enlisted in the WAVES the year before, finished her service and came home for a visit. Alleta topped the list of nominees for Iowa Mother of the Year.[20]

Len Fried, who ran the Paramount Theatre, widely advertised the opening. Two weeks before the debut, two regional radio stations featured four spots of advertising per day for the movie, increasing to eight the week before. Two thousand handouts were delivered to grocery stores, and the four leading downtown department stores, including Blacks, displayed placards in their windows. 20th Century-Fox, in "The Selling Approach on New Product," advised all theaters to corral naval service families, war workers, residents named Sullivan, or the Red Cross as "tie in[s]" to endorse the film. Exhibitors in other cities proclaimed that a "medium amount of exploitation" would benefit the "campaign" for customers. Later in the year, movie houses in places such as Astoria, New York; Buena Vista, Georgia; Ft. Branch, Indiana; Hay Springs, Nebraska; and Galena, Kentucky, reported that *The Fighting Sullivans* "just fits" or was "a grand picture for" or was "extra good" for small towns in the United States. But we also have rough attendance figures for audiences in big cities with movie palaces comparable to the Paramount. In Baltimore, Minneapolis, Philadelphia, St. Louis, Cincinnati, Pittsburgh, Kansas City, Cleveland, and Chicago the exhibitors played up patriotism. *The Fighting Sullivans* was playing for a second or even a third week, with something like an average take of well over $1,000 per day.[21]

Of course, in Waterloo the real Sullivan parents would appear, and nearing the debut, the *Courier* pulled out all the stops in describing the festivities that would supplement the opening. At the Paramount, Len Fried arranged for area dignitaries to be present. A twenty-five-member chorus of WAVES would sing a selection of patriotic songs, and an orchestra would perform. Quarter-page ads for the event repeatedly appeared in the newspaper: IOWA'S OWN HEROIC FAMILY; THE NAME THAT'S ON THE LIPS OF THE NATION. The people of Waterloo could now view for themselves the movie that dramatized the courage and adversity of common men and that put the town in an international spotlight in the long global crisis: SEE THE PICTURE THAT ALL WATERLOO WILL BE PROUD TO BE A PART OF.

Proceeds for the first showing would all go to the Sullivan Fund, which had gone into hibernation, but which the *Courier* now wanted to reawaken. The Paramount "brisk[ly]" sold ordinary tickets at $1.10, and special "loge" seats ran $5. Promoters spoke over and over about a "capacity" crowd that might raise something like $3,000 for the fund. Through the newspaper, the town's Sullivan Fund Committee told likely patrons that they might get turned away if they did not put their money down early. The theater sold only actual seats and would not provide standing-room tickets. Elaborating on how the Sullivans had brought the town an American and even universal renown, one member of the fund committee proclaimed that the Sullivans "have carried the name Waterloo, Iowa, to all parts of the nation and to all fighting fronts of the war."[22]

Tom and Alleta for a second time, and Gen and Keena for the first time, saw the film March 9 in Waterloo. One cannot help but wonder how they felt about seeing their idealized family; or the depiction of the shocking notification of the drowning of the boys. After leaving the movie house, Mother and Dad Sullivan said the movie was "just like having the boys right here again." The townsfolk agreed, staying away in droves.

Late in the afternoon on the next day, Friday March 10, the *Courier* pictured a fund committee member handing over a check to the newspaper for $493, one-sixth of what was expected. For the first of only two times in seventy years of its treatment of the Sullivans, the newspaper spoke about how the citizens of Waterloo had rejected the family. "From their cold watery graves of the south pacific," said the *Courier*, the five brothers had come back to their native city. But they did not return "in the flesh," and their arrival was disrespected because "Waterloo's thousands sent fewer than 500 people to welcome them home." The number came closer to 400 in that 1,800-seat auditorium, although those who did show up praised the movie. The same day, the paper reported that the Red Cross drive in Waterloo had met almost half of its 1944 goal of $87,500; it was only March, and benefactors had amassed $41,000. Although attendance was well below that in other towns and cities, *The Sullivans* ran at the Paramount for a week, and the numbers

Soldier Field, October 1944. Tom, daughter Gen, Alleta, Mayor Kelly, and FDR in Chicago (AP).

picked up when the profits went to 20th Century-Fox, and the family did not benefit.[23]

The historian must stop here and reflect once more about the feeling in Waterloo. Some unforgiving dislike gripped the natives. What sins—even beyond those I have ferreted out—had the Sullivan boys committed to engender the disdain that left at least 75 percent of the seats in the Paramount empty? An enormous gap existed between what leaders and elected officials wanted and what the public was willing to give in Waterloo. Its citizens were content that the Sullivan brothers had simply gone away and would never be seen again.

In 1944 Franklin Roosevelt ran for his unprecedented fourth term as president. The Sullivans were Roosevelt Democrats, most assuredly War Democrats. In July, four months after the gala Waterloo opening, Gen went to the Democratic National Convention in Chicago, and in

October Tom and Alleta were invited as special guests to a huge Roosevelt rally—again in Chicago, at Soldier Field. FDR and Mayor Ed Kelly, the nation's strongest big-city political boss, greeted the parents and introduced them to the gigantic audience. "Who's all right?" the crowd shouted, "Who's all right?" "The Sullivans! The Sullivans! The Sullivans!"[24] The admiration for the Sullivans nationally contrasted dramatically to the aversion for them in their birthplace.

# CHAPTER ELEVEN

## THE SULLIVANS AND

## *THE FIGHTING SULLIVANS*

While some historians of film have praised *The Fighting Sullivans* as one of the great movies of World War II, I find much of it mawkish and mainly of interest for cultural history. Unsurprisingly, the story glamorized the family. The Sullivans had to exemplify middle-class propriety. The crucial question is not whether the movie romanticized them, but how it transformed the truth, and to answer this question we need to explore more precisely the intentions of the moviemakers. From a comparison of the various screenplays of the film itself we can gauge the expectations of the film people in making *The Fighting Sullivans*. We also receive help from the censors and from the written correspondence among the producer, the director, and the studio.[1]

First, let us look at material that the film did *not* contain or misleading material that it did contain. The family was not living on Adams Street when the boys were growing up in 1928 and 1929. Bystanders saved Al from drowning, not his brothers; he did not go to high school. George and Frank served in the navy from 1937 to 1941, and for almost the entire second part of the movie, when the film showed them in Waterloo, they were away. Red rode a motorcycle in the first instance, and not George, who spent most of this time on a ship. The two oldest siblings sailed the ocean when little brother Al was courting Keena and when the movie pictured the continued bonding of George and Frank with their three younger brothers.

Sharp-eyed critics have also pointed out that some naval insignias are incorrect, that the motorcycles are the wrong models, and even that there are telltale signs of moviemaking equipment in the film.[2] Yet such problems have a negligible impact on our understanding of the family. Some issues are more problematic. Consider the absence of George and Frank for four years in the navy; the film does not mention this. But the fact that the two older brothers had spent 1937–1941 away intimated a greater independence than teammates might have had. The movie had a reason to ignore the first round of national service if *The Fighting Sullivans* did not merely simplify a complicated family life but also tried to convey a certain kind of stick-together family life.

Other "simplifications" have a different weight. All the shooting scripts had the performers using coarser colloquialisms than those that appear in the film, and in particular Bacon and Jaffe made Alleta's speech more refined. With prompting from Joe Breen, they excised a scene in the scripts in which a neighbor called the family "Shanty Irish" and in which Alleta retaliated by calling the detractor and others "bog-trotters . . . on all fours," an ethnic slur applied to poor farmers in Ireland that has since faded from the English language. In the scripts, Al and Katherine Mary get together at a party at the motorcycle clubhouse. Yet in the film it is an upscale dance hall, and there is no mention of a clubhouse. In the movie a puzzled Alleta asks Joe if he is still going to the World Series, and when he answers "yes," there is no further discussion of Alleta's puzzlement. Cut from the film is her response in the script: How can he afford to go when he is losing all his money at the pool hall? The movie, finally, eliminated some fighting and roughhousing scenes. The Sullivans on paper had less breeding than the family on the screen.

So far as I can tell, no official censoring body, but Bacon and Jaffe themselves (or Zanuck), cut these scenes; and the Production Code Administration had not given an order but a recommendation about the bog-trotters line.

Of equal importance, more scenes of the family eating meals together and more scenes about the family's faith made it into the film than Mary McCall had originally called for. Indeed, the Production Code Administration advised that because *so many* religious ceremonies occurred, Jaffe and Bacon should seek "technical advice" from the Catholic Church about the theological correctness of the renderings. Alleta never said to her boys in the picture what repeated scripts had called for on the morning of Sunday, December 7: "Pity you couldn't get your lazy carcasses out of bed in time for Church"; instead she says to George that he should not "be lolling over the funny papers." Jaffe recalled that although the Sullivans were "not a religious family at all," he and Bacon "ma[d]e them religious"—with christenings, communion, marriage, and going to heaven. "We thought for dramatic purposes this was a good idea."[3]

Three other crucial alterations (or simplifications) of domestic dynamics occur. The first concerns how the film portrayed Al's wedding, the birth of little Jimmy, and the nine-month-old baby when we see him as the Sullivans get together on the morning of Pearl Harbor. From the point of view of the Hollywood Code and conventional morality, the real Jimmy may not have been conceived in a proper marriage bed. Alleta's public fudging about the date of his birth hinted that the conception discomfited the family.[4] Hollywood felt Alleta's pain, and *The Fighting Sullivans* sweated to make Jimmy born in wedlock. "Mr. Zanuck" directed Bacon and McCall to put in some new material between the wedding and the birth to suggest the passage of time. Said Zanuck: "Otherwise it's going to seem that she is having the baby *much, much* too soon!"[5] The film mainly accomplished this goal by inserting a scene announcing a ten-month hiatus between Al and Katherine Mary's wedding and the doctor's announcement that they were going to have a baby. There is, however, no way to make the dates come out right if a moviegoer is a stickler for propriety with a competence at arithmetic.

To understand the second and third alterations we begin with Alleta's mother, May Abel. She was written into the earliest script and had a principal role in the childrearing, but she did not appear in the movie. The real May Abel was a daily presence for the six children. Here Hollywood's simplification of the family structure was not merely an ignorable misrepresentation. Tom never has a drink in the film, and Alleta as played by Selena Royle never takes to her bed or chews tobacco when she gets up. The movie presents Tom and Alleta as hands-on, conscientious parents. The movie brothers do not need May Abel to raise them, and the two other notable simplifications concern the parents.

The first is about Tom. Anyone who has looked at movies of the 1930s and 1940s knows that Hollywood cleverly pictured drinkers and drunks. Bacon and Jaffe did not try this with Tom, despite their repeatedly seeing him inebriated in March 1943 when the parents signed a contract. A shot in the movie shows Tom smacking George, and we do get a sense of paternal authoritarianism. But even this scene adulterates Mary McCall's screenplay. According to the shooting scripts, Tom actually hits George and "Gen whimpers, Ma is sickened."

The last simplification—with Alleta—is astonishing. Selena Royle's lack of physical similarity to Alleta is dramatic, a Cinderella effect. The film presented an amazing contrast between the faithfulness of the other members of the cast to the Sullivans they played, and the lack of fidelity in the depiction of Alleta. Mitchell bore some resemblance to Tom Sullivan. The ten actors who portrayed the Sullivan boys had a pleasant appearance, and so had the boys themselves. The actresses who played sister Gen and sister-in-law Katherine Mary (Keena) were comely young women, and so were the real Gen and Keena.

At least five other actresses were considered for the role of Alleta, born in 1895, who was forty-seven years old in 1942 and early 1943. Dorothy Vaughan was born in 1890; Fay Bainter, Phyllis Povah, and Dale Winter all in 1893; Mary Phillips in 1901.[6] Selena Royle was born in 1904 and was thirty-nine in 1943 when she played Alleta in 1942. Bacon and Jaffe deliberately cast Royle to differ from Alleta. We would never mistake the imposing Royle for the heavy and sloppy Alleta, out of her league in managing the family, and Royle never attempted to play Alleta Sullivan. When Royle had the role, Jaffe and Bacon repeatedly exchanged worries by phone and mail, as the script called for someone with a "stout, motherly body." Too "earthy," Royle had an "excellent, slim figure"; she might be "too chic-looking." More than once Jaffe told Bacon that they might do something to make her look heavier, "put something around her waistline." It appears that they did, though much less than necessary were Royle to resemble Alleta Sullivan.[7]

Covering up Jimmy's possible illegitimacy, ignoring Tom's alcoholism, and translating Alleta's dowdiness into Selena Royle's grace distorted basic realities in the Sullivan family. Bacon and Jaffe would not reveal the family's shortcomings in respect to middle-class proprieties. At the Waterloo premiere, the film's deficiencies in the way of facts did fluster friends and relatives. Eddie Doherty, who had written the initial story and who could sugarcoat with the best of them, liked the film. But, he said, Bacon and Jaffe had changed much in his original, and "a lot of gags and Hollywood touches have been inserted." One friend said the

Selena Royle. This publicity still dates from 1946 when Royle was forty-one or forty-two (Everett Collection).

movie was "enhanced" and "unrealistic." Keena Rooff Sullivan thought the movie was "embarrassing" and "BS." "Some of it was accurate, but for the most part it wasn't."[8]

Hollywood converted the Sullivans into something they were not, although we can easily comprehend why it generated the spurious treatment. Otherwise, government censors, Breen's Code office, and

Alleta and Marlene Dietrich. Beginning in World War II, the United Service
Organizations provided entertainment and programs for servicemen and
their families. In Hollywood in 1944, the movie star and the gold-star mother
help out (AP).

audiences might conclude that the brothers deserved their fate—and
Hollywood might never have released the film. Everyone shared the
values of the movie capital. The producer and director suggested that
Americans were an expendable resource if they could not be defined
according to a series of stereotypes.

Perhaps as he filmed, Bacon learned that the Sullivans were more
upright than he had first thought. More likely, he labored to make them
more upright than he discovered them to be. Bacon wanted the Sullivans to have far fewer deformities than they had. An argument can be
made that the more he consciously buffed up the Sullivans, the more
he had to make their deaths compensatory. That is to say, Bacon and
Jaffe may have added the ascent into another life to the film *because*
Hollywood worked so hard to make the Sullivans perfect embodiments

of middle-class ideals. The more acceptable the family, the more Hollywood had to do to counterbalance the loss.

There is another dimension to *The Fighting Sullivans* that must be explored but that runs in a different direction from the analysis above. The Great Depression and the worldwide collapse of capitalism gave life to the radical left in the United States. But the run-up to World War II and the Nazi-Soviet pact disturbed American supporters of international revolution and in particular of the Soviet Union. Then, when the United States and Russia became formal allies in 1942, communist sympathizers fostered a "united front" attitude with the USSR as a democratic and trustworthy collaborator. This attitude was for the most part consistent with run-of-the-mill Americanism. Nonetheless, the attitude went beyond standard Americanism to commit citizens to a universal and altruistic peoplehood and to a brave new world that would include the Soviet Union. In Hollywood, many differences were submerged as everyone eagerly made films that villainized Japan and Germany, glorified American and Russian warriors, and praised an improved American way.

Ten years after *The Sullivans* was released, an anticommunist "red scare," led by Senator Joseph McCarthy of Wisconsin, gripped the United States. Many Hollywood people whose politics had been acceptable during the war became suspect a decade later. The messages of a few wartime movies thought too accommodating to Russia were condemned, while many writers, actors, producers, and directors sympathetic to Russia in the 1930s and 1940s had more or less serious problems in their jobs. At the extreme, some of these people were blacklisted; others had their reputations besmirched, and hidden procommunist implications were sought in films from World War II.

The core individuals responsible for *The Fighting Sullivans* were left-liberals, some of whom had their troubles in the 1950s. Screenwriter Mary C. McCall Jr. and actress Selena Royle had their anticommunism questioned and their working careers abbreviated. Producer Sam Jaffe and director Lloyd Bacon were associated with performers on the left; Thomas Mitchell avoided much of a taint but continued to perform in movies that were often decoded as anti-anticommunist. I believe that the collaboration of the five on *The Fighting Sullivans* displayed a bland form of the popular-front mentality. The film spoke to how we the living in the United States might properly bear the death of loved ones for a greater cause. This was not just the sort of patriotism that might appeal to Joe Breen or the Office of War Information or the US Navy. In dealing with the death of the Sullivan men, the film also had in mind a different sort of concern about the virtue of individual suffering for a collective good. For the left, "the defeat of fascism" might demand that we forego private bourgeois allegiances.[9]

One historian evaluating *The Fighting Sullivans* found it one of the great propaganda films of the war and the "All five" scene "one of the greatest propaganda scenes in motion picture history."[10] Hollywood wanted audiences to accept martyrdom in World War II, and this accurately gets at what Bacon and Jaffe sought to achieve. Nonetheless, learning the purpose of the filmmakers and pronouncing it propaganda don't do the trick. We can decipher the intent of filmmakers, but capturing that intent tells us only part of what we need to know.

To understand *The Fighting Sullivans* we must also grasp what audiences found in the film. A gap may exist between what viewers were supposed to *take in* and what they actually *took from* the movie. More is at stake than examining intent.

To figure out how viewers in the past construed a movie, historians have hitherto relied almost entirely on newspaper articles by critics or on random reports describing how people reacted. Sometimes target groups who screened a film filled out questionnaires preserved in studio archives. In a few instances scholars have received private showings of films. This has led to historians giving supreme weight to their own individual screenings. Books have even depended on distant memories of how someone felt about seeing an old movie, which for various reasons could not be looked at when it turned up as an item of learned scrutiny. These limitations have propelled into being disputable theories of "reception" that especially flourish in the absence of evidence.

Matters have dramatically changed with the age of digitalization when, through various preservation projects, we have on DVD or on the Internet so many more films available for anyone who wants to watch. In addition to being able repeatedly to see most of the World War II movies frame by frame, at our leisure, we now can also access detailed responses of people who have watched these films. These appraisals often include recollections of emotions when Hollywood screened a movie for the first time. Of course we cannot duplicate the milieu in which 20th Century-Fox first released *The Fighting Sullivans*, and we cannot mimic the experience in a darkened hall with a mass of customers. Watching *The Fighting Sullivans* on a big-screen TV in 2008 does not replicate watching it in the summer of 1944 in a movie house in Muncie, Indiana. But as a phenomenon and as an item of historical inquiry, film has a transtemporal and transcultural resonance. We have many lengthy responses to viewing *The Fighting Sullivans* over the past twenty years, and I have greedily used them to comprehend the movie. I have also regularly asked friends to watch the motion picture and tell me what they make of it.

Theorists of art and of interpretation have undermined the view that a cultural product universally conveys a single message. However, among works of art—popular or not—the movies reflect an "overwhelming" "sensuous experience," as one commentator has written, and the experience often imposes itself on audiences.[11] I am not the first person to be struck by the power of the cinema to influence people, and to influence them in a more or less single direction. Moviegoers absorbed messages that, while subject to argument, constrained argument. No one, for example, would claim that from the mid-1930s to the mid-1950s Americans found Hollywood a champion for civil rights, for an unrestrained sex life, or even for families without dogs.

Hollywood's sense of the appropriate and its expectations of the censors' demands shaped the filmmakers' intent, and Jaffe and Bacon additionally resolved that the deaths of the Sullivans would have a transcendent meaning. Nonetheless, audiences did not entirely buy what Hollywood, at least on the surface, was selling.

In judging what audiences took from *The Fighting Sullivans*, we must juxtapose the collective biography contained in the first 100 minutes of the movie to the 12 minutes of the last three scenes—the revelation to the family and Tom's farewell; the naming of the ship; and the entrance of the boys to the pearly gates. How did viewers assimilate the way Hollywood put these parts of the film together?

For the most part, moviegoers took, or take, at face value the story of the lives of the Sullivan brothers, which occupies nine-tenths of the film. Viewers accepted the unrealistic version of family life. They then found the declaration of the deaths of the five Sullivans overwhelming. The scene in which the film tells us of their passing—defined as the pronouncement of "All five" and Tom's salute on the caboose—has a core interest, as Darryl Zanuck pointedly saw before the script became the film. People occasionally find that the scene of the christening of the USS *The Sullivans* helps to make sense of the drama, but more likely they do not mention it, while they ridicule the scene stolen from *The Iron Mask*. Viewers register the domestic details of the Sullivans growing up. They focus, however, on the tribulations of an American family caught up with death in war, and filmgoers are evidently and primarily concerned to show their shock and sympathy with the demise of the young men. The audience places in a secondary role the nation's and the admiral's tribute and dismisses the brothers' jogging to heaven. The magnitude of a family's forfeit to the state overshadows everything else in the film, and no explanation of the forfeit—a ship christening or a trip to the promised land—suffices as justification for the deaths. What sticks with viewers is that the Sullivans lost their boys.

Hollywood intended to tell the audience that if your five sons die in battle, it will be a revered and warranted sacrifice in a worthy cause: the navy will name a destroyer after them, the nation will defeat its enemies, and the children will land in paradise. All of that forms a justification for what has taken place. But all of that does not make the damage done to the Sullivans acceptable for people who watch the movie. Hollywood made every effort to render palatable the unpalatable, but these efforts do not succeed. Nothing can balance the state's demand for the souls of your offspring. Nothing validates this cost of war. Hollywood cannot cover up what it has displayed to us. Once the viewers see Tom and Alleta learning of the deaths, the scale cannot be tipped back.

We memorialize the death of soldiers—their gift to the nation. We make heroes of those who have "died for their country." We idolize those who have "served," or made the "supreme sacrifice." We accept the principle that citizens should willingly "give their lives." Death for the country is touted as a matchless virtue. *Dulce et decorum est pro patria mori*. The state essentially surrenders all resources—human and material—to preserve the state itself. We are proud to kill and be killed for the ideals that the state represents. We are devoted to such ideals, which encompass a great common loyalty.

The nation for which a soldier dies may be called Germany, or Great Britain, or France, or America, or Japan, or Russia. The ideals of these states may differ, but the principle of sacrifice remains the same. Lincoln's Gettysburg Address most eloquently renders this aesthetic—we must preserve the unique people's governance of the United States at all costs. Yet a seditious lesson of *The Fighting Sullivans* teaches that views of statesmen such as Lincoln cannot contain the whole truth. The interests of the individual self may be limited, but it does not follow that the demand of the state for allegiance trumps other loyalties—to one's church, ethnic group, or community—or, more momentously, to one's family. The nation cannot fully legitimate the destruction of one's children.[12]

*The Fighting Sullivans* has the typical artistic troubles of popular cinema and does its best to make defensible the imperatives of politics among nations. Nonetheless, the film opens the possibility that families cannot consent to these imperatives. Upon inspection, the film delivers an ambivalent judgment about even the nature of a good war. The rights of the state became problematic even in a time of crisis. Despite itself, Hollywood alerted citizens to the power of government, and audiences were not blind to this alert.

Critics often deplore the Hollywood film as a heady form of mass entertainment without depth. Yet the medium has a nature such that in adhering to certain conventions it paradoxically subverts them. Film—and *The Fighting Sullivans*—has an insubordinate quality that allows it to question issues at the foundation of human experience. The movie also exemplifies the way in which the big screen gives Americans their sense of history: sentimental but complex. In 1944 *The Fighting Sullivans* exhibited the surprising aspect of Hollywood, past and present. This people's entertainment, which panders to the worst aspects of American society, can probe human relationships and social inequities with great seriousness. This Hollywood narrative of heroism and salvation was more nuanced than it might appear.

Hollywood, finally, delivered a peculiar piece of *evidence* useful in the construction of a more adequate history of the family, to the extent that greater accuracy is important. In telling Americans about the Sullivans, Bacon and Jaffe systematically left out information that they thought would make the family look bad, and they gave us spurious information that would redound to the Sullivans' benefit. The movie concealed Al's possible shotgun marriage, Tom's drinking, and Alleta's fragility. Because we have some fragmentary knowledge of these realities, Bacon and Jaffe's dissembling gives us more reason to believe the allegations of illegitimacy, boozing, and depression.

# CHAPTER TWELVE

# THE BATTLES OF WATERLOO, 1944–1964

One viewer of *The Fighting Sullivans* wrote that the film "in its Midwest corn fed way" was as manipulative as *Triumph des Willens*, Leni Riefenstahl's notorious Nazi propaganda movie of 1935. This appraisal overlooks the subversive aspect of *The Fighting Sullivans*, but the Germans also learned from this American family spectacle. Propaganda minister Joseph Goebbels believed that the Third Reich must Germanize Hollywood. But the Jews who presided over cinema in the United States taught Goebbels about moviemaking, and he loved American films. During World War II he smuggled Hollywood wares into Germany, and in July 1944 the Nazis released their own upscale version of *The Sullivans*, titled *Die Degenhardts*. Nazi authorities designed this drama of household life to bolster German morale, and both movies aimed at the same message of persevering on behalf of the state. Aside from structural similarities to *The Sullivans*, *Die Degenhardts* also showed how German filmmakers adopted Hollywood conventions.

The movie presents a two-part story of a bourgeois family of four sons and a daughter. The first part depicts a sometimes amusing but more or less empty and proper German household before the outbreak of World War II. A common-law marriage has estranged one son, but Mother and the other four children channel their interests around Father Degenhardt. He expects a promotion to inspector in the municipal government of Lübeck, but instead his hometown mandatorily retires him. Degenhardt then hides his shame at an otherwise joyful celebration of his supposed elevation—one of many occasions on which the family congregates around a dinner table. Later, he pretends to go off to his new executive position, but he finally sinks into depression. In the second part of the movie, however, the pater familias finds a new vocation in the patriotism Germany demands after September 1939.

Soldiers marching off to fight move Degenhardt, and for a while he tramps along with the troops, just as Jimmy Cagney, playing George M. Cohan, had done at the end of *Yankee Doodle Dandy.* The English bomb Lübeck; the bombing recalls a favorite series of scenes of the burning of Atlanta from Goebbels's favorite American film, MGM's *Gone with the Wind.* All of the Degenhardts now participate in the war effort, and the parents embrace the alienated son. Papa gets a fresh lease on life with an important government job when Lübeck mobilizes its civilians. Although one son dies in battle, the death symbolizes the importance of service to a greater good, and at the end of the film, signifying the renewal of the state and the family, a grandchild joins the dining table of Vader and his Frau.[1]

The war in Europe ended with the unconditional defeat of the Germans in May 1945, and Japan surrendered a few months later after the United States dropped two atomic bombs on the country. During the early part of the occupation of Germany in 1945 and 1946, the United States selected *The Fighting Sullivans* as a film that would inculcate into the Germans an appreciation of American democratic values.[2] At the same time, America banned *Die Degenhardts* before the movie fell from notice. The catalogue of proscribed films totaled 175, but they dated from the early 1930s. The inclusion of *Die Degenhardts* on the list intimated that Allied censors believed in the power of the movie to indoctrinate Nazi notions.

Back in the United States *The Fighting Sullivans* after the war had a more lengthy and complicated history than *Die Degenhardts.* The US film was, after all, intertwined with a real family. But *The Fighting Sullivans* took on a life of its own in characterizing the heroism of the boys for audiences across America. Moreover, the navy was unabashed in using the Sullivans to forward the admirals' interests long after World War II ended. The service embroidered its early narrative of salvation and adopted the film story as truth. Waterloo got involved. Resident opinion makers, in a multifaceted interchange with the townsfolk and with the particular aid of the *Courier*, established the city's own narrative in a give-and-take that lasted well over fifty years. Politicians in Waterloo were recurrently at odds with their electorate in the moral condemnation of the supposedly disreputable family. In short, in the second part of the twentieth century and beyond, the navy, the movie, Waterloo and the nation, and the remaining Sullivans were all complexly intertwined.

In 1944 *The Fighting Sullivans* had only modestly succeeded. The movie had cost approximately $950,000, about the price of a standard first-run film, and had brought in just over $1 million at the end of its first fiscal year. That means a 5 percent profit, as best as we can figure, in 1944. But the film intermittently made it back to theaters and had a longer extended life than most World War II pictures. By 1950 it had made almost $4.3 million, well over four times what it had cost, and revivals continued.[3] Over the next seventy-five years Americans regularly returned to the movie, the most durable tribute to the Sullivans. Once old movies became a staple on television, *The Fighting Sullivans* recurrently appeared on holidays like Veterans Day. Aesthetically good or bad, accurate or not, *The Fighting Sullivans* so forcefully renders the five brothers that the film must affect anyone who thinks about the family.

Tom and Alleta were most in the public mind in 1943 and 1944. Yet while they became yesterday's news after World War II, they periodically came to national and neighborhood attention. Journalists, politicians, and the navy never entirely lost sight of them, and naming ceremonies and memorial services often paid homage to them. Did the remaining Sullivans show up at re-releases of the movie to stare at the past? One hardly knows how to conceive of the family's agony. The appalling notoriety could hardly have benefited Tom, Alleta, Gen, and Keena. The parents must have paid a psychic price to appear brave and smiling at the events at which their wretchedness was again and again and again evoked in memory. One wonders what went on at home before and after these events, when they prepared themselves for an occasion, and later settled back to their routine. As an old man, grandson Jim, in tears, lamented, "I don't know how they stood it. I really don't."[4] And what was the routine? We know that death in combat fundamentally reshapes families and that multiple deaths usually destroy them. Otherwise normal people are driven to extremes. We don't know if the already shaky Sullivans suffered a greater or lesser emotional toll. War is for the health of the state; it is far less good for the individuals called upon to undergo war. Said one commentator, "Five children taken from one family equals enduring misery."[5]

The postwar anxieties of the Sullivans naturally began in Waterloo. In the years after the *Juneau* sank, the litany of nasty-minded complaints about the family interminably circulated sub rosa. People in the town did not have the moral resources to accept that battle might have altered the boys, or that immense loss might earn Tom and Alleta a pass in their dealings with the world. Upright people, who presumed to have families like the one depicted in *The Fighting Sullivans*, contrasted themselves to the real Sullivans, who were not those of the movie. Many of these more decorous types had sons or husbands or fathers or nephews killed in the war. Their families did not get a trip around the country, or a personal letter from FDR. The newspaper and a constantly revived movie did not venerate these ordinary but respectable people.[6]

The detractors came particularly and unfairly to despise Alleta. They thought she only sought fame, fortune, and publicity for her children. This perspective was cruel and untrue. It takes little imagination to understand that parents find no good to come out of the deaths of their sons. Nonetheless, Alleta did believe that by making a somebody of herself she would in Waterloo rid the boys of the opprobrium they had shared in life. The five Sullivans got such vindication beyond the city, although reconciliation within its confines continued to elude the sons and their mother.

To some extent the troubles in Waterloo showed the stress between East Side Catholics and West Side Protestants, unsavory immigrants versus old-stock WASPs. But plenty of ethnics from the East Side didn't like the Sullivans. More significantly, the high-ranking citizens of Waterloo would never speak against the boys. These leaders did not want to wash the city's dirty linen in public, especially when the exalted brothers, a golden bequest to Waterloo, could lift up the city nationally. In opposition to many voters, officials ignored moral niceties when it came to polishing the reputation of Waterloo or raising money for its coffers.

When Tom and Alleta had made their first trip to Hollywood in April 1943, Alleta had confided by mail to her good friend Nell Turner: the people in Los Angeles "have been wonderful to us. It sure puts Waterloo to shame." At the end of January 1944, in New York for the premiere of the movie, Alleta wrote an extraordinary letter to Nell after the two Sullivan parents had their private showing of *The Sullivans*. She told Nell that it was a "grand picture" but said nothing about its substance. Nor did Alleta convey to Nell any of her emotions about the film. Instead, Alleta related that she had "cryed many times since we left home about what Myrtle [a Waterloo friend] said about me," and about what the Waterloo Navy Mothers, whose Chapter 66 she had helped to create in 1938, thought of her. In January 1944 the gossip had "so hurt" Alleta that she didn't know if she would go near the organization again. Alleta had told her story about these hurts to naval authorities, she wrote to Nell. Well, "Washington" now knew what was going on. The Sullivan-handlers from the capital had advised Alleta "not to pay any attention" to enemies like Myrtle or to the hometown Navy Mothers. In one of the more striking psychological aspects of this entire story, Alleta said that the navy had told her "it was just jealousy."[7]

On VJ Day—August 14, 1945—the *Courier* ran a story and sent a reporter around to Adams Street to interview Tom and Alleta. The boys in the Pacific were coming home in triumph. How did Mother and Dad Sullivan feel? The couple did not talk to the press that day, but daughter Gen spoke for them: Alleta was happy that other mothers would have their sons returned "but hers won't be back."[8]

Alleta doggedly supported every opportunity in Waterloo to acknowledge her boys in death to make up for their problematic lives. She yearned for distinctions, and they came to her. For example, many veterans' associations named new World War II chapters after the five sons. Alleta accepted many commemorative invitations. She reported items of note to the *Courier*–like the gift of the silver service of the USS *The Sullivans* when the navy temporarily decommissioned the ship at the end of 1945; she exhibited the silverware in one of the display windows of Blacks in the center of town. Her name appeared as a byline over essays in national magazines documenting her trials.[9]

Foes in Waterloo had an uphill fight, for who would say out loud: we don't want to recognize these wastrels? The disparagers could never vocalize their truths, and *The Fighting Sullivans* made complaint seem base, worse than petty. Enemies never censured the Sullivans directly but observed that other area families tolerated unheralded tribulations. Alleta's antagonists never relinquished their resentment at the celebrity given, in their eyes, to a notorious litter, and their actions spoke louder than words. A series of dubious battles—a struggle of passive resistance and the combat of terminologies—grew up between Sullivan-haters in Waterloo and the Waterloo marketers of the Sullivan name.

Waterloo had failed to rejuvenate The Fighting Sullivans Memorial Fund after the discomfiting premiere of the movie in 1944 and left the fund in limbo. But the *Courier*, the chief carrier of the salvific narrative promulgated by the town's authorities, never gave up.

We heard nothing about the fund in the newspaper for over four years, and then at the end of 1948 officials announced that Waterloo would erect a new hospital. A community industrialist had left $600,000 for such a facility, and the additional $925,000 would be raised through voluntary contributions. Within four months patrons promised over two-thirds of this extra money—more than $630,000. In February 1949, the Sullivan Committee revealed that it would donate the proceeds from the fund to the hospital as part of the push to raise the final $300,000. The committee had put the money in war bonds, and in early 1949 their value was almost $7,000. For this the hospital provided the Sullivan Fund with a plaque in one wing that commemorated all the Waterloo vets who lost their lives in the war *and* the five brothers. The brothers themselves received "their room" in the facility, as did the Business and Professional Women in Waterloo, who had bequeathed a similar amount.[10]

Alleta could not find even a tiny victory here, although not because the plaque went "unnoticed."[11] An entire hospital named after the boys could not temper her pain. Slowly the Sullivans still among the living were themselves being destroyed, collateral damage from the sinking of the *Juneau*. Little Jimmy, as a man, remembered that "everybody in town" knew that Tom drank, and now his grandfather drank openly on the job. He favored fifths of Wild Turkey Kentucky bourbon, and IC workers would see him on his freight run with the drink; he "had the turkey by the neck." But the IC would not punish the father of American idols and looked the other way. A self-proclaimed acquaintance of

Jim's said that "his grandfather was not just a friend of the bottle, but its best pal." We know less about Alleta, although neighbors recalled her melancholy. Reclusive, she lost her extra weight, and this "high-strung" woman shrank into silence. Gen made a couple of very public marriage engagements that were broken off. She did wed but joined the ranks of Sullivan drinkers. Only Keena was able to move on. One commentator testified that "inconsolable darkness burdened the parents' last years and reached across generations."[12]

Meanwhile, unalloyed national tributes continued. Authorities planted Sullivan trees in Washington and built a Sullivan Auditorium in Sampson, New York. In 1956 the contributions of Sullivan families across America resulted in the construction of a statue of Mary, "Our Lady of Peace." Dedicated to George, Frank, Red, Matt, and Al, the monument stood at the front of their sometime parish school, Saint Mary's in Waterloo. At this time, one oldster recalled, incriminating records about the family located in the school went missing. The Sullivans' friends did not want such information in the hands of enemies, or waiting "like a bomb to go off"; "the Catholics buried that stuff."

The statue *in* Waterloo was not, however, a statue *from* Waterloo. The first homegrown tribute for which I can find no evidence of protest came in 1959. At Maxwell and Stratford Streets, the city opened Sullivan Memorial Park, renaming and refurbishing the old Maxwell Park; a sign explained the new name, and a district veterans' organization installed a commemorative inscription. I have almost no information about this naming ceremony.[13] The park lay far from the center of town, in a peripheral district on the nonelite West Side. The site, however, soon fell into a state of disrepair.[14]

The quickly decrepit condition of Sullivan Memorial Park in the early 1960s—and the budding shabbiness of Waterloo—reflected what was occurring in many metropolitan areas across America. Particularly in the Midwest, cities large and small decayed as massive demographic shifts and changes in the economy of the United States took place in the postwar period. Old inner-city America lost population and industry, and vandalism in some areas became widespread. Waterloo, however, so dependent on its well-to-do center-city area on both sides of the river, did not go down without a series of fights. In the 1960s the town participated in a set of programs created by President Lyndon Johnson to solve urban problems often called the "war on poverty."

The Sullivans could help in this war. The town's politicians may not have disagreed with their constituents about the supposed deficiencies of the family. Nonetheless, leaders did not repudiate the national reputation of this valiant clan or look in the mouth the gift horse of *The Fighting Sullivans*. Pragmatic executives would use the name time and again in service to Waterloo. With the *Courier* at their side, they eagerly commemorated the Sullivans. While the townspeople shook their heads, civic principals had only to allude to the advantages that doffing Waterloo's collective patriotic hat to the family would bring. The elite of Waterloo, often scheming at cross purposes from its citizens, used the movie about the town's most famous residents to fight for national and state financial resources. Provincial politicians pitted the boys not against the Japanese but against the forces of inner-city deterioration—and their mother's old homegrown adversaries.

Around the time the city opened Sullivan Memorial Park, Tom and Alleta moved out of their sinking blue-collar neighborhood. According to fearful whites, African Americans were "invading" from just to the south, breaching the Black Triangle. Then, in 1961, the couple sold 98 Adams and a big adjoining lot. Under the aegis of the urban renewal impulses of the era, experts designated the area as "blighted." The city tore down 98 Adams and other properties, and grants came through for a large playground and adjacent "residential development" (i.e., public housing). Waterloo's movers and shakers attracted money for the project on the basis of the sacred spot immortalized in the movie, overlooking the moral imperfections of the family in favor of municipal improvement. The leaders made it impossible for the anti-Alleta group even to raise its voice, let alone be effective.[15] In 1964, Waterloo changed the name of Sullivan Memorial Park to Galloway Park. On the other side of town, the city then created a new and more elaborate Sullivan Brothers Memorial Park that encompassed the former site of 98 Adams Street. Construction workers converted eight acres into an expansive common with a ball field and basketball court. Waterloo also set two monuments in place—a large granite pentagon with one of the boys' names on each of its five sides, and a smaller plate recalling their sacrifice.

The planning documents pronounced that the new park—and other suitable experiments—would halt the city's decline. Politicians found federal money easier to come by if they advertised such projects as marks of respect to the Sullivans. Such undertakings, said the organizers, would remedy the perception across the United States that Waterloo had not taken enough initiatives to remember the boys.[16] As Tom and Alleta had done so many times in the past, they dutifully attended the inaugural ceremonies for Sullivan Brothers Memorial Park in 1964. But what turned out to be their last dedication only began a new sort of remembrance of the five brothers.

# CHAPTER THIRTEEN

## TOWN AND COUNTRY

The making of Sullivan Brothers Memorial Park began what seems now like the endless task of saving Waterloo from an ongoing downward spiral. Over and over, the city fathers reaped the benefits of the fame of the family but fought their constituents while doing so. Homage to the boys was both unceasing and contested. After Tom's death in 1965 and Alleta's in 1972, Albert's son, Jim, now grown up, took over the role of performing at dedicatory events. Later his daughter, Kelly Sullivan Loughren, an elementary school teacher in Black Hawk County, became an effective, intelligent, and articulate spokesperson for the family mythology. In time, the reputation of the family and the boys benefited, although most people forgot about the parents' decades-long pain, which was beyond words. It was less clear, however, if the Sullivans did much to salvage Waterloo.

By early 1966—two years after the début of the park—hooligans had wrecked its monuments.[1] Mini-warfare erupted over what had literally been the Sullivans' turf. Then, crushed into its ghetto for years, Waterloo's black community blew up in fury in the late 1960s. African Americans broke through the geographical boundary with which white Waterloo had surrounded them. Demonstrations were so frightening and extensive that they prompted an article in New York City's *Wall Street Journal:* WHY WOULD NEGROES RIOT IN WATERLOO? In a series of Waterloo hearings in 1967, white leaders learned about the realities of segregation and racism in their town. Among other things, blacks' anger at not being allowed to swim in the Cedar River surprised the whites. Five years later, in 1972, when more racial animosity disrupted East High, black parents met at Sullivan Park before deciding to pull their children out of school.[2]

In the North End, according to graybeards, young black men delighted in "crapping on the pentagon" in "the Irish boys' park." These acts shocked and disgusted white residents of the North End. They had heard that the five brothers were "pretty creepy back then [in the 1930s]," but even the Sullivans were "not so bad so they should get treated like that." "Pissing on their graves," said one aged white neighbor, "might be OK if they were really racial, but doing number two went too far." Blacks who had made it out of the ghetto had been told by their grandparents that the Sullivan boys were "troublemakers" long ago, and "that was why we went after the park."

The disturbances immediately shook the affluent center-city area of East Side Waterloo. Large retail stores essential to the district fled. The planning documents tell us that white commerce critically feared black pollution or violence. It would not just work its way north through the Sullivans' old neighborhood but also spread south across the North End tracks toward the Cedar. But the situation was more complicated. Anxiety about black people pushed establishments in downtown East Waterloo to leave, but a pull came from Waterloo's near suburbs, which had bargain-priced land and a growing population with money to spend. Businesses did not just move *from* the East Side but *to* the suburbs.

Moreover, by the early 1970s businesses on the *west* side of the river were also departing, and the West Side was lily-white. No one worried that African Americans would cross the river, one westsider recalled: "We knew they couldn't swim." Nonetheless, West Side enterprise near the river was losing out to shopping malls on the edge of town just as the East Side was hurting. The *Courier* worried about its "attractive city with a worn-out heart"; the paper did not want winds blowing through "empty, derelict buildings in a decaying downtown." Waterloo's center city needed "open heart surgery" "to revitalize the entire community." "You can't expect new industry to settle here," said one labor leader, "if the city appears to be dying."[3]

Faced with a crisis, politicians and urban specialists in the early 1970s generated a complicated plan that evinced both a novel racial egalitarianism and a concern for economic development on both sides of the Cedar. The West Side of Waterloo had a population that was 100 percent white. The East Side had a poorer population, 20 percent black, although the percentage of African Americans was far higher in a few neighborhoods where blacks were still penned in. The plan first called for an elaborate concourse over the Cedar—more than the bridge spanning 4th Street at the river—to join the two halves of the town and to encourage integration. To foster mingling of the races *and* to rejuvenate the downtown, a restaurant and shopping corridor on East 4th Street would rehabilitate the east side of the river; on West 4th Street near the river, investments would foster the arts and culture, positioned around a convention center. This building would host gatherings of businesses and professionals from across Iowa, especially from the "corridor" of towns that ran atop the north of the state along US Highway 20. This convention center with an adjacent hotel would anchor a remade district on both banks of the Cedar. The vaulted sheltered arcade-bridge would take Waterloo's citizens and tourists back and forth above the river to shops, restaurants, and cultural institutions.

Despite grand drawings and verbiage, the large structure received the plain-Jane designation of Conway Civic Center. In the minds of planners, the unglamorous but carefully thought-out title amalgamated ideas of connection, convention, confluence, congregate, corridor, and even concave—for the shape of the promenade that on one end would debouche at the center. In the one open discussion I have found about the name, professionals changed the title to ConWay, instead of Conway.[4] Sponsors of the Sullivan family do not appear to have lobbied for a name. The mayor of Waterloo was an energetic and effective figure— Leo Rooff, Keena's cousin and the best man at Keena and Albert's wedding. Rooff probably did not want another airing of gripes about the family to jeopardize a critical governmental initiative. In any event, as part of the whole effort, when Rooff dedicated the ConWay Center in 1975, he gave Sullivan Memorial Park on the East Side another elaborate makeover, although the hotel with a walkway to ConWay was not completed until 1983.[5]

The project did not turn out well. Waterloo lacked a major airport to bring conventions to ConWay. More important, all the midwestern cities like Waterloo persisted in their downhill slide in a way that renewal programs could not arrest. The city center did not rebound and, in the late 1970s soon after the refurbishing of Sullivan Park, the facility had again deteriorated. Delinquents tore the memorial sculpture from its concrete base, and it lay on the unkempt grounds, which in any case became a home to drug dealers and the homeless.[6] Sub voce critics said that the state of Sullivan Park fit its namesakes. Downtown, one resident complained that the domed walkway had become "a restroom over the river." Although the police argued that the reports of crimes committed on the bridge were "not factual," one witness at a City Council meeting declared that Waterloo was in a lot of trouble. There were "many negative happenings in the city," and while the cops and firemen should be retained, the rest of City Hall should be "reduce[d]."[7]

Matters got even worse, as the full effects of "deindustrialization" hit Waterloo. "By 1980," as one historian has written, "unemployment figures began a steady and frightening climb." By the mid-1980s Rath Packing went belly-up; the railroad shut many of its operations; and John Deere instituted extensive layoffs, which at first stabilized but then continued into the twenty-first century.[8]

We can see in retrospect that, by the 1980s, the attempts that started in the 1960s to stem the population movement to America's suburbs and to revitalize downtown neighborhoods had miscarried. The 1990 census registered a drop in Waterloo's population from the city's high of 87,500 in 1980 to 62,500, a 28.6 percent decrease. The 10 percent population increase in the United States in the same decade made the decline more dramatic. Although Waterloo reached its low point in the late 1980s, the city did not bounce back as America grew. In the first half of the twentieth century, the town was an industrial center; in the second half, it registered as just one of many urban trouble spots.

A lot of people simply left. Some who stayed in the region moved to the outskirts of Waterloo and shopped at the huge malls, which had lower prices. In the formerly prosperous hub of some 100 square blocks that sat astride the Cedar, the pace of abandonment quickened. Six- to eight-story office buildings went unoccupied. Business vacated elegant old hotels, and department stores emptied. The Paramount was torn down after a fire. Blacks opened a suburban branch while it also tried to hang on in the center of town. When that emporium gave up its prime location at 4th and Sycamore in 1981, and closed its doors, thoughtful Waterlooans knew the game was up. The attractive old building still remains as a monument to what the city once was.

Deurbanization did not spare the 1930s–1940s Waterloo of the Sullivans either. In writing this book, I tried to visit every one of their haunts for which I had even an approximate address. Some had been demolished; others were closed; none had lasted. The Waterloo of the family was gone, and it had been replaced by various monuments to the boys that were themselves aging.

Who departed Waterloo? The young, the adventurous, the talented. Who hung on? The halt and the elderly; and the poor—whites, African Americans, Asians, Hispanics.

Waterloo, and those in it who used the Sullivan label, did not surrender. In May 1987, an Iraqi jet attacked the USS *Stark*, and a few days later President Ronald Reagan eulogized the thirty-seven sailors who were killed. Reagan's stirring address, done in his standard Hollywood style, again called national attention to the Sullivans:

> My own mind has turned many times to the great war of 46 years ago. Few of us who lived through it can ever forget those opening months of conflict, when our nation and our fighting men were so sorely tested.
>
> In later years, in the South Pacific campaign, American sailors would speak often of the bravery of the marines they put on the beaches to fight and die; but one night, especially, off a place called Guadalcanal, as the shellfire lit the darkness in one of the most violent surface actions ever seen, it was the marines who stood in awe and in silent tribute to the men of the United States Navy. Hopelessly outnumbered and outgunned, a small group of U.S. ships had taken on a powerful enemy fleet. . . . And though . . . the enemy was turned back and Guadalcanal was saved, the price was so high and the burden so heavy—nine ships and hundreds of young lives. And none of us who were alive then can forget the special burden of grief borne by Mr. and Mrs. Thomas Sullivan of Waterloo, Iowa.

"They would remember forever," Reagan concluded, "the autumn afternoon they learned that their sons, the Five Sullivans as we knew them then, would not be coming home."

Then, in November 1987, six months later, the Iowa Humanities Board refused Waterloo a grant to promote public dialogue about the Sullivans. Was the board composed of Sullivan-haters? The humanities folks explained that the proposal for a small sum of money did not make a sufficient case for the significance of the death of the five brothers. The explanation prompted an unilluminating treatment of historical significance and some unpleasant exchanges in the *Courier*. The newspaper quoted President Reagan several times. Most of all, the incident propelled the chair of the Black Hawk County Board of Supervisors into action. John Rooff was the nephew of recently retired mayor Leo Rooff and was a cousin of Jim Sullivan. John Rooff wanted the Sullivans rightly treasured. The same month that the humanities panel made its decision, a recently formed Waterloo American Legion Post, in part named after the Sullivans, sponsored a commemoration of the sinking of the *Juneau* on its forty-fifth anniversary. Waterloo's mayor, Bernard McKinley, proclaimed Sullivan Day.[9] No one voiced objections, but John Rooff had bigger ideas, and these ideas animated those in Waterloo who, in their last stand, could not suffer the Sullivans or anything about them.

The next year, under Supervisor Rooff's leadership, and with the support he garnered from various veterans' organizations, the Waterloo Park Commission voted funds for yet another rehabilitation of Sullivan Park. At the same time that politicians agreed to smarten it up, these city leaders settled on renaming the ConWay Civic Center for the Sullivans. The foes of the family at last made an overt attempt to sabotage a Sullivan tribute.

Waterloo conducted two open hearings at City Hall on changing the name. At the first, in June 1988, Rooff proposed a resolution that would provide documentation for another title for the convention center. The resolution, he said, culminated his five-year effort to preserve the memory of his relatives. The Ancient Order of the Hibernians offered up Five Sullivan Brothers Civic Center by way of a new name. The tourism council of Black Hawk County spoke in favor, as did the AMVETS, the American Legion, and a history professor at the neighboring University of Northern Iowa. Don Miller, whom I mentioned in my introduction, protested: two "poor decisions" produced the tragedy of the Sullivans—their own choice and the authorities' agreement with that choice. Overriding the objection, the City Council voted to prepare the documentation for the change but called for a further public discussion in a second town assembly.[10]

This meeting, a month later, appears like the earlier one to have been carefully scripted by Rooff, although, as we have seen, Miller and others were ready for a fight. The mayor declaimed that some opponents did not want to speak publically, but Miller made his way to the podium, and it is unclear if he breeched "the General Rules" to "refrain from personal, impertinent or slanderous remarks." He again called attention to the "bad judgment" of the five Sullivans. He argued that they should not be considered heroes. ConWay should remain ConWay. Miller concluded by telling the City Council that the whole business was only Supervisor Rooff's hobbyhorse.

Mayor McKinley allowed that "the Sullivan brothers are probably Waterloo's most famous citizens." Someone else remarked that it would help tourism in the community and "allow the tourist to identify Waterloo as the home of the five Sullivan[s]." The members of City Council added their voices. One orated that it was important to him growing up around the park to be reminded of the exploits of the family. Another said the town needed "to educate our youths of the community on the story of the Sullivan brothers." Someone else noted that today's generation lacked heroes and that the boys "would be an appropriate role model." A final council member who disagreed with Miller still wanted "to commend" him "for his courage to stand up for what he believes."

Waterloo officials had on their side the symbol of Hollywood's *The Fighting Sullivans*. Waterloo had produced no more consequential people than the boys. They surely put to shame other celebrities who hailed from Waterloo—Lou Henry Hoover, wife of the failed Depression president, Herbert Hoover, and professional wrestler Thunderbolt Patterson. If Waterloo hoped to avoid the deurbanization that beset so much of the Midwest, the town should lead with its trademark. Foolish it was not to employ their name. The moral obligation to honor the blood gift of the Sullivans reinforced the notion that their "brand" would attract more business than the old name of ConWay.

Once before, in early 1944, when natives declined to go to the premiere of the movie, the *Courier* had admitted that a lot of people in Waterloo did not like the Sullivans. Now, over forty-three years later—for only the second time in its history—the paper recorded visceral dislike of the family. The *Courier* reported that "a number of comments were received in opposition to the change." Officials suggested that some antagonists "did not feel comfortable speaking before the council with a possibly partisan audience opposed to their views."[11] Nonetheless, it was the final time the paper would even intimate criticism of the Sullivans, and thereafter—so far as I can tell—no one criticized the family in the open. Time was carrying off aged critics; veterans groups stepped up to defend their own. In a mix of admiration and patriotism, the *Courier* championed the Sullivans. City Council voted 6–0 in favor, with one absence, and the building got retitled.[12]

Reagan's America had forsaken Waterloo; the town had been cast aside. The nation's leaders—liberal or conservative, flag-wavers or skeptics—could or would not salvage small Rust Belt cities like Waterloo. As the country left it behind in the postindustrial era, the municipality made its own desperate attempt at self-rescue by asserting its nationalism via the Sullivans. The *Courier* focused Waterloo's heroic and newly dominant story of the family.

The 5 Sullivan Brothers Convention Center was born on Veterans Day, November 11, 1988. In addition to a new name, the building had a plaque, some memorabilia, and meeting rooms named after Tom and Alleta's boys.

After a Mass at the Sullivans' putative church, Saint Mary's, VIPs led a parade. They marched through the North End, south over the tracks, and crossed the Cedar to the rededicated center just on the West Side. Jim Sullivan—"little Jimmy"—spoke as an esteemed guest. He emotionally told a large audience that he had questioned how much Waterloo remembered or cared about his father and uncles. But today, he concluded, "I have no doubts." A speaker at the ceremonies said to the assembled guests, "The brothers, wherever they are, are as proud of you Waterlooans as you are of them."[13]

Altering the name of the building came easily. But leaders could not make the Sullivan Center profitable, or even keep Sullivan Park cleaned up. Laborers only minimally accomplished renovations to the center by 1990, and these changes did not do the trick. "Throwing money down a rat hole," grumbled one employee. The latest chapter in the tale of Sullivan Park was filled with more dramatics. The *Courier* editorialized that "brazen and arrogant" drug dealers gathered around the former 98

Adams Street. The city patrolled with extra cops, but as soon as they left, the illegal businessmen returned. People living around the park said the black teenagers took special delight in "messing with all the Irish stuff." In the summer of 1990 church groups tried to reclaim the playground with an endeavor called Sunday at Sullivan. Each week a black church (from the East Side) or a white church (from the West Side) would hold a recreation day with free food. The churchgoers wanted to ease racial tensions, bring the two parts of town together, and show off Sullivan Park as an amenity. After a couple of well-attended outings, drive-by shootings in July 1990 undermined the program.[14]

Two years later the town had again cleansed and tidied up the park, and on the fiftieth anniversary of the sinking of the *Juneau*, November 13, 1992, Waterloo once more mounted a parade to accompany an official reopening. The *Courier* pronounced the procession the largest such affair in Waterloo's history. There were tributes all around as the town hosted the naval reunions of the USS *The Sullivans*; of a second USS *Juneau*; and of a tiny group from the first *Juneau*. Seven hundred attended the banquet at the Sullivan Center. It was a momentous day of remembrance.[15]

The bad memories and malicious stories also fought an overwhelming national inclination to glorify the boys. By 1995, Kelly Sullivan Loughren had taken up the familial role that had briefly occupied her father, Jim, but that had fundamentally belonged to Alleta. That year Loughren christened a second USS *The Sullivans*, and in yet another incongruity Loughren wished the vessel "the luck of the Irish."[16]

In 1997 a popular rock group, Caroline's Spine, released what turned out to be the group's most popular single, "Sullivan." Caroline's Spine singer and main songwriter, Jimmy Newquist, wrote the song after reading the book *Hollywood Goes to War*,[17] though clearly his reading also inspired him to see *The Fighting Sullivans*, by then available for home viewing. Indeed, the "Sullivan" music video—the short film and pictures that now often go along with the words and music when artists distribute a pop tune—featured footage of the band performing, as well as excerpts from *The Fighting Sullivans*.

Newquist recalled that "coming from a big family, the story of five brothers really struck home with me. . . . I saw a news clipping with a photo of Mrs. Sullivan holding a banner with five gold stars—one for each of her dead sons. It's a really sad story with incredible loyalty and courage." "The song was an act of love. . . . I sleep well at night knowing that I brought attention to something that shouldn't be forgotten." He counted "Sullivan" among his favorites of Caroline's Spine's recordings.

The song narrative begins

> It's not hard to reach back
> To that day, underneath the Iowa sun
> Running to the tower of Waterloo
> Looking for the Sullivans' train to come
> And his five boys would run to the top
> And salute him as he went by
> First we wave hello, then we waved goodbye

The song then focuses on the letters Alleta and the boys exchanged after they join up. The first verse and the mention of Alleta's smile in a subsequent verse on receiving mail from her boys tell us that the source of the song is the movie. Newquist has recalled to mind the opening and closing scenes at the water tower in *The Fighting Sullivans* and the warmth of actress Selena Royle.

The songwriter recognized that the experience of war "overnight [turned] my buddies . . . into men / Running out of time for games and girls." The choruses also feature messages from the military to Alleta, and the last line of each chorus encourages her to "keep her Blue Star in the window." The navy declares the boys dead, and Alleta "change[s] her Blue Star to Gold." Newquist grasped the fundamental point that, compared to the lives of children, the country's regrets do not suffice: "When the war finally came home / Uncle Sam'll send you a telegram / So he doesn't have to tell you over the phone."

In 1998, soon after "Sullivan" made the charts, the Hollywood genius Steven Spielberg added to his directing triumphs with *Saving Private Ryan*, which called the Sullivans to mind. Hollywood had done this before after *The Fighting Sullivans*. In *Christmas in Connecticut* (1945), Barbara Stanwyck fell in love with a sailor who survived much time on the open sea after his ship was sunk and he was adrift. As Admiral Bull Halsey, Jimmy Cagney in *The Gallant Hours* takes personally the news of mid-November 1942.

*Saving Private Ryan* differed, as it was simultaneously more direct and more oblique in its reference to the Sullivans. While the movie fiction begins with the storming of the Normandy beaches on D-Day, the film traces the movements of a group of soldiers after June 6, 1944. General George C. Marshall, Chief of Staff of the US Army, has ordered them to find and pull out of combat a James Francis Ryan, three of whose brothers have already been killed in the war. In a notable performance, Tom Hanks played Captain Paul Miller, who died during the rescue of Ryan.

The writer of *Saving Private Ryan*, Robert Rodat, first came up with the idea for the film in 1994 when he saw a monument dedicated to four sons of Agnes Allison of Port Carbon, Pennsylvania. These brothers were killed in the American Civil War, and their mother was a more genuine Mrs. Bixby. The film's premise, however, depended on what people thought had happened during World War II to the Niland brothers from Tonawanda, New York. The Normandy beaches claimed two of the four siblings on D-Day and the day following. Although the War Department thought a third was dead, he came back from a Japanese POW camp in Burma; and a fourth survived D-Day, but officials returned him to the United States to serve out his enlistment presuming him to be a sole surviving son. The military mistakenly believed three Niland sons had been killed, and only one safely dispatched to the United States.

At the same time, Spielberg and Rodat paid their respects to the Bixbys and the Sullivans and indeed directed attention back to *The Fighting Sullivans*. In the early minutes of *Saving Private Ryan*, army headquarters learns that the mother of the three Ryan brothers is going to be informed of their deaths on the same day in 1944. One of General Marshall's staffers explains to his chief that the army had separated the Ryan brothers to avoid a repeat of what had happened to the Sullivans. General Marshall then reads the Bixby letter to his assistants to enlighten them on why he wants the only living Ryan son rescued. In the middle of these deliberations a striking and moving scene is reminiscent of what happened at the end of *The Fighting Sullivans*. Mrs. Ryan, seen in the kitchen and on the porch of her Iowa farm, collapses when a car arrives carrying a general who will inform her of the death of three of her boys.[18] Finally, the opening and closing of the movie take us to the American cemetery at Normandy as the now elderly James Ryan contemplates the meaning of loss. These scenes more intensely begin and end the movie than Lloyd Bacon's initial efforts in *The Sullivans*, although the flashback framing of *Saving Private Ryan* may have derived from the original *The Sullivans*.

In 2000—two years after *Saving Private Ryan*—the History Channel, the nation's chief teacher of popular history, did a show on the Sullivans. "The True Story of the Fighting Sullivans" formed an episode of the *History's Mysteries* series, and fixed on the Battle of Guadalcanal, the survivors of the *Juneau* on the open sea, and George's death particularly. One question shaped the documentary: Had the navy been negligent? The show implied a complex answer and left one wondering about what had occurred, a "mystery of history." This was accomplished reporting of the wartime issues.

At the same time, the start and finish of the documentary established the bona fides of the Sullivans as good Americans. Kelly Sullivan Loughren made several appearances as a talking head and amplified some basic fictions of *The Fighting Sullivans*. Loughren told the cameras that the Sullivans went to church every Sunday; they did not. She also reported that they sat down every day to eat together as a family; we really don't know anything about this, and I can imagine only with difficulty that Loughren could. By the time she was born in 1971, Tom had died; Alleta died the next year and Genevieve in 1975. Although May Abel died in 1980 at 102, she had suffered some form of dementia for years. Loughren's grandmother, Keena Rooff Sullivan, was still thriving, but Keena knew the family only after 1939 and did not live with them until after the boys went off to war.[19]

We do know that Loughren often watched *The Fighting Sullivans* as a child—her father said "I don't know how many times"—and that every year as an adult she showed the movie to her grade-school class. Of course, that movie made the family into pious Catholics and showed the eight Sullivans repeatedly at the kitchen table. A friend also confessed that Loughren was so busy appearing at commemorative events that she did not have time to examine primary sources about her grandfather and great uncles.[20]

We easily understand why the granddaughter had a vested interest in convincing herself that the Sullivans were an authentically "All-American family," as she put it. Yet one of the History Channel's consultants had conducted interviews that made clear the family did not have middle-class attributes. Almost sixty years after the boys had died, television still determined to commend them only if they were conventionally respectable.[21] Over the years, Waterloo politicians had ignored ethics and swallowed the truth when they made heroes of the five brothers. Ordinary Americans, however, had less ability to entertain or tolerate ambiguity in moral judgments, and the History Channel was directed at such viewers.

Meanwhile, by the end of the twentieth century, the latest generation of citizens of Waterloo had changed their minds about the Sullivans. In the postwar period, residents would not credit the Sullivans because they were blemished; as the blemishes passed out of memory, the boys were defined as unblemished, and so they became candidates for credit. Local inhabitants, in entirely fantastic recollections, could "recall" the positive role of the Sullivan boys in the community.[22] Alleta's foes were passing from the scene, and while black Waterloo would not respect the park, the disrespect seemed no longer to be specific to the "dead Irish boys." In the center of town, businesspeople of African American, Hispanic, and Asian heritage claimed not to know anything about the Sullivans, in fact not to have heard of them at all.

How many ironies can the historian find! As the spokesmen for the Sullivan Center prevailed in a fight over renaming the structure, they were losing the fight against the uninterrupted decay of their city. In the mid-1990s, one sympathetic witness wrote that downtown Waterloo was a "worn-out grid of buildings, many empty now, that signify a remembrance of better days long past."[23] Waterloo's *decline* entailed that more *honors* would come to the Sullivans. In the first part of the twentieth century, when the town was up, the family was down; at the end of the century, when Waterloo was down, the Sullivans were up. In the 1930s prim locals believed that the derelict Sullivans were emblematic of the city's problems. From the 1960s onward, the family was continually called upon to turn the tide against a sinking Waterloo. Into the twenty-first century, as the old-time local opposition to the Sullivans disappeared, the family simultaneously did not enter the minds of newer Waterlooans at all.

In 2002, an independent planning group found the Sullivan Convention Center in such a state of disrepair that it recommended closing the "shabby" place—or rehabilitating it. John Rooff had ascended from chair of the county supervisors to mayor; faced with shuttering a Sullivan memorial, the city again put money into tarting up the building. Yet Waterloo had little ability to attract clients, and the center, although managed by a hotel chain, attracted few conferences and could not pay for itself.[24] Often empty, it catered to weddings and parties, business meetings, and inevitably veterans who might come to Waterloo for naval reunions.

The latest makeover in 2003 had been incorporated into a larger project, Waterloo's Downtown Master Plan, which originated under Mayor John Rooff in 2000. Between 2000 and 2010, the state of Iowa and Waterloo leaders, with the sponsorship of the *Courier*, expanded on the notions that had produced the original ConWay Convention Center in the 1970s. The politicians demarcated the Waterloo Cultural and Arts District and took up yet another set of efforts at a renaissance. To one reflective inhabitant, made cynical by the overall collapse of old midwestern urbanism, the leaders "were blowing smoke . . . and we all know what kind." Although developers, contractors, and middlemen would make money from government subsidies, did not politicians know that rescuing the downtown—after so many flops—was unlikely to work? Nonetheless, leaders would not give up even if real-estate people would line their pockets while the tax dollars of the poor might not benefit the nucleus of Waterloo.

The idea for the Cultural and Arts District derived from the load of artifacts that Henry Grout, a well-off Waterloo native, had collected. In 1956 these objects had found a permanent home in the Henry W. Grout Historical Museum, a building just over the river on the West Side. Grout had been a hoarder of Waterloo memorabilia and, among other things, the museum had naturally accumulated odds and ends about the Sullivans. Over the second half of the twentieth century, people added to his store of treasures. The city purchased historical residences around the Grout Museum, which itself formed separate divisions. Among other things, the Grout went after items pertinent to the Sullivan family and, indeed, entered the bidding for autographed Sullivan letters in auctions and later on eBay. At the turn of the century, museum managers purchased a 1942 letter from Red to the Tic Toc Tap for $1,900.[25] By 2008 authorities had final proposals about an enlivened museum neighborhood—the Cultural and Arts District. Developers created a new exhibition hall, the Sullivan Brothers Iowa Veterans Museum, close to the Sullivan Convention Center. The politicians hoped—credulously?—that the convention center, the war museum, the related institutions around it, a riverfront park, and plaza, all in close proximity, would draw people downtown. Little opposition arose over the name for the new museum, although the planners doffed their hats to a vanishing opposition by including "Iowa Veterans" in the title.

Caroline's Spine often sang "Sullivan" at concerts, and when the Sullivan Brothers Museum opened in 2008, Jimmy Newquist performed it. The program added this special rendition at the last minute. Two nights earlier Caroline's Spine had coincidentally played at Spicoli's Bar and Grill in Waterloo. Kelly Loughren spoke at the museum event and later praised the show: "That was really special to hear that song. . . . He just brought me to tears."[26]

The Downtown Master Plan did not work out, and both the Sullivan Center and the Sullivan Museum saw limited use. In part the continuing troubles were attributed to the drying-up of money from the state in the first decade of the twenty-first century. Later, however, the city sponsored a revised master plan, the Waterloo Downtown Master Plan Update, which was a work in progress.[27] Critics joked that it was part of the city's "Planning and Dreaming Department," but now the city's failure to provide cash was blamed. When Waterloo cut off grants to the Sullivan Museum, donations were not enough to keep it solvent. As the museum fell into debt, and had to dip into its small endowment to pay expenses, it curtailed some of its activities and cut back the hours of employees. With the support of the *Courier*, politicians tried to resolve the "museum district's struggling operations." After a referendum in

The Waterloo Museum. Sullivan Brothers Iowa Veterans Museum was opened in November 2008 (Author's Collection).

2013 failed to approve monetary support, in 2015 voters approved a tax levy, with city oversight, for the Grout District, and the finances were at least settled for a time.[28]

The Sullivan Museum still did not have much traffic, and the Sullivan Center could still not draw much by way of conventions, although it hung on by providing space for smaller affairs; a witness called it one of the city's "money pits." The Downtown Master Plan Update, which Waterloo's leaders had at least put high on their list of projects, noted that the convention center had "lost its edge in the marketplace." Nonetheless, the authors of the plan reserved a vacant plaza opposite the center for an even bigger Sullivan Center, a "larger exhibit space" that would be needed when Waterloo's development took off. One schematic drawing (a "high priority") showed a bridge from the underused convention center to an imaginary building that would be part of an expanded gallery but that was in 2015 an empty lot.[29] People believed what they wanted to believe about the Sullivans, no matter what the facts; city officials also had capricious dreams about the downtown district that bore so many Sullivan names.

The old center of Waterloo looked as if a neutron bomb had struck it. Because of the low occupancy rate, public agencies conveniently rented low-cost halfway housing for alcoholics, the homeless, or the noncriminal mentally impaired; they made up the bulk of pedestrians on the streets. The situation prompted an appalling joke about the meaning of Iowa: **I**diots **o**utside **w**alking **a**round. The acres of empty parking lots and parking garages, and streets with unused parking meters, enhanced the loneliness of the area. In early 2016, however, the city fathers approved a $750,000 makeover of the 4th Street Bridge that led to the convention center and the museum named for the Sullivans. One frustrated official said of the overpass, "It's the world's longest urinal, in my experience. That it's become an icon of our community is a sad commentary."[30] The rest of the city's Sullivaniana was not faring much better. The Sullivan Park was a drug den at night. Miscreants endangered the statue of Mary Mother of Peace, which memorialized the Sullivans in front of the boarded-up Saint Mary's Parish School. In 2012 concerned citizens moved it to another part of town, to grace the Knights of Columbus building, presumably out of harm's way, far to the southeast of its original location. But even there, the statue overlooked a pornography shop; one very old citizen who claimed (dubiously) to have known the Sullivan children mused, "Appropriate . . . the boys would have loved it." That was Waterloo in the early twenty-first century, "a virtual shrine" to the Sullivans, as the History Channel documentary had put it.

# CONCLUSION

In 1931 James Thurber, who would go on to become a premier comedic short-story writer of the twentieth century, wrote a piece of fiction for *The New Yorker* magazine. "The Greatest Man in the World"[1] was obviously based on the feat of Charles Lindbergh, a hitherto unknown but talented US airmail pilot who became the first person to fly over the Atlantic Ocean, alone and nonstop, in May 1927. He was soon awarded the nation's highest military decoration—the Congressional Medal of Honor. But Thurber's brief tale took a dour view of American hero-worship.

"The Greatest Man in the World" is told in 1950 about the first round-the-world flight of 1937, made by Jack Smurch, a garage mechanic's helper from Westfield, Iowa. Smurch comes from a mean and marginal family. The Smurches are "despised and feared" in their hometown, and Jack, the product of two stretches in reform school, is considered "a nuisance and a menace." But in the weeks after his triumphal flight, when he is kept from public sight because of exhaustion, authorities instruct him "in the ethics and behavior of heroism." Smurch resists, however, being "a national hero of insufficient intelligence, background, and character successfully to endure the mounting orgies of glory"; he is a "congenital hooligan, mentally and morally unequipped to cope with his own prodigious fame." At a secret meeting with leading politicians and newspapermen at the rest home where he is recovering from the week in the air, he is thrown out of a window to his death, as the president makes a stealthy exit. A cover story follows, as does an elaborate funeral at Arlington Cemetery and the construction of a magnificent monument there.

Although close to one another, the Sullivan family had serious problems. Tom drank, and Alleta could not cope; Grandma Abel kept the group together. The Sullivans had no interest in education, and the unoriginal intelligences of the boys did not lead them to look for success

in business or professional endeavors that required training or education. They also lacked the work ethic that people often attributed to the
poor but estimable. In any event, during the Great Depression men did
not easily find jobs. Simultaneously, Tom's remunerative trade elevated
the Sullivans economically, and his income gave the boys a cushion
and a disincentive to seek occupation; they had no desire to hang on to
whatever lowly employment they may have been able to obtain.

In the late 1930s the Sullivan boys were growing up as habitués of
saloons and dance halls, drinking and brawling. Although the brothers
were more run-of-the-mill than remarkable in their social niche, the
motorcycle club to which they belonged only underscored a not particularly admirable existence. Pearl Harbor and World War II gave their
lives an object and shape that they did not have before December 7,
1941. The Sullivan men answered to a majestic purpose. Nonetheless,
we do not know much about their response to the South Pacific and if
or how war altered them. In November 1942, they were in the wrong
place at the wrong time, put in harm's way by a US government with a
righteous cause but unprepared to realize its goals in a sparing manner.
In the way of medals—the common measure of wartime courage—the
Sullivan parents collected for each son only a Purple Heart, indicating
injury or death to a combatant. The five were casualties, but not worthy
of higher commendations such as the Medal of Honor.

In the aftermath of the destruction of the *Juneau*, the navy—for reasons both base and laudable—made up a narrative to give beneficial
meaning to the tragedy that had befallen the siblings. We also find an
encrustation of fiction about the family in Waterloo—in popular song,
museum exhibits, widely held beliefs, and most of all in *The Fighting
Sullivans*. But 10 percent of the film conveys the most important fact entailed by the call to duty in even a democratic nation in a good war. The
five brothers surrendered their lives to the state. FULL STOP. For those
who lose their children in war, no closure exists. FULL STOP. Such deaths
defeat families. FULL STOP. It is hard to combine the sentimentality of
90 percent of the film with the shocking 10 percent, just as no path
guides us from the Sullivans in life to the Sullivans in death.

We need heroes. But how we identify them is unclear, as is why we
must elevate them beyond the human. We may confer heroism on in-

dividuals because of the special burdens they bear, but the demand for perfection is puzzling. The Sullivans could not be remembered unless people deemed their social origins as worthwhile. We had to see travail as unmerited in order to appreciate it—and it could be unmerited only if the victims were upright. If we thought the Sullivans deserved their fate, then we could not give them respect. Why is pain not tragic if its victims are flawed? America recognized the need for moments of silence only if bad things happened to good people. If such things happened to people whom a conventional middle class suspected, commemoration was beside the point, or the culture had to fabricate the nature of these people. This was true for the Hollywood filmmakers who made paragons of the family, and also true for the community that dismissed the Sullivans because the boys did not conduct themselves as paragons. In this context Waterloo's officials showed a refreshing cynicism and allowed their politics to override their ethics.

Normal people lost sight of our common humanity, our own failings, and our own weaknesses. Instead, we put our faith in our own provincial ideals, which none of us really lives up to. On the contrary, William James got it right when he said we all share "common clay with lunatics and prison inmates."

Truth is supposed to break myth. But nothing has penetrated the shell of invention that has enveloped the Sullivans. Over and over again basic facts about them have been ignored and fundamental realities dismissed. We are so single-minded in wanting heroes of an acceptable sort that we will reject whatever we must to get pristine creatures. Thinkers who believe that truth must out, or that erroneous belief will lead us astray, have gotten something wrong. Human beings often live by the sham; on these occasions they cannot face accuracy—and do not want the genuine. Thus we don't just *need* heroes. To obtain heroes we habitually commit ourselves to the false or the impossible or the pretend. Rather than striving after the authentic, people from time to time can survive only with the fictitious. Heroes receive definition as part of this counterfeit realm. A tendency to accept artifice seems hardwired in the mind, and the deep consideration is that such fantasy may be desirable. Human life is at best a patchwork, and we may be able to go on only through a belief in the heroic that is necessarily illusory.

The five brothers will never "swell the rout / Of lads that wore their honours out, / Runners whom renown outran / And the name died before the man." Instead, fate left their lives unfinished. We can never know individuals from seeing them in their twenties; they have to grow up for us to know what their youth portended, how their lives realized their early humanity. For that reason the sons will always remain enigmatic and strange. They live in the shadow of a great name: *The Fighting Sullivans*. On the fiftieth anniversary of their demise, in 1992, one of the many navy admirals who had spoken over the years in support of the family told a Waterloo crowd that George, Frank, Red, Matt, and Al had stature as "giants among men."[2] From the perspective of history, the weightiest thing that happened to the children was the opportune manner of their deaths.

## ACKNOWLEDGMENTS

Every year I spend a good part of the summer in Elkhorn, Wisconsin, at the vacation home of my wife's family. Elkhorn is in the heartland of the United States, in the congressional district that produced the conservative Republican vice presidential candidate in 2012 who later became Speaker of the House. For four years, while writing this book, I would make a four-hour trip farther west to spend a week, or the inside of a week, in Waterloo. The drive is an arrow's straight shot into the very heart of the heartland. If you go toward the end of the day, you will have the sun in your eyes for the entire trip, but you can always follow the American flags from place to place. After Beloit, I have gone through small Wisconsin towns many times. Gratiot, Shullsberg, Benton. You cross the Mississippi at Dubuque. WELCOME TO IOWA. Once you get out of Dubuque, it is seventy-seven miles to Waterloo on Highway 20, the shaft of the arrow. The landscape is farmland and becomes progressively less hilly. About fifteen miles out of town, a sign announces BLACK HAWK COUNTY.

I feel I know Waterloo well. I have my favorite places to eat, have tried a movie, and gone to a minor league baseball game. I have repeatedly walked the streets of Waterloo, and not just where the Sullivans lived. Downtown, I have again and again pressed my face up to empty ground-floor windows of some beautiful old buildings, including, many times, Blacks.

I have no friends in Waterloo, and have had one unfortunate encounter with a waitress, and my attempt to contact Kelly Loughren Sullivan was rebuffed. But I have met a lot of helpful and pleasant people in the city, and over the years they have gossiped with me a lot about their town. Waterloo's citizens have been good and kind to me.

I have thought a lot about how my writing might be received in Waterloo, and about what my moral obligations are, and what are my obligations as an historian. This book definitively answers these questions. But first of all in these acknowledgments, I want to say thanks to the people of Waterloo.

For readings of the book I would like to thank: Elizabeth Block,

Thomas Childers, Steve Conn, Richard Freeland, David Hollinger, Stephanie McCurry, Leo Ribuffo, and Susan Schulten; and especially Chuck Myers of the University Press of Kansas.

Mark Quigley of the UCLA Cinema Studies Archive was uncommonly helpful in explaining to me the issues of film preservation. Michael McGee of Waterloo was invaluable.

D'Alba Cartography has produced and copyrighted the original maps of Waterloo and of the Pacific War. As ever, Rosemarie D'Alba has been precious.

# NOTES

ABBREVIATIONS

The following abbreviations appear in the Notes and Bibiographical Essay to help readers identify sources cited by the author.

| | |
|---|---|
| BCW | Black Hawk County Court House, Waterloo, Iowa |
| MHL | Margaret Herrick Library of the Motion Picture Academy of Arts and Sciences, Los Angeles |
| NA | National Archives, College Park, Maryland |
| NHC | Naval Historical Center, Washington, DC |
| SM | Sullivan Brothers Iowa Veterans Museum, Waterloo, Iowa |
| UCLA | Library at the University of California–Los Angeles |
| USC | Cinematic Arts Library at the University of Southern California |
| WCH | Waterloo City Hall |
| WPL | Waterloo Public Library |

INTRODUCTION: THE SULLIVAN BROTHERS IN AMERICA AND
IN WATERLOO, IOWA

1. See the treatment in the *Courier* from June 24 to August 18, 1988.

CHAPTER 1. GROWING UP SULLIVAN

1. My narrative is indebted to that of Sean Nicholson, "The Sullivans," an unpublished speech written for a celebration in Trafrask in 2003.

2. *Courier*, Thomas Sullivan obituary, March 2, 1965, pp. 1, 2; the 1900 US Census has him in Harpers Ferry, but he cannot be found in the 1910 US Census (the 1890 US Census is unavailable). My own guess is that he mined in South Dakota, where his grandfather Tom was living in 1903. See the probate of the older Tom's will, September 9, 1903, Deadwood, Lawrence County, South Dakota. Deadwood had been a gold-rush town in the 1870s, and mining was an important feature of its economy into the 1900s. Although over 600 miles distant from Harpers Ferry, Deadwood was far closer to home than locations in Montana or Colorado.

3. See Barbara Beving Long, *Waterloo, Factory City of Iowa: Survey of Architecture and History* (Waterloo, IA: City of Waterloo, 1986); *Negro-White Relations in the Waterloo Metropolitan Area* (Iowa State Teachers College, Louis Bultena, Instructor, 1955) (copies in WPL). Also: Charline J. Barnes and Floyd Bumpers, *Iowa's Black Legacy* (Charleston, SC: Arcadia Publishing, 2000), p. 93; and

Glenda Riley, *Cities on the Cedar: A Portrait of Cedar Falls, Waterloo, and Black Hawk County* (Parkersburg, IA: Mid-Prairie Books, 1988), pp. 42–43.

4. Although I have done my own reconstruction of the family life of the Sullivans, I am indebted to John R. Satterfield, *We Band of Brothers: The Sullivans in World War II* (Parkersburg, IA: Mid-Prairie Books, 1995), and Dan Kurzman, *Left to Die: The Tragedy of the USS* Juneau (New York: Simon and Schuster, 1994). Both authors conducted interviews in the late 1980s with people who knew the Sullivans. This material is no longer available, and the people who contributed have died.

5. Kurzman, *Left to Die*, pp. 13–14.

6. *Courier*, March 6, 1933, p. 5. Riley, *Cities on the Cedar*, pp. 52–53.

7. See the US Censuses of 1920, 1930, and 1940; and the Iowa Census of 1925.

8. *Courier*, February 19, 1926, p. 4.

9. *Chicago Herald-American*, January 20, 1943, p. 7.

10. This incident is mentioned by Red in a letter to his mother [n.d./fall 1942], Five Sullivans Binder, SM; and in stories that came out in the newspapers in 1943 before the film. See especially *Chicago Herald-American*, January 18, 1943, p. 2.

11. Jennifer Jacobs, "Red Letter Occasion," *Courier*, March 17, 1999, Five Sullivans Binder, WPL.

CHAPTER 2. DEPRESSION TROUBLES

1. *Courier*, January 12, 1943, p. 3.

2. This educational history is far from definitive and subject to differing accounts; the limited information is available in: the 1940 Census (where Tom and Alleta's schooling went from previously reported fourth grade to eighth); *Courier*, October 26, 1931, p. 3; January 21, 1932, p. 7; May 12, 1932, p. 8; and Waterloo East High School Yearbooks, 1933–1939, WPL. There is even evidence that George began tenth grade in the fall of 1933 (1933 Yearbook).

3. *Courier*, August 20, 1933, p. 5.

4. See the letter from George Sullivan to the US Navy, ca. December 26, 1942, reprinted on pp. 38–39 (chapter 3).

5. On the Hundleys see, for example, *Courier*, January 5, 1926, p. 14, and January 7, 1926, p. 4; ads for the Merry Garden in the *Courier* for September 1933; and *City of Waterloo v. Mary K. Hundley*, No. 5734 (1935), BCW.

6. John Cosden, "Remembering the Sullivan Brothers," *Irish American Magazine* (March 1992), pp. 46–50; Matt to Boots, posted February 7, 1942, Sullivan Brothers, Letters, SM; Mullen to Matt and Red, postmarked Brooklyn,

March 7, 1942, Five Sullivan Brothers Binder, WPL. I cannot account for how this letter was preserved.

7. I was repeatedly told stories like these from people who had evidently heard them from much older friends or relatives.

8. On the issue of film genre, Jeanine Basinger, *The World War II Combat Film: Anatomy of a Genre*, Wesleyan ed. (Middletown, CT: Wesleyan University Press, 1986, 2003), is exceptional.

9. Lawrence H. Suid, *Guts & Glory: The Making of the American Military Image in Film*, rev. and expanded ed. (Lexington: University Press of Kentucky, 2002), pp. 7–8, 42–44; and *Sailing on the Silver Screen: Hollywood and the U.S. Navy* (Annapolis, MD: Naval Institute Press, 1996), pp. 17–55.

10. See the movie ads in the *Courier* for June 11 and December 3, 1933, and February 6 and November 3, 1935; and the pamphlet *Historical Tours of Black Hawk County Iowa* (Cedar Falls, IA: Cedar Falls Historical Society, 1996).

11. John R. Satterfield, *We Band of Brothers: The Sullivans in World War II* (Parkersburg, IA: Mid-Prairie Books, 1995), p. 37.

12. *Chicago Herald-American*, January 20, 1943, p. 7.

13. See Alleta's letter to the Navy of January 1943, reprinted on pp. 68–69 (chapter 5).

14. US Census, 1940. The 1940 US Census is the first to give us salary figures (for 1939), but the continuing rise in the value of the family's housing from the 1920s on testifies to Tom's comparatively high income over the years. See also Diane Petro, "Brother, Can You Spare a Dime? The 1940 Census: Employment and Income," *Prologue*, vol. 44, no. 1 (Spring 2012) (online).

15. Jonathan Faley, "Love into Money," *Forbes*, January 7, 2002, p. 62; and for a later history, see Randy D. McBee, *Born to Be Wild: The Rise of the American Motorcyclist* (Chapel Hill: University of North Carolina Press, 2015), pp. 2–7, which notes the dispute on when bikers gained notoriety.

16. *Courier*, July 7, 1932; January 2, 1933; and August 16, 1940, in McGee Collection.

17. In addition to the Black Hawks' bar, there may also have been a clubhouse near Rath's. See Satterfield, *We Band of Brothers*, pp. 44, 54. And for the distinction between bar and clubhouse, see Daniel R. Wolf, *The Rebels: A Brotherhood of Outlaw Bikers* (Toronto: University of Toronto Press, 1991), pp. 164–166, 180–183.

18. Cosden, "Remembering the Sullivan Brothers," pp. 46–50. On Brokaw see the *Courier*, October 22, 1933, p. 5, and May 20, 1934, p. 12; on the membership, see *Courier*, March 14, 1943, p. 11.

19. See William L. Dulaney, "A Brief History of 'Outlaw' Motorcycle Clubs,"

*International Journal of Motorcycle Studies* (November 2005) (online), which has the quotation; we have pictures of the Tic Toc, some description of what it was like, and letters to it, but the detailed depiction is generic.

20. "The Fighting Sullivans," *Chicago Herald-American*, January 18, 1943, pp. 1–2.

21. Estate probate record, George Sullivan, Box: The Sullivans, SM.

22. A careful examination of the criminal cases in the Black Hawk County court records from 1934 to 1941 shows no mention of the Sullivans. While the extant records do not include juvenile cases or Waterloo city cases, the county records take account of offenses as common as driving while intoxicated. The material is in BCW.

23. On Marshall, see Justus D. Doenecke, "Vern Marshall's Leadership of the No Foreign War Committee, 1940," *Annals of Iowa* 41 (1973): 1153–1172.

CHAPTER 3. IN THE NAVY

1. See my discussion in the Bibliographical Essay.

2. I have been unable to find the original of this letter, although it is available on many websites. If it was indeed typed, and not handwritten, it is likely that Gen—who had learned typing and how to compose a business letter in her commercial course at East High—was a partial author.

3. Metrotone News, quoted in John R. Satterfield, *We Band of Brothers: The Sullivans in World War II* (Parkersburg, IA: Mid-Prairie Books, 1995), p. 174; *Washington Post*, January 25, 1945, clipping in File: Juneau, Box 41, Records of the Bureau of Naval Personnel, Casualty Assistance Branch, RG 24, NA.

4. *Courier*, January 2, p. 6; January 4, pp. 1, 4, 1942.

5. *Des Moines Register*, January 4, 1942, p. 1; a similar story appears in the *Courier*, January 4, 1942, p. 6.

6. The story is from Lynn Harned, from nearby Cedar Falls, interviewed August 11, 2015.

7. Joe to Joe, circa January 1942, McGee Collection; Joe to Ham and Gary, postmarked January 26, 1942, Sullivan Brothers, Letters, SM; one letter is reproduced in Satterfield, *We Band of Brothers*, p. 63.

8. Thomas Arthur Rapp, "Blue Heaven, or, Saving Sergeant Shaffer," *American Road* 4 (Autumn 2006): 15.

9. Joe to Ham and George [circa February 1942], McGee Collection; the visit is featured in an early script of the movie—First Draft Continuity Script, *The Sullivans*, July 10, 1943, Folder 1, Script Collection, USC.

10. George Baer, *One Hundred Years of Sea Power: The U.S. Navy, 1890–1990*

(Stanford: Stanford University Press, 1994), pp. 142–144, 212–222, 225–226; and Craig C. Felker, *Testing American Sea Power: U.S. Navy Strategic Exercise, 1923–1940* (College Station: Texas A&M University Press, 2013), pp. 121–137, 141. For a view from one expert: Eric Hammel, *Guadalcanal: Decision at Sea, The Naval Battle of Guadalcanal, November 13–15, 1942* (New York: Crown Publishers, 1988), p. 323.

11. Matt to Nell and Charlie [n.d.], McGee Collection.

12. *Chicago Herald-American*, January 22, 1943, p. 5.

13. *Courier*, March 4, p. 2; March 15, p. 1; April 26, p. 1; May 25, p. 7; June 21, p. 1; June 28, p. 1, 1942.

14. One can follow the *Juneau* through October of 1942 in the [Captain Lyman Knute] Svenson War Diary, Microfilm NRS 1973–71, NHC.

15. *Courier*, May 24, p. 12; May 31, p. 1, 1942.

16. See Red to Paul Hamilton, and Red to Gang, undated, in McGee Collection (reprinted in Satterfield, *We Band of Brothers*, pp. 79–80); *Courier*, October 29, 1942, p. 5; January 15, 1943, pp. 1–2. Also: "Love and War," by Pat Kinney, *Courier*, January 1999; and Red to Folks, July 2, 1942, reprinted in Jennifer Jacobs, "Red Letter Occasion," *Courier*, March 17, 1999, clippings in Five Sullivans Binder, WPL.

17. A good example of the growing literature on this topic is William Merrill Decker, *Epistolary Practices: Letter Writing in America before Telecommunication* (Chapel Hill: University of North Carolina Press, 1998).

18. V-Mail was not in standard use until after the *Juneau* went down, although the Sullivans at home at one time had some from the boys: *Chicago Herald-American*, January 21, p. 5; January 22, p. 5, 1943.

19. Red to Alleta [fall 1942], Five Sullivans Binder, SM; Gen to Red, October 28, 1942, McGee Collection; and Jennifer Jacobs, "Red Letter Occasion," *Courier*, March 17, 1999, clipping in Five Sullivans Binder, WPL.

20. See for example, Joe to Gang [n.d., but written on Saint Patrick's Day 1942], McGee Collection.

21. For example, *Courier*, September 27, 1942, p.16.


CHAPTER 4. GUADALCANAL

1. Samuel Eliot Morison, *The Struggle for Guadalcanal*, vol. 5: *History of United States Naval Operations in World War II* (Boston: Little, Brown, 1949, 1953), pp. 3–4.

2. *Juneau*, Action Report, October 30, 1942, Operational Archives, NHC.

3. Navy report in McGee Collection.

4. Satterfield interview with Madaris, in John R. Satterfield, *We Band of Brothers: The Sullivans and World War II* (Parkersburg, IA: Mid-Prairie Books, 1995), p. 122; *Courier*, January 14, p. 3; February 11, 1943, p. 2.

5. *Courier*, November 1, 1942, p. 8.

6. John McDowell, "The Terrible Ordeal of the U.S.S. *Juneau*," *Sea Classics*, 19 (March–April 1986), p. 18.

7. See Hoover's report, November 13, in USS *Helena* Report; and November 15 action report, *San Francisco* Commanding Officer to Commander in Chief, US Pacific Fleet, both in Microfilm NRS 1973–71, NHC.

8. Dan Kurzman, *Left to Die: The Tragedy of the USS* Juneau (New York: Simon and Schuster, 1994), p. 168, and especially the quoted George Walker Diary, November 13–17, 1942.

9. A recent study is Ian W. Toll, *The Conquering Tide: War in the Pacific Islands, 1942–1944* (New York: Norton, 2015), esp. pp. 146–174.

10. On this issue see William Halsey, *Admiral Halsey's Story* (New York: Whittlesey House, 1947), pp. 133–134.

11. Allen Heyn, Interviews with Survivors of *Juneau*, Microfilm NRS 1973–71, NHC.

12. Halsey to Nimitz, December 4, 1942 (received December 10), Microfilm NRS 1973–71, NHC; and the documents in Folder: Juneau, Box 41, Records of the Bureau of Naval Personnel, Casualty Assistance Branch, RG 24, NA. See also Heber A. Holbrook, *The U.S.S.* Juneau *(CL-52) of World War II* (Dixon, CA: Pacific Ship and Shore-Books, 1994, 1995); and *The Loss of the U.S.S.* Juneau *(CL-52) and the Relief of Captain Gilbert C. Hoover, Commanding Officer of the U.S.S.* Helena *(CL-50)* (Dixon, CA: Pacific Ship and Shore-Books, 1997), esp. p. 6.

CHAPTER 5. NATIONAL HEROES

1. *Courier*, January 14, 1943, p. 3.

2. The original, which differs slightly from the usual printed versions, is found in Folder: Juneau, Box 41, Records of the Bureau of Naval Personnel, Casualty Assistance Branch, RG 24, NA.

3. Alleta Sullivan, "I Lost Five Sons," *American Magazine* 137 (March 1944): 92–95.

4. Various stories were printed in the *Courier:* January 12, 13, 15, and 16 and February 2, 1943. Syndicated stories by Basil Talbott first appeared in the *Chicago Herald-American*, January 15 and 17–22, 1943.

5. *Courier*, January 14, 1943, p. 1.

6. Metrotone News, quoted from John R. Satterfield, *We Band of Brothers: The Sullivans in World War II* (Parkersburg, IA: Mid-Prairie Books, 1995), p. 174.

7. *Courier*, January 22, p. 10; January 24, p. 18, 1943.

8. *Courier*, January 15, 1943, pp. 1–2.

9. Lowell (Massachusetts) *Sun*, January 21, 1943, McGee Collection.

10. For the older notions see Joseph Campbell, *The Hero with a Thousand Faces* (Princeton, NJ: Princeton University Press, 1949); Thomas Carlyle's famous lectures originally delivered in 1840, *On Heroes, Hero-Worship, and the Heroic in History* (Berkeley: University of California Press, 1993); and Sidney Hook, *The Hero in History: A Study in Limitation and Possibility* (Boston: Beacon Press, 1943). For a contemporary overview about which readers will have their own ideas: Scott Allison and George R. Goethals, *Heroes: What They Do and Why We Need Them* (New York: Oxford University Press, 2011). The phenomenon I ruminate about here—the heroic in America—is part of a more general change that became apparent in the aftermath of the war. See Angela Brintlinger, *Chapaev and His Comrades: War and the Russian Literary Hero across the Twentieth Century* (Brighton, MA: Academic Studies Press, 2012); Neil Diament, *Embattled Glory, Veterans, Military Families, and the Politics of Patriotism in China, 1949–2007* (Lanham, MD: Rowman & Littlefield, 2009); John M. Kinder, *Paying with Their Bodies: American War and the Problem of the Disabled Veteran* (Chicago: University of Chicago Press, 2015); and James Orr, *The Victim as Hero: Ideologies of Peace and National Identity in Postwar Japan* (Honolulu: University of Hawai'i Press, 2001).

11. *Courier*, January 20, 1943, p. 6.

12. The series appeared in the *Chicago Herald-American* from January 18 through January 23, with an initial story without Talbott's byline on January 15.

13. I have reconstructed Tom and Alleta's radio statements from the report in the *Courier*, February 1, 1943, p. 1.

CHAPTER 6. A NEW MRS. BIXBY

1. See Harold Holzer, *Lincoln and the Power of the Press: The War for Public Opinion* (New York: Simon and Schuster, 2014).

2. Garry Wills, *Lincoln at Gettysburg: The Words That Remade America* (New York: Simon and Schuster, 1992).

3. Sandburg's ruminations are found in *Abraham Lincoln: The War Years*, vol. 3 (New York: Harcourt Brace, 1939), pp. 665–669. For the scholarship on the Bixby letter, see Michael Burlingame, ed., *At Lincoln's Side: John Hay's War Correspondence and Selected Writings* (Carbondale: Southern Illinois University Press, 2000), pp. 169–184.

4. *Courier*, January 12, pp. 1–3; January 20, p. 6; February 1, p. 1, 1943.

5. The original of this letter was apparently lost by the remaining Sullivans,

although a copy of the January 13 draft is available: http://www.archives
.gov/exhibits/a_people_at_war/war_in_the_pacific, as well as an image of the
February 1 final: http://www.fdrlibrary.marist.edu/_resources/images/sign
/fdr_50.pdf, which is located in the Presidents Personal Files, 8293, FDR Library, Hyde Park, New York. The Associated Press photo of Alleta reading the
letter is dated January 20, 1943.

## CHAPTER 7. THE NAVY TOUR AND AFTER

1. For the "Seaman Izzi" example see File: Izzi, Box 118, General Correspondence, Industrial Incentive Division, RG 80, NA.

2. Jacobs to Taylor, July 5, 1944 (quoted), and, for example, Atkinson to
Grycky, September 9, 1946, and Semmes to Klausmeyer, September 27, 1946,
Folder: Juneau, Box 41, Records of the Bureau of Naval Personnel, Casualty As-
sistance Branch, RG 24, NA. See also James D. Hornfischer, *Neptune's Inferno:
The U.S. Navy at Guadalcanal* (New York: Bantam Books, 2011), p. 375.

3. *Courier*, February 8, 1943, p. 1.

4. For Taylor's travels with the Sullivans see Folder: Taylor, Box 110C, General Correspondence, Industrial Incentive Division, RG 80, NA.

5. *New York Times*, February 28, 1943, p. 1.

6. Tom and Alleta both reconstructed from the *Courier*, February 5, 8, 10,
1943, all p. 1.

7. *Courier*, February 8, p. 3; February 9, p. 6; February 14, pp. 11–12, 1943.

8. *Courier*, April 5, 1943, pp. 1–2. And see John R. Satterfield, *We Band of
Brothers: The Sullivans in World War II* (Parkersburg, IA: Mid-Prairie Books,
1995), p. 190.

9. *Courier*, April 5, 1943, pp. 1–2.

10. For this correspondence, the appraisals, and quotes, see Folder: P20-1(1),
Box 141, General Correspondence, Industrial Incentive Division, RG 80, NA.

11. Forrestal to Knox, March 22, 1943, Folder: P20-1(1), Box 141, General
Correspondence, Industrial Incentive Division, RG 80, NA.

12. *Courier*, March 23, p. 1, April 11, p. 11, April 12, p. 1, May 4, p. 1, June 13,
p. 1, 1943; Ripley to Henry Sullivan (uncle of the six siblings), June 16, 1943,
McGee Collection.

13. *Dubuque Telegraph Herald*, June 14, 1943, p. 1; *Courier*, August 27, 1943,
p. 3; *Motion Picture Herald*, July 17, 1943, p. 48.

14. Newspaper clipping, circa May 1943, McGee Collection; *Courier*, December 23, p. 5, 1943; January 10, p. 10, February 9, p. 7, 1944.

15. *Courier*, January 12, 1943, p. 3; for a sample of the poetry, see April 13,
1943, p. 1.

16. *Courier*, February 9, p. 6; February 10, pp. 1–2, 4; February 11, pp. 1–2; February 12, p. 1; February 19, p. 2; March 31, p. 1; May 30, p. 11, 1943.

17. See especially *Courier*, February 13, p. 11; April 11, p. 11, 1943. It is possible to track every dollar that was given to the fund by following the newspaper reports.

18. *Courier*, March 1, p. 1; March 12, p. 1, 1943.

19. *Courier*, March 8, pp. 1–2; March 19, pp. 1–2, 1943. Other sources claim that the Paramount seated 2,000; if this is true, the rejection was greater.

20. *Chicago Herald-American*, January 15, 1943, p. 3; January 23, 1943, p. 5.

21. *Courier*, April 4, p. 11; April 15, p. 1; May 6, p. 1, 1943.

22. Carolyn Anspacher, "The Sullivans," clipping from *San Francisco Chronicle*, April 3, 1943, in McGee Collection.

23. *Courier*, January 17, 1943, p. 2.

CHAPTER 8. HOLLYWOOD IN WAITING FOR THE SULLIVANS

1. On these matters in World War II see M. Todd Bennett, *One World, Big Screen: Hollywood, Allies, and World War Two* (Chapel Hill: University of North Carolina Press, 2012), pp. 32–34.

2. A sophisticated but formal and philosophical treatment, with relevance to the Sullivans, is Jason Stanley, *How Propaganda Works* (Princeton, NJ: Princeton University Press, 2015).

3. There are some outstanding treatments of the economic history of the film, including John Izod's synthetic *Hollywood and the Box Office, 1895–1986* (New York: Columbia University Press, 1988). Mae D. Huettig's still essential *Economic Control of the Motion Picture Industry* (Philadelphia: University of Pennsylvania Press, 1944) focused on the late 1930s and early 1940s.

4. David Bordwell, *The Way Hollywood Tells It: Story and Style in Modern Movies* (Berkeley: University of California Press, 2006), p. 4.

5. On this issue see Laura Heins, *Nazi Film Melodrama* (Urbana: University of Illinois Press, 2013).

6. While it does not cover 20th Century-Fox, Thomas Schatz, *The Genius of the System: Hollywood Filmmaking in the Studio Era* (New York: Pantheon Books, 1988), is outstanding in analyzing movies in the 1930s and 1940s. See also Ethan Mordan, *The Hollywood Studios: House Style in the Golden Age of the Movies* (New York: Alfred A. Knopf, 1988); for his description of Hollywood executives, see p. 11.

7. This is a hot topic. Begin with Saverio Giovacchini, *Hollywood Modernism: Film and Politics in the Age of the New Deal* (Philadelphia: Temple University Press, 2001). Alexander McGregor, *The Catholic Church and Hollywood:*

*Censorship and Morality in 1930s Cinema* (London: I. B. Taurus, 2013), pp. 116–138, argues that Hollywood's own censors effectively sided with the Germans because they opposed Russian communism; Ben Urwand's *The Collaboration: Hollywood's Pact with Hitler* (Cambridge: Harvard University Press, 2013) argues that Hollywood itself was more than cowardly. Less controversial is Thomas Doherty, *Hollywood and Hitler, 1933–1939* (New York: Columbia University Press, 2013). For a more general interpretation see Mark Harris, *Five Came Back: A Story of Hollywood and the Second World War* (New York: Penguin Books, 2014).

8. These pressures are taken up in two essays in an outstanding collection, Peter C. Rollins and John E. O'Connor, eds., *Why We Fought: America's Wars in Film and History* (Lexington: University Press of Kentucky, 2008): John Whiteclay Chambers II, "The Peace, Isolationist, and Anti-interventionist Movements and Interwar Hollywood," pp. 196–225; and Cynthia J. Miller, "The B Movie Goes to War in *Hitler, Beast of Berlin*," pp. 226–241.

9. The violence allowed was still more than muted. See George H. Roeder, *The Censored War: American Visual Experience during World War Two* (New Haven, CT: Yale University Press, 1993), esp. pp. 22–23, 35.

10. Several essays in Lewis A. Erenberg and Susan E. Hirsch, eds., *The War in American Culture: Society and Consciousness during World War II* (Chicago: University of Chicago Press, 1996), make this point. See the work by Perry Duis, Larry May, and particularly Gary Gerstle, pp. 110, 113–114, and 121. More recently, the complexities of this issue are reviewed in Steven Casey, *When Soldiers Fall: How Americans Have Confronted Combat Loss from World War I to Afghanistan* (New York: Oxford University Press, 2014), esp. pp. 38–39, 46–64.

11. Helpful on the OWI is Alan M. Winkler, *The Politics of Propaganda: The Office of War Information, 1942–1945* (New Haven, CT: Yale University Press, 1978), but it has little to say about the movies. See esp. pp. 57–60.

12. See George F. Custen, *Bio/Pics: How Hollywood Constructed Public History* (New Brunswick, NJ: Rutgers University Press, 1992).

13. Frank Walsh, *Sin and Censorship: The Catholic Church and the Motion Picture Industry* (New Haven, CT: Yale University Press, 1996), has an excellent and extended appraisal of this film at pp. 36–45.

14. Les and Barbara Keyser, *Hollywood and the Catholic Church: The Image of Roman Catholicism in American Movies* (Chicago: Loyola University Press, 1984), is uncritical but also treats *The Sullivans* at pp. 159–162. Christopher Shannon, *Bowery to Broadway: The American Irish in Classic Hollywood Cinema* (Scranton, PA: University of Scranton Press, 2010), is more up to date. Wider in scope is Anthony Burke Smith, *The Look of Catholics: Portrayals in Popular*

*Culture from the Great Depression to the Cold War* (Lawrence: University Press of Kansas, 2010). See also Wyatt Wells, "Research Note: Appointment of Catholics during the New Deal," *Journal of the Historical Society* 13 (2013): 361–413.

15. An extraordinary scene in *The Human Comedy* (1943) displays the Protestant consensus in America that Jewish Hollywood confirmed: an entire railroad car of soldiers joins in the singing of "Leaning on the Everlasting Arms," a popular hymn originally written in 1887 by Anthony J. Showalter and Elisha Hoffman. Anthony Burke Smith, in "America's Favorite Priest," argues that *Going My Way* was the breakthrough movie in *Catholics in the Movies*, Colleen McDannell, ed. (New York: Oxford University Press, 2008), pp. 107–126.

CHAPTER 9. THE FILM IS BORN

1. For an overview see H. Avery Chenoweth, "Combat Artists of Guadalcanal," *Naval History Magazine* 21 (2007) (online); and Brian Lanker and Nicole Newnham, *They Drew Fire: Combat Artists of World War II* (New York: TV Books, 2000), esp. pp. 92–93.

2. *Courier*, January 17, p. 2; March 7, p. 11, 1943.

3. *Hollywood Reporter*, February 18, 1943, p. 3; *Los Angeles Examiner*, March 6, 1943, clippings, Folder 33, Box 1, Lloyd Bacon Papers; Sam Jaffe Oral History (February—July 1991), pp. 67, 226–236, MHL.

4. For Doherty's role see *Courier*, March 10, 1944, p. 3. For the navy, Schermer to Bacon, March 17, 1943, Folder 34, Box 1, Bacon Papers, MHL.

5. Woodward to Bacon, September 9, 1943, Folder 34, Box 1, Bacon Papers, MHL.

6. Thomas Schatz, *Boom and Bust: The American Cinema in the 1940s* (New York: Scribner's Sons, 1997), p. 50.

7. The most sympathetic treatment of Bacon's abilities is found in Martin Rubin, "1933: Movies and the New Deal in Entertainment," pp. 100–103, 108–109, in Ina Rae Hark, ed. *American Cinema of the 1930s: Themes and Variations* (Rutgers, NJ: Rutgers University Press, 2007); and in David Bordwell, *Narration in the Fiction Film* (Madison: University of Wisconsin Press, 1985), pp. 186–188. Most expansive is Ehsan Khoshbakht's Internet appraisal, "Notes on Cinetomograph: A Guide to Lloyd Bacon."

8. On Bacon's navy movies see Lawrence H. Suid, *Sailing on the Silver Screen: Hollywood and the U.S. Navy* (Annapolis, MD: Naval Institute Press, 1996), pp. 38–55.

9. This narrative derives from the Bacon statement in Sullivans Legal, Folder 38, Box 1, Bacon Papers, MHL.

10. *Film Daily*, March 25, 1943, p. 10; for Jaffe's recollections see Jaffe Oral

History, pp. 226–236; for the legal arrangements, Sullivans Legal, Folder 38, Box 1, Bacon Papers, MHL.

11. *Courier*, March 14, 1943, p. 1; John R. Satterfield, *We Band of Brothers: The Sullivans and World War II* (Parkersburg, IA: Mid-Prairie Books, 1995), p. 188.

12. Jaffe Oral History, pp. 67, 226–236, MHL. Copies of the legal documents can be found in Folder 38, Box 1, Bacon Papers, MHL. For the estate records, see Estate Probate Records, Box: The Sullivans, SM.

13. *Motion Picture Daily*, April 8, p. 6; May 10, p. 2, 1943; *Motion Picture Herald*, June 26, 1943, p. 33.

14. Alleta to Nell Turner, April 15, November 6, 1943, Sullivan Letters, From Alleta, SM.

15. *Courier*, April 16, p. 1; April 28, p. 1; May 12, p. 1, 1943.

16. I have constructed my account from *Film Daily*, May 26, 1943, p. 6; Jaffe Oral History, pp. 226–236; and an eighteen-page deposition by Bacon, circa 1943, which was apparently prepared in case there would be a contest with Schermer for rights to a movie, Sullivans Legal, Folder 38, Box 1, Bacon Papers, MHL; see also *Motion Picture Herald*, June 26, 1943, p. 33.

17. *Hollywood Reporter*, July 12, 1943, p. 6.

18. On Zanuck see George F. Custen, *Twentieth Century Fox: Darryl F. Zanuck and the Culture of Hollywood* (New York: Basic Books, 1997), esp. pp. 261–267; and Mel Gussow, *Don't Say Yes until I Finish Talking: A Biography of Darryl F. Zanuck* (New York: Doubleday, 1971), esp. pp. 13–18, 75, 80–82, 120.

19. *Motion Picture Herald*, July 17, 1943, p. 37.

20. Indirectly relevant to the atmosphere of *The Sullivans* are Kenneth MacKinnon, *Hollywood's Small Towns: An Introduction to the American Small-Town Movie* (Metuchen, NJ: Scarecrow, 1984), esp. pp. 114–116; and Emanuel Levy, *Small-Town America in Film: The Decline and Fall of Community* (New York: Continuum, 1991), but there are no discussions of the physical setting of this kind of movie. See also John E. Miller, *Small-Town Dreams: Stories of Midwestern Boys Who Shaped America* (Lawrence: University Press of Kansas, 2014), although it does not include Zanuck.

21. See the memos of three discussions on the script, July 13, July 26, and August 30, in Folders 1, 2, *The Sullivans*, Script Collection, USC; and Tom Stempel, *Framework: A History of Screenwriting in the American Film* (New York: Continuum, 1988), pp. 77–79.

22. Zanuck to Jack Warner, February 16, 1944, in Rudy Behlmer, ed., *Memo from Darryl F. Zanuck: The Golden Years of Twentieth Century-Fox* (New York: Grove Press, 1993), p. 72.

23. See John Izod's *Hollywood and the Box Office, 1895–1986* (New York: Columbia University Press, 1988), pp. 127–128. On Zanuck's interventions: Conferences with Zanuck, July 13, July 26, August 30, 1943, Folders 1, 2, *The Sullivans*, Script Collection, USC.

24. Suid, *Sailing on the Silver Screen*, p. 71; and Woodward to Bacon, September 9, 1943, Folder 34, Box 1, Bacon Papers, MHL.

25. Information about the shooting in Santa Rosa comes from *Hollywood Reporter*, July 16, pp. 1–2, and July 22, p. 9, 1943; and Folder 36, Box 1, Bacon Papers, MHL. There may be a back story to the shooting of this and other films in Santa Rosa, for the exterior scenes did not benefit from being filmed "on location" and not in a studio; but this is only a guess. Apparently Waterloo was also considered for filming the "on location" portions of the movie (*Hollywood Reporter*, July 22, 1943, p. 9).

26. *Hollywood Reporter*, July 15, p. 4; July 26, p. 6; August 4, p. 8; August 15, p. 6; September 24, p. 6, 1943.

27. *Hollywood Reporter*, November 9, p. 9; November 15, p. 2, 1943; Alleta to Nell and Charlie Turner, November 6, 1943, Sullivan Letters, From Alleta, SM; *Courier*, October 22, 1943, p. 10.

28. *Motion Picture Daily*, November 23, 1943, p. 7; Alleta to Nell and Charlie Turner, January 28, 1944, Sullivan Letters, From Alleta, SM.

## CHAPTER 10. *THE SULLIVANS* AND *THE FIGHTING SULLIVANS*

1. A collection of reviews of *The Sullivans* is in the Film Files, Box 26, The Sullivans, Lawrence Suid Papers, Special Collections, Georgetown University, Washington, DC. The quote is from Sherwin Kane's review, *Motion Picture Daily*, February 3, pp. 1, 3. See also *Hollywood Reporter*, February 3, pp. 3–11; and February 14, p. 12, 1944.

2. Sam Jaffe Oral History (February—July, 1991), pp. 226–236, MHL.

3. For Driscoll's especially unhappy story see Thomas G. Aylesworth, *Hollywood Kids: Child Stars of the Silver Screen from 1903 to the Present* (New York: E. P. Dutton, 1987), pp. 208–211.

4. George F. Custen, *Bio/Pics: How Hollywood Constructed Public History* (New Brunswick, NJ: Rutgers University Press, 1992), pp. 184–186.

5. See the *Chicago Herald-American*, January 15, 17–18, 1943; and *New York Times*, February 2, 1944.

6. I have taken these examples from Jeanine Basinger, *The World War II Combat Film: Anatomy of a Genre*, Wesleyan ed. (Middletown, CT: Wesleyan University Press, 1986, 2003), p. 28. An accessible consideration of Basinger's

ideas is Robert Eberwein, *The Hollywood War Film* (Chichester, West Sussex, U.K.: Wiley-Blackwell, 2010), pp. 11–13, although the treatment of *The Fighting Sullivans* is flimsy, pp. 20–21.

7. There is even a scholarly essay on the topic: Geoff Mayer, "'A Stab in the Back on a Sunday Morning': The Melodramatic Imagination and Pearl Harbor," in Tony Barta, ed., *Screening the Past: Film and the Representation of History* (Westport, CT: Greenwood, 1998), pp. 83–92.

8. See *The Sullivans*, Second Revised Final, August 9, 1943, Script Collections, MHL and USC.

9. Santa Rosa for some reason was a popular spot for moviemaking. It played itself in *Shadow of a Doubt* (1943).

10. The best account of these movies is in Clayton R. Koppes and Gregory D. Black, *Hollywood Goes to War: How Politics, Profits, and Propaganda Shaped World War II Movies* (Berkeley: University of California Press, 1987), pp. 154–175.

11. Conference with Mr. Zanuck, July 13, 1943, *The Sullivans*, Folder 1, Script Collection, USC.

12. Robert Fyne, *The Hollywood Propaganda of World War II* (Metuchen, NJ: Scarecrow, 1994), p. 128.

13. Conferences with Zanuck, July 13 and July 26, *The Sullivans*, Folder 1, Script Collection, USC.

14. *Hollywood Reporter*, April 4, 1944, p. 8.

15. My extended description of *The Sullivans* is to some extent speculative and relies on the *Courier*, February 13, 1944, pp. 13, 15, which told readers in detail about the movie that had premiered in New York.

16. I have constructed this part of the narrative from *Los Angeles Evening Herald*, April 2, 1943, clippings, Folder 33, Box 1, Lloyd Bacon Papers, MHL; *Vassar Miscellany News*, vol. 28, no. 7 (October 14, 1943), p. 6; and *Motion Picture Herald*, November 6, 1943, p. 55.

17. See the exchange of letters in *The Sullivans*, Motion Picture Association of America, Production Code Administration Records, MHL.

18. Willa Cather, *One of Ours* (New York: Vintage, 1991), pp. 222–223.

19. Summaries of many of these sorts of films, though not those with an ending like *The Fighting Sullivans*, may be found in James Robert Parish, *Ghosts and Angels in Hollywood Films: Plots, Critiques, Cast, and Credits for 264 Theatrical and Made-for-Television Releases* (Jefferson, NC: McFarland, 1994).

20. *Courier*, January 24, p. 2; February 9, p. 7; February 20, p. 10, 1944.

21. The reports (overwhelmingly from small towns) come from the column "What the Picture Did for Me" in *Motion Picture Herald*, February 26 to De-

cember 16, 1944; the Fox selling approach is at March 4, p. 57; and the Waterloo advice, April 22, p. 50. The figures for the gross take for the film in selected cities come from *Motion Picture Daily*, February 16 through August 10, 1944.

22. This narrative can be traced in the *Courier* from mid-February 1944 until the March opening.

23. I estimate that the theater had 300 loge seats and 1,500 regular seats, and an algorithm tells us that the maximum number at the opening was 493; the minimum, 110. From what I can figure out, maybe 420 were in the Thursday audience; for Friday and Saturday the audiences for individual showings numbered about 500, peaked that Sunday at 1,200, and then dropped off to under 300 the following week. These are probably overestimates, because the newspaper always exaggerated the positive when it came to the Sullivans. *Courier*, March 10, pp. 1, 2; March 13, p. 7, 1944.

24. *Courier*, October 29, p. 1; October 30, p. 3, 1944.

CHAPTER II. THE SULLIVANS AND *THE FIGHTING SULLIVANS*

1. Some commentators have argued, contrary to my view, that because of the collective nature of the endeavor and the vagaries of intentionality, we cannot make sense of what Hollywood hopes to accomplish with its products, the meaning it plans for a movie to bear. The issues raised are explored with illumination in Richard Maltby, "'A Brief Romantic Interlude': Dick and Jane Go to 3 1/2 Seconds of the Classical Hollywood Cinema,'" in David Bordwell and Noël Carroll, eds., *Post Theory: Reconstructing Film Studies* (Madison: University of Wisconsin Press, 1996), pp. 434–459. This volume has many instructive essays. Various extant versions of the script of *The Sullivans* have allowed me to reconstruct how the tale of the Sullivans was elaborated, and they are listed in the Bibliographical Essay. These screenplays can be compared to the two versions of the film itself, although I have been able to locate only a lengthy written description of the first version, *The Sullivans*, in the *Courier*, February 13, 1944, p. 1; less detailed reviews of the first version can be found in the Film Files, Box 26: The Sullivans, Lawrence Suid Papers, Special Collections, Georgetown University, Washington, DC.

2. A catalogue of these "errors" can be found in the Bibliographical Essay.

3. Breen to Joy, July 29, 1943, Production Code Administration Records, *The Sullivans*; Sam Jaffe Oral History (February—July, 1991), pp. 226–236, MHL.

4. See Alleta's statements in the *Courier*, February 1, p. 1, and February 8, p. 1, 1943.

5. Conference with Zanuck, July 26, 1943 (underlining in original), *The Sullivans*, Folder 1, Script Collection, USC.

6. Povah and Winter are mentioned in *Hollywood Reporter*, August 5, 1943, p. 6; Vaughan in Vaughan to Bacon, September 6, 1943, Folder 32, Box 1, Lloyd Bacon Papers; Bainter in Jaffe Oral History, pp. 226–236, MHL; and Phillips in Conference with Zanuck, July 13, 1943, "The Sullivans," Folder 1, Script Collections, USC.

7. Jaffe Oral History, pp. 226–236; Jaffe to Bacon, September 7 and 11, 1943, Folder 36, Box 1, Bacon Papers, MHL; and *The Sullivans*, First Draft Continuity Script, July 10, 1943, *The Sullivans*, Folder 1, Script Collections, USC.

8. John R. Satterfield, *We Band of Brothers: The Sullivans in World War II* (Parkersburg, IA: Mid-Prairie Books, 1995), has a good summary of the reactions of those who knew the family at pp. 197–198; see also "Albert Sullivan's Widow Looks Back," *Courier*, November 11, 2012.

9. McCall and Royle's troubles have been documented. There are only hints about the other three. See, for example, Larry Ceplair and Steven Englund, *The Inquisition in Hollywood: Politics in the Film Community, 1930–1960* (Garden City, NY: Anchor, 1980); Paul Buhle and Dave Wagner, *Radical Hollywood* (New York: New Press, 2002) (n. 51, p. 258 is the only citation I have been able explicitly to find on Bacon); and also Buhle and Wagner, *Hide in Plain Sight: The Hollywood Blacklistees in Film and Television, 1950–2002* (New York: Palgrave Macmillan, 2003). Drew Faust in *This Republic of Suffering: Death and the American Civil War* (New York: Knopf, 2008) addresses how survivors in a good cause deal with the dead.

10. Robert Fyne, *The Hollywood Propaganda of World War II* (Metuchen, NJ: Scarecrow, 1994), p. 182. See also his *Long Ago and Far Away: Hollywood and the Second World War* (Lanham, MD: Scarecrow, 2008), p. 8.

11. M. Todd Bennett, *One World, Big Screen: Hollywood, Allies, and World War II* (Chapel Hill: University of North Carolina Press, 2012), p. 17.

12. These issues are pointedly addressed in Paul W. Kahn, *Putting Liberalism in Its Place* (Princeton, NJ: Princeton University Press, 2005), pp. 228–230, 244, 288–289.

CHAPTER 12. THE BATTLES OF WATERLOO, 1944–1964

1. My view that Goebbels answered *The Sullivans* with *Die Degenhardts* is speculative and far from conclusive, based on a comparison of the movies, and not on documentary evidence. It is also likely that Goebbels had in mind *Mrs. Miniver* (1942), a Hollywood movie about an English family during the war, generally regarded as the best film about civilian life during the conflict. Interested readers ought to look at *Die Degenhardts* and consult Laura Heins, *Nazi Film Melodrama* (Urbana: University of Illinois Press, 2013),

esp. pp. 178–191; and Mary-Elizabeth O'Brien, *Nazi Cinema as Enchantment: The Politics of Entertainment in the Third Reich* (New York: Camden House, 2004), pp. 144–150. For an up-to-date scholarly bibliography and an even more speculative interpretation see Cary Nathanson, "The Last Laugh: *Die Degenhardts* as Nazi Redemption of *Der letze Mann*," in *Reworking the German Past: Adaptation in Film, the Arts, and Popular Culture*, Susan G. Figge and Jenifer K. Ward, eds. (New York: Camden House, 2010), pp. 15–38.

2. See Jennifer Fay, "Constructing America for German Reconstruction: American Films and Reeducation in Occupied Germany, 1945–1947," *Southern Quarterly* 39 (Summer 2001): 94; and Fay, *Theaters of Occupation: Hollywood and the Reeducation of Postwar Germany* (Minneapolis: University of Minnesota Press, 2008), pp. 36, 176.

3. Jaffe to Cohn, August 26, 1950, Folder 41, Box 1, Lloyd Bacon Papers, MHL.

4. *Courier*, November 11, 2015, p. 1. Tom and Alleta changed their address though not their house, I believe, to avoid the notoriety of 98 Adams. The house sat at the corner of Adams and Ankeny; and for the public they no longer resided at 98 Adams but at 101 Ankeny. See *Courier* clipping, October 26, 1946, and Alleta to Anna, January 24, 1953, both in McGee Collection.

5. Thomas Arthur Rapp, "Blue Heaven or, Saving Sergeant Shaffer," *American Road* 4 (Autumn 2006): 15.

6. For a summary of Waterloo's vision of the Sullivans see the email, Satterfield to Jill, January 11, 2001, Five Sullivan Brothers Binder, WPL; and McGee interviews.

7. Alleta to Nell and Charlie Turner, April 15, 1943; January 28, 1944, Letters: From Alleta, SM. The original reads "jialousy."

8. *Courier*, August 15, 1945, pp. 3, 16.

9. Alleta Sullivan, "I Lost Five Sons," *American Magazine* 137 (March 1944): 92–95; "A Letter to Mothers," *Good Housekeeping* (November 1945): 21.

10. *Courier*, October 6, p. 1, December 23, p. 3, and December 24, p. 3, 1948; February 2, p. 8, and February 20, p. 13, 1949; July 2, 1950, p. 13.

11. *Courier*, May 8, p. 4, and November 11, p. 6, 1962 (which has a picture of the plaque).

12. John R. Satterfield, *We Band of Brothers: The Sullivans and World War II* (Parkersburg, IA: Mid-Prairie Books, 1995), pp. xiv, 195.

13. See *Courier*, May 1, p. 5; July 12, p. 13, 1959. There is little about the various Sullivan family dedications in the city council minutes from 1959 to 1971; see WCH.

14. Clippings in McGee Collection, June 5 and November 28, 1961.

15. Clippings from the *Courier* are assembled in the McGee Collection: June 5 and November 28, 1961; September 8, 1963; July 23, 1964; September 20, 1964; June 27, 1988.

16. See the *Courier*, September 8, 1963, pp. 13–14; and Alvin Sunseri and Kenneth Lyftogt, *The Sullivan Family of Waterloo, Iowa* (Cedar Falls, IA: M&M, 1988).

### CHAPTER 13. TOWN AND COUNTRY

1. See in particular, *Des Moines Daily Register*, April 19, 1966, McGee Collection.

2. *Hearings before the Waterloo Commission on Human Rights* (September 7, 1967), mimeograph, WPL; *Courier*, May 25, 1972, p. 3; Glenda Riley, *Cities on the Cedar: A Portrait of Cedar Falls, Waterloo, and Black Hawk County* (Parkersburg, IA: Mid-Prairie Books, 1988), p. 73.

3. City Planning Binders, November 12, 1972; January 24, 1973, WPL. For the quotes and long analyses of the city's troubles see *Courier*, September 5, 1971, pp. 9–10; and December 7, 1972, p. 4.

4. *Courier*, May 3, 1971, pp. 1, 6.

5. See Urban Planning, 1970s, Binder, WPL; Margaret Corwin and Helen Hoy, *Waterloo: A Pictorial History* (Rock Island, IL: Quest, 1983; 2nd printing, 1994), p. 189.

6. See, for example, Leo Roof, obituary, *Courier*, January 6, 2004, p. 1.

7. Minutes of City Council, March 15, p. 2; May 9, p. 1; May 16, 1988, p. 1, WCH.

8. John D. Donnell, *Why the Rath Packing Company Failed* (Waterloo, IA: Grout Museum of History and Science, 1993), esp. pp. 23–29; Riley, *Cities on the Cedar*, pp. 71–72; *Courier*, August 16, 2015, pp. A-1, 3. The Rath company's records, with an outstanding online shelf list, are located in the Special Collections Library at Iowa State University in Ames.

9. For an overview see *Courier*, November 8, 1987, p. A-7; for a sense of John Rooff, see John Rooff, Oral History Interview, July 28, 2012, WPL.

10. Minutes of City Council meeting, June 27, 1988, p. 8, WCH.

11. See the various articles in the *Courier* for June 24, 26, and 27, 1988; March 13, 1993, p. A-9; and Minutes of Dedication Committee, September 28, 1988, SM.

12. Minutes of City Council, July 25, 1988, pp. 3–4; General Rules, from August 17, 2015, p. 1, WCH.

13. *Courier*, November 12, 1988, p. 1; *Des Moines Register*, November 12,

1988, p. 3A: John R. Satterfield, *We Band of Brothers: The Sullivans in World War II* (Parkersburg, IA: Mid-Prairie Books, 1995), pp. 208–209.

14. *Courier*, July 18, 1989, p. D-1; June 7, B-1; August 9, B-1, 1990.

15. See the *Courier*'s extended coverage of these events for November 11 (Veterans Day), 12, 13, 14, and 17, 1992.

16. See "The True Story of the Fighting Sullivans" (2000), *History's Mysteries* series, DVD, 2009.

17. Edward F. Dolan Jr., *Hollywood Goes to War* (New York: Gallery Books, 1985), see pp. 50, 188.

18. This sequence from *Saving Private Ryan* may also have derived from Mickey Rooney's announcement to a Mrs. Rose Sandoval (played by Ann Ayars) of her son's death in *The Human Comedy*. See also Jennifer Fay on *The Sullivans* and *Saving Private Ryan* in Fay's *Theaters of Occupation: Hollywood and the Reeducation of Postwar Germany* (Minneapolis: University of Minnesota Press, 2008), p. 176.

19. See the spirited interview, "Albert Sullivan's Widow Looks Back," *Courier*, November 11, 2012.

20. *Courier*, November 13, 1988, p. B-1; Justine Elias, "Dreaming Private Ryan," *US* (August 1988): 75 (clipping of article in McGee Collection); McGee interviews. An outstanding example of Loughren's affective story telling is a standard lecture she gave in Arkansas at the Clinton School of Public Service in 2012, available at: http://clintonschoolspeakers.com/content/fighting-sullivans.

21. See the *History's Mysteries* episode, "The True Story of the Fighting Sullivans."

22. See, for example, the recollections of an usherette at the Paramount opening of the film, *Courier*, November 8, 2011.

23. John R. Satterfield, *We Band of Brothers*, p. xi.

24. *Courier*, November 10, 2003.

25. *Courier*, November 29, p. A-1; December 6, p. C-2, 1998.

26. Lana Fanelli, "Caroline's Spine's Jimmy Newquist Talks with JAMtv," *Rolling Stone* (October 30, 1997); Tom Spinelli Interview with Caroline's Spine, Melodic.net (September 20, 2008); Isaac Josephson, "Caroline's Spine Hits the States Like a Monsoon," *Rolling Stone* (October 7, 1997); Andrew Wind, "Displays of Patriotism," *Courier*, November 16, 2008, Five Sullivans Binder, WPL.

27. *Master Plan Update* (Waterloo, IA: [n.d]), p. 8; the version available in 2015 is at the Waterloo Planning Department, WCH.

28. Minutes of City Council, March 15, 1988, p. 4, WCH; *Courier*, August 16, 2015, pp. A-1, 3; November 4, 2015, p. 1. The most extensive coverage of the Grout's problems is in the *Courier*, October 25, 2015, from which comes the quote.

29. *Master Plan Update* (Waterloo, IA: [n.d.]), pp. 33, 34, and map insert following p. 56.

30. *Courier*, February 16, May 16, 2016.

CONCLUSION: HOW WE REMEMBER AND WHY

1. Originally published in *The New Yorker* on February 21, 1931, the story has been frequently reprinted and is available on the Internet.

2. The rhyming quote is from A. E. Housman, "To an Athlete Dying Young," and Pat Kinney, "Reflections on the Five Sullivan Brothers," *Courier*, November 15, 1992, Five Sullivans Binder, WPL.

# BIBLIOGRAPHICAL ESSAY

SOURCES AND METHODS FOR FAMILY HISTORY

I have re-created the lives of the Sullivans by reviewing primary sources from Waterloo, Iowa, from the 1920s to 2015; the US Census from 1900 to 1940 (particularly the last); the Iowa Census of 1925; and various Waterloo directories. There are public records, collected letters and interviews, various newspaper reports, and other documents from the period of the torpedoing of the *Juneau* and its aftermath at the Sullivan Brothers Iowa Veterans Museum and the Waterloo Public Library. The records of Waterloo's City Council are found in the office of the City Clerk in the Waterloo City Hall, while the available court records are found in the Black Hawk County Court House in Waterloo. The *Waterloo Courier*, which had various titles in the twentieth century, is mainly searchable online and entirely accessible on microfilm at the Waterloo Public Library. I have identified the newspaper, an exceptional source of information, as *Courier*. For recent years, I have quoted the paper online, where there are no page numbers. I have also used the collection of primary sources that Waterloo genealogist Michael McGee has assembled. The notes single out this material as McGee Collection, and McGee is the "researcher" mentioned in my text. I spoke to him at length in Waterloo on August 13 and 14, 2013; July 21 and 23, 2014; and August 19, 2015. I have also had a lengthy email correspondence with him. On trips to Waterloo, I talked to many people casually about their city and the Sullivans, attempting to elicit opinions, some of which the text quotes. Readers should never take these opinions as fact or elevate my elicitations to the status of interviews. I have rather tried to indicate the aura of the Sullivans among various Waterlooans, most of whom refused to give even their first names.

I have also quoted several letters in full; they are all widely known, and I have not provided any further provenance for them.

While not all of material cited in the Notes is listed in this essay, in my reconstruction of the history of the family, I have centrally employed John R. Satterfield, *We Band of Brothers: The Sullivans in World War II* (Parkersburg, IA: Mid-Prairie Books, 1995), as well as Dan Kurzman, *Left to Die: The Tragedy of the USS Juneau* (New York: Simon and Schuster, 1994). Both authors conducted interviews, no longer available, in the late 1980s with various people, now dead, who knew the Sullivans in the 1930s. Any information about the family not specifically cited derives from the relevant parts of these two books. I have enormous respect for the research that Satterfield and Kurzman carried out, without which my own efforts would have far less depth. Nonetheless, I have examined the interviews in their books more searchingly than did the two authors, questioned competing memories, and compared the interviews to other evidence. Although I have repeatedly noted how rickety the reconstruction of the Sullivans' lives is—both in the books of Satterfield and Kurzman and in mine—Kurzman, especially, has far more detail about the young Sullivans (e.g., pp. 11–26, 37–42). Much of it, however, appears to me made up.

Hanging over most of the evidence—and certainly the interviews—is the movie *The Fighting Sullivans*, easily the most important history of the family, even though it is an account with little basis in reality. As an example of the movie's power, I relate my own story. One Saturday morning I was watching an old movie in which Edward Ryan had a minor part. When I saw him, my first thought was: *What is Albert Sullivan doing in a film?*

Even a sketch of the Sullivans is an exercise of the historical imagination, and no neutral language exists to describe the family. We can dissect the facts as well as what the historian makes of them; hugely charged silences mainly face us. Those scholars who define reality as only about an elastic idea of "texts" will find much—though not, I think, enough—to back up their views if they subject the Sullivans' history to scrutiny.

On the Internet, readers can find endless narratives about the family and the film. My account is rock-solid by comparison.

Readers should finally note that I have regularly exploited an interpretive form of logical inference: *abduction*. From early 1943, when the people of Waterloo rejected a day of prayer for the missing sailors, to 1988, when a later generation fought the naming of the convention center after the Sullivans, I have a list of instances when Waterloo's citizens expressed disrespect for the family. I have tried to explain this repeated phenomenon by presuming that, before 1943, the Sullivans had infuriated much of the local public, and I used this presumption to make intelligible much otherwise sparse and fragmentary evidence from the earlier period.

I did not set out to paint the portrait of Waterloo and its inhabitants that is now on these pages. I would repeat, however, that any telling of the story of the brothers, including my own, remains unsettled, although I have ruminated for several years over every piece of evidence I could lay my hands on—and over the way I have construed it.

POLITICAL HISTORY

The political (and cultural) history of the 1930s to the 1980s is often in the background of this book. On the 1930s and 1940s: Bruce M. Russett, *No Clear* and *Present Danger: A Skeptical View of the U.S. Entry into World War II* (New York: Harper and Row, 1972); two books by Robert A. Divine, *Second Chance: The Triumph of Internationalism in World War Two* (New York: Atheneum, 1967), and *The Reluctant Belligerent: American Entry into World War II* (New York: Knopf, 1979); Maurice Isserman, *Whose Side Were You On? The American Communist Party during the Second World War* (Middletown, CT: Wesleyan University Press, 1982); and Richard H. Pells, *Radical Visions and American Dreams: Culture and Social Thought in the Depression Years* (New York: Harper and Row, 1973). On the 1960s: Michael W. Flamm, *Law and Order: Street Crime, Civil Unrest, and the Crisis of Liberalism in the 1960s* (New York: Columbia University Press, 2007); Charles Murray, *Losing Ground: American Social Policy, 1950–1980* (New York: Basic Books, 1984); Thomas J. Sugrue, *Sweet Land of Liberty: The Forgotten Struggle for Civil Rights in the North* (New York: Random House, 2008); and a number of books by Jon C. Teaford, including *Cities of the Heartland: The Rise and Fall of the Industrial Midwest* (Bloomington: Indiana University Press, 1993). On the 1970s and 1980s: Jefferson Cowie, *Stayin' Alive: The 1970s and the Last Days of the Working Class* (New York: New Press, 2010); Andrew Highsmith, *Demolition Means Progress: Flint, Michigan, and the Fate of the American Metropolis* (Chicago: University of Chicago Press, 2015); Philip Jenkins, *Decade of Nightmares: The End of the Sixties and the Making of Eighties America* (New York: Oxford University Press, 2006); Peter Rachleff, *Hard-Pressed in the Heartland: The Hormel Strike and the Future of the Labor Movement* (Boston: South End Press, 1999); John W. Sloan, *The Reagan Effect: Economics and Presidential Leadership* (Lawrence: University Press of Kansas, 1999); Judith Stein, *Pivotal Decade: How the United States Traded Factories for Finance in the Seventies* (New Haven, CT: Yale University Press, 2010); and Patricia A. Turner, *I Heard It through the Grapevine: Rumor in African-American Culture* (Berkeley: University of California Press, 1993).

NAVAL HISTORY

My narrative of the travels of the *Juneau* derives from Satterfield, *Band of Brothers;* and Kurzman, *Left to Die,* although I have augmented these sources with information about the Sullivan brothers' activities derived from primary sources. Pertinent naval records of the Sullivans' service and their parents' tour are located at the National Archives in College Park, Maryland. The Naval Historical Center in Washington also has material on the navy's study of the sinking, which microfilm reel NRS 1973–71 has collected, but the Clark Woodward Papers there are unhelpful. The story of the battles for the Solomon Islands draws from standard sources in military history. An excellent bibliography can be found in Charles F. Brower's *Defeating Japan: The Joint Chiefs of Staff and Strategy in the Pacific War, 1943–1945* (Basingstoke, U.K.: Palgrave-Macmillan, 2012); a recent account is James D. Hornfischer, *Neptune's Inferno: The U.S. Navy at Guadalcanal* (New York: Bantam Books, 2011). I have given my own flavor to the description of the overall strategy of the United States and Japan in the Pacific because I wanted readers inexpert in military history (like myself) to grasp the larger issues, and also because I wanted to convey what this strategy meant to the Sullivans and their families.

FILM

As a novice to cinema studies, I have been overwhelmed by the enormous literature, although I have tried to sample it deeply. I have laid out my understanding in an elementary manner so as not to lose the reader whose grasp of Hollywood might resemble my own. This scholarly literature has broken down for me into three branches: the history of the industry and of the films themselves; American history on film; and finally film theory.

A fundamental book that I have mastered and would recommend is Bruce F. Kawin, *How Movies Work* (New York: Macmillan, 1987). Other such texts of both more and less recent vintage exist, but I have formulated views that, I hope, put the Hollywood film of the 1930s and 1940s into historical perspective but do not tilt toward movies produced in the past thirty years. For my comprehension of the studio system, filmmaking, and Hollywood in the 1930s and 1940s see the material cited in the Notes. Recommended on the cultural history of American film are: M. Todd Bennett, *One World, Big Screen: Hollywood, Allies, and World War Two* (Chapel Hill: University of North Carolina Press, 2012); Clayton R. Koppes and Gregory D. Black, *Hollywood Goes to War: How Politics, Profits, and Propaganda Shape World War II Movies* (Berkeley: University of California Press, 1987); and Frank Walsh, *Sin and Censorship: The Catholic Church and the Motion Picture Industry* (New Haven, CT: Yale University Press, 1996).

On the connection of historical movies and written history see: Leger Grindon, *Shadows on the Past: Studies in the Historical Fiction Film* (Philadelphia: Temple University Press, 1994); Robert Brent Toplin, *Reel History: In Defense of Hollywood* (Lawrence: University Press of Kansas, 2002); the second edition of Toplin's *History by Hollywood* (Urbana: University of Illinois Press, 2009); Robert A. Rosenstone, *History on Film/Film on History* (Harlow, U.K.: Pearson Educational, 2006); and Robert Burgoyne, *The Hollywood Historical Film* (Malden, MA: Blackwell Publishing, 2008). An interesting variant is Mary L.

Aquila, *Movies as History: Scenes of America, 1930–1970* (Jefferson, NC: McFarland Publishing, 2014).

The book inevitably looks at issues of "film theory," but I have encountered a paradox. Movies are central to American popular culture, and many are intelligible to most children. But theorists have studied film in a way that is unintelligible to many of those writing about cinema and to 99.99 percent of the reading public. This project has attempted to avoid the unintelligible.

To sample film theory see David Bordwell, *Making Meaning: Inference and Rhetoric in the Interpretation of Cinema* (Cambridge, MA: Harvard University Press, 1989); and Janet Staiger, *Perverse Spectators: The Practices of Film Reception* (New York: New York University Press, 2000). To the extent that I have absorbed cinematic philosophy, I have relied on the writers in what I call the Harvard tradition of aesthetics and film criticism: Hugo Münsterberg, Susanne K. Langer, Nelson Goodman, and Stanley Cavell.

In one sense this book is about the cultural imprint of World War II movies and their connection to prewar films: there are fundamental themes repeatedly depicted. While I have commented on these themes in the text itself, interested readers are encouraged to examine the notes to chapters 8 through 11, where I have written in a more detailed way about Hollywood's rendering of some of the verities of American life.

MAKING THE MOVIE

To grasp how Lloyd Bacon and Sam Jaffe made *The Sullivans* we have various records of 20th Century-Fox located in Los Angeles, California, libraries: that of UCLA; the Cinematic Arts Library at the University of Southern California; the Margaret Herrick Library of the Motion Picture Academy of Arts and Sciences; and archival material from the Production Code Office in Hollywood at the Herrick Library. 20th Century-Fox has removed some of its records from UCLA, and they are not open to the public, and Fox records have been misplaced and are not available at USC. The American Film Institute in Los Angeles has no relevant material. A number of Hollywood trade publications proved useful, and they are cited in the notes. I have been unable to locate documentation about the movie in naval records or in the records of the Office of War Information, both at NA.

I have examined various versions of Mary McCall's screenplay of *The Sullivans*: A First Draft Continuity Script, of July 10 (Script Collection, USC); a Final Screenplay, July 21, 1943 (Script Collection, USC); a Revised Final, July 28 (Script Collection, USC); a Second Revised Final, August 9, 1943 (Script

Collection, USC, and Script Collection, MHL); and a Shooting Final, August 27 (Script Collection, USC, and Folder 32, Box 1, Lloyd Bacon Papers, MHL). The Shooting Final has a number of additional or altered scenes dated in September and October 1943.

20th Century-Fox released two versions of the movie—*The Sullivans* of January 1944 and *The Fighting Sullivans* of April 1944. 20th Century-Fox does not have a copy of the earlier print, and I have been able to see only the later film, although, as my notes indicate, I have seen extended written descriptions of the earlier one. I have located an intermediate version at UCLA, a film titled *The Sullivans*, but with all the emendations of *The Fighting Sullivans*.

I have vigilantly watched *The Fighting Sullivans* many times. The impact of its final scenes is never diminished for me, and their authority has grown, even as I have become more self-conscious about the fraud, artifice, or magic—the reader should choose the correct word—involved. A central topic of the book is figuring out just how the cinematic effect is achieved. For readers who do not know the movie and wish to get a sense of it, the first and last ten minutes are critical. The entire film is sometimes available on YouTube, and clips from it are always there. There is a commemorative 2005 edition with extra material available on DVD.

Readers can also purchase on DVD *How Green Was My Valley*, *The Human Comedy*, *Saving Private Ryan*, *Die Degenhardts*, and many other movies that I have used in appraising *The Fighting Sullivans*. The end of the 1929 *Iron Mask* can be accessed on YouTube. Students can also buy the History Channel's "The True Story of the Fighting Sullivans" on DVD, and I have taken quotations from it.

Trawling the Internet will provide interested readers with scores of reviews, formal and informal, of the movie, as well as of other movies of the 1930s and 1940s that I have referenced.

VIEWING THE MOVIE

*The Fighting Sullivans* is the only movie that I have watched carefully and repeatedly, and so my evaluation must be taken with a grain of salt: Lloyd Bacon slovenly crafted the movie. While the substance of this book does not burden the reader with the blemishes of the film, I want to note those in addition to the ones mentioned in the text.

First, there are the "technical" mistakes. In one shot the shadow of the overhead microphone appears on the kitchen table. When the boys are racing to the water tower to see their father off to work, a wooden fence over which they climb changes into a wire hurdle. During the sequence in which the boys get into a fight, George clutches his stomach when a stone hits him in the head. When the boys rip through the water pipe in the kitchen with their saw, the water mysteriously stops pouring out from underneath the sink as Tom and Alleta get to the kitchen. When Tom educates the boys about smoking, he manages to light five cigars on a single match. The postman also delivers the mail to two different places, but the Sullivans had two different addresses for the same house: 98 Adams and 101 Ankeny. It seems unlikely that Hollywood would have attended to this detail, but one never knows.

After George runs away from home, one shot shows his mother looking out the kitchen window for him. The view is from the outside, and the camera looks in at her. But after she leaves the room, I first thought that the next scene shows George outside, looking in at the now empty kitchen. But this is not a reverse shot. Instead, it is Al wandering around the kitchen in snow gear, long after he has gone to bed. This scene is just a muddle.

In addition to these mechanical troubles, the editing that produced *The Fighting Sullivans* and the continued rewriting of the shooting script compromised the movie. Early written scenes for *The Sullivans* related Tom's desire to make wine and to trick the boys into doing the garden work to weed the grapevines: he suggests that they dig for fishing worms. But all of these scenes about wine-drinking vanish in *The Fighting Sullivans*, where we simply see the boys rummaging in the garden for no understandable reason. In the second part of the movie one theme gets confused and unsuccessfully abbreviated. Bacon and Jaffe had at first wanted a part in the movie for a Bill Bascom, the proxy for Gen's sometime real-life boyfriend, Bill Ball. He had been serving in Hawaii on the *Arizona*, and his fate motivated the Sullivans to join the navy after December 7, 1941. In the shooting scripts many scenes establish the friendship between Ball/Bascom and the Sullivan boys; they even ask him to join their football team. Later, when everyone has grown up, he appears at a dance in his navy uniform, mentions that he is serving on the *Arizona*, and waltzes off with Gen; and in another scene Alleta presses him on Gen. None of these scenes made it into the movie to foreshadow what did get in.

On December 7, 1941, the boys mention Bascom when the radio announces the news of Pearl Harbor, and Alleta tells the family that she will phone Mrs. Bascom to offer support. The movie shows Alleta making the call, reporting on it to the family, and suggesting that everyone visit Mrs. Bascom. Finally the family agrees to go off to church to light a candle for Bill. Somewhere along the line, the moviemakers dropped the earlier foreshadowing scenes, and the post—Pearl Harbor bits simply hang out in the completed film.

In addition to these mishaps, many fans of the film have catalogued a variety of what I would call minor "factual" errors. Up though 1939, Indian motorcycles, the main rival of Harley-Davidson, had open fenders on their Chief models, and from 1940 through 1953 they sported large skirted fenders, but the company built no new models in 1943 (or 1944). Yet one of the bikes in the 1939 motorcycle race was a 1940, 1941, or 1942 model. When Al meets Katherine Mary after the race in 1939, the band is playing "You'll Never Know," although 20th Century-Fox did not introduce this song until 1943 in the film *Hello, Frisco, Hello*. The naval insignias at the recruiting office are incorrect, and the USS *The Sullivans*, the ship christened at the end of the film, has the wrong number on it.

Finally, I have brooded over a related matter. In readying his movie, Lloyd Bacon reported that when the boys left for the war, Tom Sullivan mortgaged 98 Adams to pay off their debts. But the same little essay that contains this story also contains false material, and other evidence suggests that the boys paid off their own debts. One is an interview describing Red's sale of his Harley to rid himself of encumbrances; the other the estate probate record for George, wherein he received a $25 refund for a down payment on a motorcycle, indicating that he did not have arrears when he left for the navy (Lloyd Bacon, "The Sullivans," *This Week*, March 5, 1944, n.p.; Satterfield, *Band of Brothers*, p. 59; and Estate Probate Records, Box: The Sullivans, SM). Bacon, as I have indicated, screened a scene in which Sullivan/Mitchell says he will take out a mortgage. I don't know what really happened. Did the filmmakers have evidence, not now available, but so unanswerable that they put the scene in? Perhaps it was poetic license designed to exhibit parental concern as well as control over the boys.

## POPULAR CULTURE AND AMERICAN HISTORY

On one topic of this book—how the filmed version of some historical occurrence is developed—the reader might consult: Nicholas Evans Sarantakes, *Making Patton: A Classic War Film's Epic Journey to the Silver Screen* (Lawrence: University Press of Kansas, 2012). I am particularly interested in the historical intersection between film and culture, as exhibited by Yunte Huang, *Charlie Chan: The Untold Story of the Honorable Detective and His Rendezvous with American History* (New York: Norton, 2010); Ellen Noonan, *The Strange Career of Porgy and Bess: Race, Culture, and America's Most Famous Opera* (Chapel Hill: University of North Carolina Press, 2012); Glenn Frankel, *The Searchers: The Making of an American Legend* (New York: Bloomsbury, 2013); Ernesto R. Acevedo-Muñoz, *West Side Story as Cinema: The Making and Impact of an American Masterpiece* (Lawrence: University Press of Kansas, 2013); and Paul Seydor,

*The Authentic Death and Contentious Afterlife of Pat Garrett and Billy the Kid: The Untold Story of Peckinpah's Last Western Film* (Evanston, IL: Northwestern University Press, 2015). On a related topic, Anne-Marie Scholz's *From Fidelity to History: Film Adaptations as Cultural Events in the Twentieth Century* (New York: Berghahn Books, 2013) is about the adaptations of books into movies; its up-to-date bibliography of film studies also displays their incomprehensibility and may be contrasted with Aquila, *Movies as History.*

MEMORIALIZING SACRIFICE

Emily S. Rosenberg, *A Date Which Will Live: Pearl Harbor in American Memory* (Durham, NC: Duke University Press, 2003), has an outstanding bibliography of work on national mourning, commemoration, and sacrifice. See also Erika Doss, *Memorial Mania: Public Feeling in America* (Chicago: University of Chicago Press, 2012). For cultural artifacts and their history see Karal Ann Marling and John Wetenhall, *Iwo Jima: Monuments, Memories, and the American Hero* (Cambridge, MA: Harvard University Press, 1991); James Bradley and Ron Powers, *Flags of Our Fathers* (New York: Bantam Books, 2000); and Geoffrey M. White, *Memorializing Pearl Harbor: Unfinished Histories and the Work of Remembrance* (Durham, NC: Duke University Press, 2016). Alex Kershaw, *The Bedford Boys: One American Town's Ultimate D-Day Sacrifice* (New York: Da Capo Press, 2003), deals with mourning at America's crossroads. Kyle Longley's *The Morenci Marines: A Tale of Small Town America and the Vietnam War* (Lawrence: University Press of Kansas, 2013) illustrates the scholarship on mourning the Vietnam War.

We have a large literature on the religious aspect of sacrifice. The most sustained effort is Carolyn Marvin and David W. Ingle, *Blood Sacrifice: Totem Rituals and the American Flag* (New York: Cambridge University Press, 1999). I have also found helpful Paul W. Kahn's introduction in his *Political Theology: Four New Chapters on the Concept of Sovereignty* (New York: Columbia University Press, 2011), pp. 1–27. The online magazine *The Library of Social Science* devotes much of its space to the state and sacrifice.

Alex Kotlowitz has written a community study about race that in some ways I have tried to emulate: *The Other Side of the River: A Story of Two Towns, a Death, and America's Dilemma* (New York: Doubleday, 1998). I have also been influenced by the work of my deceased colleague Erving Goffman; see, for example, Charles Lemert and Ann Branaman, eds., *The Goffman Reader* (Cambridge, MA: Blackwell, 1997).

✯   ✯   ✯

Finally, when referring to the Hollywood studios I have deliberately not used the technically correct Warner Bros., but Warner Brothers instead, and 20th Century-Fox rather than Twentieth Century-Fox. Knowledgeable readers will note that I have borrowed a few phrases from Willa Cather's *One of Ours* (New York: Vintage, 1922, 1991).

# INDEX